guc

THE RAMPARTS WE WATCH

THE RAMPARTS
WE WATCH

*A STUDY OF THE PROBLEMS OF
AMERICAN NATIONAL DEFENSE*

By GEORGE FIELDING ELIOT

FORMERLY MAJOR, MILITARY INTELLIGENCE RESERVE,
UNITED STATES ARMY: CO-AUTHOR OF "IF WAR COMES"

REYNAL & HITCHCOCK : NEW YORK

PRINTED IN THE UNITED STATES OF AMERICA

BY THE CORNWALL PRESS, INC., CORNWALL, NEW YORK

TO THE CITIZENS OF THE UNITED
STATES, UPON WHOSE WISDOM AND
COURAGE MUST, AS ALWAYS, REST
THE ULTIMATE RESPONSIBILITY
FOR THE DEFENSE OF OUR COUNTRY

Contents

Contents

Introduction

THE PURPOSE of this book is to place before the citizens of this republic a clear presentation of the military principles upon which their security rests, and of the military instruments by which that security may be conserved.

If his work shall in any degree contribute to that enlightened public opinion which must, in a free country, be ever the ultimate source of national safety, the author will feel well repaid for what labor and time he has expended upon its compilation.

The author desires to extend his most sincere thanks to the many friends, most of them officers of one or the other of our armed Services, who have so generously aided him with their counsel; to them is due, in great measure, whatever of merit the book may be found to possess.

For the opinions expressed and the conclusions drawn, however, the author assumes entire responsibility; these opinions and conclusions are not to be taken as representing in any degree the views of the military departments of the Government, or of the Services at large.

GEORGE FIELDING ELIOT.

Brooklyn, New York,
September 9, 1938.

Chapter I

FORCE REMAINS THE FINAL ARBITER OF NATIONS

"The Congress knows that for many years this Government has sought in many capitals, with the leaders of many governments, to find a way to limit and reduce armaments. . . . The Congress is also aware that these efforts . . . have failed up to the present time. . . . It is with the deepest regret that I report to you that armaments increase today at an unprecedented and alarming rate. It is an ominous fact that at least one-fourth of the world's population is involved in merciless, devastating war."

FRANKLIN D. ROOSEVELT,
PRESIDENT OF THE UNITED STATES,
Message to the Congress of the United States,
January 28, 1938

TWENTY YEARS have gone by since, from Switzerland to the shores of the Channel, the bugles sounded "cease firing" and the War to End War came to an end.

Along the American portion of the line, approximately from Sedan southeastward to Verdun, three-quarters of a million young Americans, the first American army ever to fight on the ancient battlefields of Europe, heard those bugles, and rent the echoing silence which followed with their cheers for victory and peace. Behind the line, in rest and billeting areas, in camps of instruction, in the various busy centers of the Services of Supply, a million-odd more Americans joined their Allied comrades in wild celebration — "Now we can go home!" They had all done their part, and they well knew how great a part in sum total, in the winning of that victory, in the gaining of that peace.

Yet many among them believed, and many more of their countrymen at home believed, that the war they had fought, the victory they had won, were indeed the War to End War, the victory which should assure the new reign of Eternal Peace.

Nor was this hopeful view confined to Americans, although perhaps it was more widely cherished in the hearts of a people ever ready to put their faith in miracles and little experienced in the practical application of the arts of war and diplomacy. Many men in many countries believed and hoped for a new day. The League of Nations came into being, an American concept — and was rejected by the representatives of the American people, determined, in accordance with their historic tradition, to avoid commitments which might automatically engage them in European strife and send American armies again across the Atlantic to fight in quarrels not of our making. Yet the hope of peace persisted, and a great political party espoused the cause of American participation in the League, refusing credence to the cynics who maintained that the League was indissolubly linked to the Versailles treaties and was in fact a system designed to perpetuate the conditions brought about by the Allied victory — to assure the permanent hegemony in Europe of Great Britain and France, and to keep the German people in eternal chains.

It is fruitless, now, to conjecture what might have been the future of the League had the United States joined it and striven to guide its course by the idealistic concepts of Woodrow Wilson, whose brain and heart had given it birth.

That did not happen; nor can any man today say with

certainty that, had it happened, the fate of the League would have been different. There are too many imponderables, too many ifs, ands, and buts in that sort of speculation to make it profitable.

What did happen was the slow disintegration of the League, a disintegration precisely proportionate to the spread of the realization that its authority, if challenged, could be supported only by force; and that the sources of force, the possessors of the instruments of force, which were the member powers, were not ready to plunge into a new war to uphold the orders of the League; that none of the great powers would, in fact, sacrifice in any degree its individual interests to an international ideal. Thus the formation of the League had done nothing whatever to upset the eternal principle, which had existed since the dawn of international relationships on this planet and which still governs those relationships, that force underlies all diplomacy, all international adjustments, "as a possible final arbiter."[1]

It was perhaps inevitable that many good and well-meaning men, shocked by the horrors and sacrifices of the war that had just ended, should seek to ensure peace by another form of international agreement — by abolishing the instruments of war, that is, the instruments of the application of force in international relationships; or if not by abolishing them altogether, by limiting the use and possession of them, or certain of them, to an international, impartial authority; or by ameliorating their nature in one respect or another.

This is, of course, an anti-logical form of reasoning which sees in the weapon a cause, whereas it is in fact an effect. "When the necessity for arms ceases, armaments will disappear. The basic causes of war are not in armaments, but in human minds."[2]

---

[1] Mahan, *Armaments and Arbitration*.
[2] Lieutenant George W. Akers, U.S.N.R., *U. S. Naval Institute Proceedings*, July, 1934.

Nevertheless, the economic pressure of the cost of armament, coupled with the hope of ending war and reinforced by a great deal of well-meaning propaganda, led to various so-called disarmament conferences during the fifteen years from 1921 to 1936. These meetings served chiefly to bring out the almost incredible complexity of the problems to be solved ere anything approaching real disarmament could be achieved, and to provide arenas in which the representatives of the participating nations struggled valiantly for partisan advantage.

Thus, during the course of the several Naval Disarmament Conferences, Great Britain was discovered as more than eager to abolish the submarine, the extensive use of which by Germany had come so near to starving the British people during the war. Meanwhile the smaller powers, to whom the use of the submarine was the one possible, if hardly complete, answer to the battleships which they were too poor to construct in any numbers, refused to consider its outlawing. Japan, on the other hand, while desirous of retaining the submarine, asserted rather stridently her complete readiness to abolish the battleship and the aircraft carrier, thus assuring her a naval dominance of the Western Pacific which could not thereafter be challenged by those who possessed no long-range weapon capable of commanding the sea, and further relieving Japan of the financial burdens necessitated by expensive types of construction, burdens which she was far less able to bear than were Great Britain and the United States.

In all of these conferences, the practical interests of the United States were stoutly upheld by the experienced career diplomats and naval officers who were charged with the duties of representing America in council. Somewhat less can be said for politicians at home and abroad; and quite a little less for popular opinion, that source of all power in democratic nations. Two examples will make this clear.

[4]

After the first Naval Disarmament Conference in Washington in 1922, the theory of "disarmament by example" was cherished in many quarters in this country. The Washington Agreement had placed definite limits on the number of capital ships and aircraft carriers to be constructed by the several powers, and fixed, in respect to these classes of ships, ratios between the powers in the proportion of 5–5–3–1.75–1.75 for Great Britain, the United States, Japan, France and Italy respectively. Limitations were also established on the size and armament of lesser warships (notably an upper limit of 10,000 tons and 8-inch guns for cruisers, a purely artificial standard imposed at the insistence of the British who desired to retain their 9750-ton, 7.5-inch gun cruisers of the *Hawkins* class); but there was no limitation as to numbers. The United States Navy was then very decidedly deficient in cruisers and it was apparent that, unless a sensible program of annual replacements for destroyers and submarines was undertaken, our large war-time fleets of those types would eventually become obsolete all at once and have to be replaced by hasty and uneconomical rush building. It was nevertheless widely held that this country must set an example to the rest of the world in the matter of naval disarmament. Consequently, America stopped building warships. In cold figures, the results of this policy were that during the years 1922 to 1929 inclusive (the years intervening between the Washington and London Naval Treaties) we laid down a grand total of 17 naval vessels (8 cruisers, 3 submarines and 6 river gunboats) totalling 83,710 tons. No vessels at all were laid down in four of the eight years (1922, 1923, 1924 and 1929). During this same eight-year period, there were laid down for the other treaty powers naval vessels totalling the following tonnages: British Empire, 325,832; Japan, 324,401; France, 271,118; Italy, 204,320. These figures hardly require further comment.

The other example of American idealism was presented

by the proposals of President Hoover to the General Disarmament Conference at Geneva in 1932, for the abolition of "offensive weapons," and particularly of bombardment aviation, heavy mobile guns, and large tanks. Quite aside from the practical impossibility in a military sense of distinguishing between offensive and defensive weapons, from the American point of view this proposal was little short of outrageous. If we should have to face an attack upon our coasts in the absence or after the defeat of our navy, our best chance of inflicting injury on the invader's warships and transports lies in the use of long-range bombing-planes, as does our best chance of preventing him from establishing the needed air bases within flying range of his proposed point of disembarkation — an imperative necessity in all future landings on a hostile shore in face of resistance. It should be noted, too, that the landing can quite well be supported by the lighter types of planes, carrying only machine-guns and small fragmentation bombs — since they will be firing largely against personnel targets rather than trying to achieve demolition effects. The destruction of ships, on the other hand, demands heavy bombs, and planes capable of carrying and discharging them. Again, in repelling an actual landing, or in attacking the ships from which it is to proceed or which are covering it by fire, the next best weapon to the bomber is heavy mobile artillery. Finally, when the landing has actually taken place, a highly useful weapon in dealing with the invading troops would certainly be the tank, capable of comparatively rapid movement and quick concentration of fire-power at threatened points; and in this weapon it is to be anticipated that the defender would have a very considerable initial advantage over the attacker, who could get such heavy material ashore only by driblets. Yet it was these several weapons which Mr. Hoover, with an eye only to European conditions, proposed in the name of the United States to abolish from the armies of the world, quite without reference to the particular military needs and security of his own country. The writer is far from desiring to attribute to Mr. Hoover any but the most noble and well-meaning intentions, nor has he any means of ascertaining the source of the advice which Mr. Hoover undoubtedly took on this subject; the facts are however beyond question, and are here presented as an example of how statesmen without adequate knowledge of military principles can imperil the safety of their fellow-countrymen by acting in such matters without giving weight to the counsel of experienced military advisers.

It should be noted, in this connection, that the three Presidents who occupied the White House from 1921 to 1933 — Harding, Coolidge and Hoover — had none of them had any personal connection with, or first-hand knowledge of, the defense forces of the nation and the problems generally grouped under the heading of national defense. With the inauguration of Franklin Roosevelt in 1933, there came into the office of Commander-in-Chief a man of life-long interest in naval affairs and one who had during the World War served as Assistant Secretary of the Navy and had in that capacity visited the American naval forces in European waters and the Expeditionary Force in France, meanwhile acquiring a considerable experience of the problems of naval operations and administration. It was to be expected, under such leadership, that a different attitude would be adopted toward the defense forces; nor was this expectation unjustified in the event. Mr. Roosevelt had the very great advantage over his predecessors of an understanding of the first principles, so to speak; it was not necessary for him to laboriously try to learn the ABC's of military policy. (His advantage in this respect was not unlike that possessed by Jefferson Davis over Lincoln in 1861, which so greatly contributed to the early successes of the Confederate armies.) There ensued a series of messages to the Congress which were promptly productive of results in increased appropriations for naval building to make up the lag of the lean years which had gone before, and were followed by increases in the army. Thus our defense forces began to revive, though, alas, with no assurance that the revival would be permanent.

Meanwhile, the international situation rapidly went from bad to worse. Italy seized Ethiopia by force of arms, in defiance of British opposition and of feeble bleatings from Geneva; civil war broke out in Spain, in which Italy and Germany on the one side, and Soviet Russia on the other, began almost openly to participate; Japan, having established herself in Manchukuo in 1931, chose what she deemed an appropriate moment for a sudden attempt to seize control of Northern China, an attempt in which her gross miscalculation of the nature and endurance of Chinese resistance led her into a long desperate struggle to destroy the existing Chinese government; Germany, after having rearmed in defiance of the Versailles treaty, made herself master of Austria by a *coup de main* and began manifesting the desire that lead to the partitioning of Czechoslovakia.

Moreover, the world was allowed to learn of an agreement for mutual support "against Communism" among the three powers who had thus constituted themselves the apostles of brutal force in the achievement of their respective ambitions — an agreement which was reported, without serious denial, to contain secret military clauses of a much more binding and formidable nature.

In answer to this threat, Great Britain and France, as well as the smaller powers of Europe, began feverishly to increase their armaments, and the two great democracies drew closer together in what has become at last a firm military alliance.

The War to End War ended twenty years ago; and today two wars are actually in bloody progress, the one in Europe, the other in Asia, while still a third — between Russia and Japan — seems in the making on the Siberian frontier, and the threat of Germany against Czechoslovakia has been occupying the sleepless attention of the chancelleries and general staffs of Europe. Nation is arming against nation as perhaps never before. New and merciless concepts of racial nationalism are arising, fired by a fierce fanaticism which seeks not only the accomplishment of national ambition, but the extinction of its enemies from the face of the earth; possessing for that purpose, as Sir Norman Angell points out, the technique of science without the least trace of the scientific spirit. New lines of division between friend and foe are cutting across the old frontiers of peoples, dividing brother against brother, adding the horrors of civil strife to the struggle for power and place.

The genius of man has brought the nations of the world closer together than ever in all his history; the wonders of modern transportation and communication link together the peoples of the six continents with bands which all but annihilate the ancient barriers of time and space. The coming of the machine age, the rise of modern industrial methods, the developments of science in a thousand fields, have combined to create a vast interlocking system of production and distribution of which the disturbance or breakage of one part affects inevitably, in greater or less degree, all the others. Yet science and the machine age and the genius of man have also improved and extended in speed and range and power the instruments of war, the means for the destruction of the wonders he has in other ways achieved; the means, perhaps, for the eventual self-destruction of man himself and all his vaunted civilization.

Nor has his genius — with all its victories over time and space, over ignorance and disease, over the innumerable threats with which nature herself menaced his primitive ancestors — been able to achieve the greatest victory of all, the victory which should abolish the curse which, since certain of those ancestors first went out with club and stone to seize by force the better cave of a neighbor, has brought desolation and death to undo the work of hand and heart and brain.

The reason must be sought in the nature of man himself, which has not changed through all the thousands of years of recorded history. Call it what you like — innate depravity, the curse of original sin, the heritage of Cain — the bitter fact remains that those still take who have the power and those still keep who can. The reign of law within civilized nations maintains a measure of peace as between individuals; among themselves the nations still follow the rule of the savage tribes who knew no law save that of might makes right.

It is with no feeling of triumph, with no martial ardor, that a soldier who has seen long years of war thus records the present failure of the labors for peace to which so much heart-breaking effort and thought and good will have been contributed by men and women of all nations of the world. Perhaps in a brighter and better day those labors will bear fruit; perhaps a generation yet to come, happy in the knowledge that the war-flags are forever furled, will find time to bow their heads in reverent memory of those who sought the light of peace amid the rolling smoke of a hundred world-scarring battlefields.

But that day is not yet, nor is it the dawn of peace which reddens the skies of Spain, of China, of — who knows what land tomorrow? It is, alas, the light of blazing cities, the pale glare of shell-bursts, the flaming meteors of falling planes which the finger of death has touched, the swinging swords of the searchlights.

And in other lands, it is the blaze of armorers' forges, clanging, clanging, day and night, that war may not come upon a people unready to meet the foe.

In such a world, there is no safety save in strength; there is no security save as that security is vigilant and armed. For him who yet doubts, let him ask of the Ethiopian who cowers today beneath a conqueror's heel; let him go to Vienna and seek that gaiety and laughter which once echoed through her streets; let him say to a Catalan mother, "Woman, where are your children?," or to a Chinese infant, "Child, where is your mother?"

Thus grimly, and sadly, is reaffirmed the maxim of Mahan, above quoted, as to the fundamental character of force, "force potential and force organized," force latent or force active, in those cynical, civilized travesties upon the tribal affairs of savages which we are pleased to dignify by the title of international relations.

Thus is made clear that those peoples who would live at peace, disclaiming all purpose of aggression, must nevertheless take note of the doings and character of neighbors perhaps otherwise minded; that for the time being the policy of peace by international agreement has failed; and that the nation which would preserve its institutions, its dignity and its rights in a world where all too obviously force still rules, must walk amongst its fellows "with sword on thigh and brow with purpose knit"; must, in the trenchant phrase of Guibert, "make its arms to be feared, though never its ambition."

Thus, finally, it becomes apparent that the time is full ripe for the people of the United States to examine with an unwonted attention the military policy of their republic, and to assure themselves that it is adequate and shall continue adequate to the heavy responsibilties which a troubled future may impose upon it.

Chapter II

MILITARY POLICY AND PUBLIC OPINION

"How hard, in a moment of real emergency, it will be for the Government to adhere to sound military principles, if there be not some appreciation of these in the mass of the people; or at the very least among the leaders to whom the various parts of the country are accustomed to look for guidance."

ALFRED THAYER MAHAN,
REAR ADMIRAL, UNITED STATES NAVY,
Armaments and Arbitration.

MILITARY POLICY has to do with the determination of the size, nature and control of the armed forces of a state and must, if adequate to its purpose, be based upon the missions to be required of those forces in peace and war — in peace, for the support of the state's foreign policy, for the protection of its interests, for the assurance, in emergency, of internal order; in war, for its defense against aggression or the maintenance of what it conceives to be its rights. It is of course impossible to foresee every exigency which the future, even the immediate future, may bring forth; but a wise military policy, correlated with a complementary foreign policy, based upon the well-weighed lessons of experience, and intelligently directed by capable and devoted public servants, will find little difficulty in adapting itself to changing conditions.

Military policy is the province primarily of the statesman, of the civil as distinguished from the military power of the state. It is for the civil power to determine higher ends of state policy and to provide the military power with the instruments necessary to support or if need be to defend the policy so adopted. It is for the soldier to advise as to the sufficiency of those instruments, but the determination of policy is not his province save in a state where the military power is supreme or nearly so, as in Japan. And even then the soldier becomes, insofar as he directs state policy, a statesman in uniform. "War," says Clausewitz, "is only a continuation of political intercourse in a new form. The subordination of the military to the political point of view is therefore the only thing which is possible."

In a democracy such as the United States, where the Government is the creature of the people and where the conduct of the civil power is in so large a measure directly responsible to, and at the mercy of the mass of the citizenry, it has become imperative — until the order of human events so changes as to relegate force as a factor in international affairs to that secondary place which hopeful human hearts have sought to assign it, but which it so persistently refuses to assume — that not only statesmen and politicians, but ordinary citizens, shall give more thought to the requirements of military policy than has been the general case in our republic in years gone by.

Herein, the first necessity is for completely realistic thinking, for the banishment of altruism and sentiment, for single-minded attention to the national interests.

Such realistic thinking is the first necessity of military policy, as it is the first necessity of the strategist in war. It is not an achievement which comes easily to most of us. Human nature is prone to deceive itself with comfortable fallacies—a legacy from childhood, which counts a punishment which cannot come until tomorrow as belonging to some indefinite and ignorable future. Just so a man who owes a debt, and is not gripped by a stern sense of duty, will perhaps spend the money due his creditor on something more attractive, meanwhile assuring himself that his creditor will not sue him until next month anyway, and by that time something will turn up. Military policy eschews this human tendency to believe that all will be well and therefore no thought need be taken for the morrow. It deals with facts, where facts are obtainable; and where they are not, it seeks to form sound judgment as to future contingencies upon the basis of past experience. Military policy does not believe in miracles. It puts faith in the promises of other states in precise proportion to the extent to which the interests of the promiser are engaged in the keeping of them; it prepares with realistic and coldly reasoned judgment against every danger it can foresee; and it always endeavors to hold some resources in reserve against the unforeseeable.

This is the sort of thinking which, it is to be hoped, American citizens will give to the military needs of their country.

Experience has made it clear that other powers are not ready to sacrifice their individual interests on the altar of internationalism; neither the great powers, which still seek their own selfish ends, nor the lesser powers, which, perceiving the utter failure of the League of Nations to protect Ethiopia, China, Austria or Spain, have shown a tendency to withdraw from the assumption of responsibilities under a Covenant from which they derive no compensatory advantage in the way of protection against possible aggression.

Americans can no longer cherish the hope that human nature is about to undergo a great awakening, that the millenium of a warless world is at hand. Force is still the final arbiter between nations.

It follows that, of the factors affecting the foreign policy of any state, the military factors, having to do with the possible or actual application of force — either in defense of the rights, interests, territorial integrity or even the existence of the state, or in the realization of its ambitions — are fundamental; and the nature of these factors, and the correct principles of their employment must be understood by those charged with the direction of policy, who else are liable to fall into irreparable error.

The errors of diplomacy can frequently be adjusted by subsequent and more enlightened negotiation; the errors of domestic policy, when perceived, can be the subject of reconsideration at any time. The one may indeed result in some loss of prestige, or other advantage; the other may impose needless burdens on the Treasury, and perhaps be disastrous to the political fortunes of parties or individuals. But errors of military policy may have a more far-reaching and sinister character, since advantage may be taken of them by those over whom the mistaken state has no control, and may proceed to lengths incapable of subsequent retrievement even at the price of war. Even if retrieved at last, they may impose penalties in blood, treasure and effort, and may entail supervening ill-consequences, out of all proportion to the original cost of correct precautionary measures.

Of this truth, American history affords a number of illuminating examples.

Thus, in 1794, Gouverneur Morris wrote, with prophetic accuracy: "I am tolerably certain that, while the United States of America pursue a just and liberal conduct, *with twenty sail of the line at sea,* no nation on earth will dare insult them. One thing I am thoroughly convinced of, that if we do not render ourselves respectable, we shall continue to be insulted." Yet succeeding Administrations continued to pay tribute to Barbary corsairs, and had in the end to fight; to endure the depredations of French privateers, and had in the end to employ frigates instead; to refuse, at last, to build any ocean-going vessels of war, relying upon a cowering policy of embargo and non-intercourse, while British warships impressed our seamen and captured our shipping on the high seas; and had in the end to see American soil invaded, the American capital burned, American coasts blockaded, and American frontiers harried with fire and tomahawk ere Macdonough's victory on Lake Champlain finally afforded the opportunity for a peace which Morris's twenty sail of the line would most assuredly have kept inviolate from the beginning.

Today, the United States is face to face with a world in which the apostles of force are rising and growing stronger on every hand. By reason of the irresponsibility of the executive to popular control, these aggressive dictator states are able to adjust their foreign and military policies each to the requirements and exigencies of the other, with that efficiency to which the unhampered labors of skilled hands so greatly conduce. Herein they possess a great advantage over a democracy such as our own. They are able to create and develop military institutions precisely adapted to the implementation of their foreign policies, unrestricted by parliamentary questions, by the whims of political faction or popular opinion, or by congressional grip upon the purse-strings. In the democracies, on the contrary, a traditional fear of undue military intrusion into political affairs has reduced the role of the soldier in the formulation of policy to that of an adviser, without power to insist upon the acceptance of his advice.

This is, of course, one of the prices to be paid for liberty. It can hardly be otherwise if liberty is to endure. But it follows that if liberty, thus protecting itself against internal dangers, is likewise to be protected against the no less real peril from abroad, some means must be found to offset the military advantage which it thus abandons to the authoritarian states. This means can hardly consist in anything save an enlightened public opinion, educated to the necessities and dangers of the moment, and prepared by intelligent understanding thereof, and of the basic principles affecting the nation's military security, for the endurance of the sacrifices which that security requires of a people if they are to retain their liberties in a world where cannon, aptly called "the last argument of kings," still speak with a decisive voice.

That American public opinion still has far to go before reaching this ideal is apparent enough from a merely cursory reading of newspapers and magazines, or even listening to the radio, wherefrom one may gather the most extraordinary collection of ideas regarding the national defense from the pens and voices of those who "have leave to print" — or talk. One gentleman would abolish "costly battleships" and put our trust in largely increased expenditures for coast fortifications; another would go "all out" for airplanes, considering these weapons sufficient for any conceivable purpose of war. Sometimes there are combinations of various themes; thus one of the most enthusiastic "No-battleship" advocates, ex-Congressman Maverick of Texas, in a radio debate at Town Hall, New York, was talking vigorously and somewhat confusedly about building more "airplanes, submarines and tanks" as insurance against invasion, when he was mildly pulled up by a lady questioner from the audience who desired information as to whether, when you got to using tanks, you had not *ipso facto* been already invaded!

Congressman Maverick, and others of like mind, are however but exemplars of our national passion for "gadgets," natural enough in a people who are almost daily dazzled by the wonders of some new invention produced by American genius. Illustrative of this is the hold which the Monitor type of warship had upon the American imagination for many years after the Civil War. Useful as this type proved for inshore operations in that conflict, it quickly became apparent that its low freeboard but poorly adapted it for seagoing work. In the Spanish War, Admiral Sampson was much hampered by having so considerable a portion of his available fighting strength tied up in four slow, sluggish monitors of little coal capacity, unstable as firing platforms and requiring to be towed in anything like a seaway. Moreover, during the period of panic along our Atlantic coast when Cervera's squadron had sailed from the Cape Verdes and its whereabouts was unknown, there was clearly demonstrated the uselessness of the monitor even for coast-defense: the Navy Department, hoping to allay the panic by suitable measures and thus release the Flying Squadron from its detention at Hampton Roads, considered employing the monitors, only to discover the insoluble problem which their use afforded — since if stationed at four separate ports, a single monitor would necessarily be inferior in force to the Spanish squadron, while if stationed (according to correct principle) at a central point, they were too slow and unseaworthy to move rapidly to whatever place the enemy might first be sighted. Incredible as it may seem, however, at the very moment when the qualities of the existing monitors were beginning to cause such anxiety, Congress authorized four more ships of this type; which were completed some years later, at a total expense of some millions of dollars, and dragged out two decades of service, largely as submarine tenders and Naval Reserve training ships.

Our tendency in military matters to confusion and inaccuracy of thought, to the eternal seeking of nostrums, of "get-rich-quick" roads to military security, is nowhere better typified than in the testimony given before the Naval Affairs Committees of the House and Senate (February and April, 1938, respectively) when hearings were being held on the Vinson bill to increase the naval establishment. Volunteer witnesses from all parts of the country flocked to

Washington, some to favor, but most to oppose the bill; and with the exception of two or three, none displayed any worthwhile knowledge of the problems involved, or was really able to contribute valuable advice to the Committees.

One had a plan for limiting by law the operations of all naval vessels to 500 miles offshore; another voiced fears that the naval increase was desired for the purpose of "policing and quarantining the world," despite the obvious fact of its entire inadequacy for such a task; a third had a marvelous bomb which was to explode at a "predetermined height" above the surface of the water and throw out a shower of "steel units" which would destroy vessels of war. There were several who talked vaguely of planes and submarines, though with little apparent knowledge of the powers and limitations of those weapons. For the most part, however, the witnesses who opposed the bill did just that—they said they didn't want a bigger navy, yet when pinned down by some of the more alert and informed members of the Committees, among whom Congressman Maas of Minnesota was outstanding, they could not claim for themselves any technical qualifications for the giving of advice on such a subject. Witness after witness repeated the same refrain: "I am not a technical expert on naval matters—I just came here to oppose this bill." To the perfectly obvious query as to why, in that case, the Committee should not rely on the advice of those who *were* experts, the volunteer witnesses had no adequate reply.

The entire performance was, of course, typically American; and it affords a key to the reasons for some of our more glaring errors of military policy in the past. It reflected the results of the insistent propaganda of the peace societies, who have for years been preaching to American ears the doctrine that "armaments breed war," though the whole record of human history is available to prove the precise converse, and though the whole record of American history bears evidence that, while we have fought four full-dress foreign wars and

[19]

one tremendous civil war, we have never, in a military sense, been armed and ready for any one of them. Indeed, there is every reason to believe that if we had been, some of those wars would never have been fought. However, it is another of our national failings that anything repeated often enough and loudly enough comes at last to attain a considerable degree of popular acceptance, however little of actual truth it may contain and however little evidence it may present of deep or accurate thinking by its proponents. This is particularly true in military matters, and is quite independent of the lessons of bitter experience; thus, for over a century nothing was able to dissuade us from our apparently ineradicable belief in the sovereign virtues of State militia forces, despite the record of all our wars; we repeated in 1812 all the errors of the Revolution, continued to repeat them in the Seminole, Mexican, Civil and Spanish wars, and were only enabled to avoid the worst of them in the World War by the good fortune of having an historian for President.

To return to the naval hearings: nothing could so clearly have demonstrated our need, at so dangerous an era of the world's history, for an enlightened public opinion on military policy, contributing not only to the support of the necessary outlays for armament, but to that intelligent continuity of purpose and practice so essential, not only to efficiency, but to economy.

It was regrettably apparent that many of the witnesses, some of them persons of prominence and indeed distinction in various walks of life, those "leaders to whom the various parts of the country are accustomed to look for guidance," in Mahan's phrase, had no idea of the true nature and functions of an army or a navy, or of the meaning and connotations of the term "national defense." This has been true, however, at every period of our history. For example, in 1898, we discover General Nelson A. Miles compelled to make vigorous protest against politically inspired orders directing him to proceed to Havana with 70,000 men and capture the city: despite the facts that he did not have transports for half that number, nor modern rifles for a third of it, nor a single modern piece of field artillery; that two-thirds of his force would have necessarily been raw volunteers, led by untrained officers; that Havana was defended by 128,000 Spanish troops armed with Mauser rifles and with many batteries of excellent guns, behind formidable fortifications; and finally that the object of the war could far less dangerously and expensively be achieved, as in the end it was, by the navy's blockade of the Cuban coast — to which the destruction of Cervera's fleet and the capture of Santiago were, in the strategical sense, but incidental.

Against this sort of aberration in war, and against the effects of indifference, false economy, and ignorance in peace, we have, it is well to repeat, but a single safeguard: the enlightened public opinion already mentioned, a public opinion which will insist upon the creation of military institutions adequate to their purpose; or, more correctly, to the adaptation in size and quality to that purpose of our existing military institutions.

Such a public opinion will, in large degree, afford its support to those military measures which are in harmony with our national characteristics, and with the examples and lessons afforded us not only by our own history, but by that of other free peoples who have had to deal with similar, though not identical, problems.

Chapter III

THE MILITARY INSTITUTIONS
OF FREE PEOPLES

". . . a military system which, recognizing the opposition to large standing armies, will still be compatible with the safety, the honor and the liberty of our people."

EMORY UPTON,
BREVET MAJOR GENERAL, UNITED STATES ARMY,
The Military Policy of the United States.

FOR THE LAST five hundred years, the political history of mankind has been in large part the history of the struggle for liberty — for the recognition of individual human rights and for the control of government by the governed.

Where liberty has been achieved, it has usually been achieved — as in the case of our own republic — by the sword; and by the sword, on occasion, it has been destroyed. Free peoples in arms — as the Swiss and revolutionary French — have maintained their liberties against external dangers; and subject peoples, like the modern Greeks and the Italians formerly subject to Austria, have won their freedom by armed revolution against their tyrants. But also, free peoples have passed beneath foreign yokes when unprepared or unable to protect their liberties by force, as the unhappy history of Poland bears witness; and freedom already established has even at times been destroyed by the military institutions created for its defense, as was the case with both the First and Second Republics of France, and as is today being attempted in Spain.

It is therefore perhaps not unnatural that there should exist, among the masses of the citizenry in the remaining free nations of the world, an instinctive distrust of strong military establishments, born of the lessons of the past when standing armies either were the instruments of established tyranny, or became the means of achieving the ambitions of those who sought to subvert the popular liberties.

On the other hand, the perils to liberty from external aggression have perhaps never, or at least not in the course of the last century, been so acute and pressing as they are today.

It seems therefore quite pertinent, and even essential, to examine the military institutions of the various modern democracies as a preliminary to the examination of a proper military policy for the United States; since it is from the lessons of experience, the experience of others as well as of ourselves, that alone can be derived an accurate appreciation of the basic principles which should guide our own course. In a department of national affairs where error is so fraught with peril, too much care cannot be exercised to profit by the example and the mistakes of those who have had similar problems to solve, and in the solution have found safety or disaster. There is a rather marked tendency on the part of American students of this subject to examine our own military past to the exclusion of that of other nations, and to seek to derive therefrom all guidance for the future; as though our history were unique and all-sufficient, and as though other nations had not encountered difficulties similar to ours and risen to prosperity or fallen to ruin by the appreciation or the neglect of those immutable principles which regulate the conduct of war and the orientation of military policy, and which have differed only in degree since the day of the cave-man.

The instinctive distrust of "standing armies" is nowhere more marked than among the smaller democracies of Europe. It is not by chance that Sweden, Norway, Denmark, Holland and Switzerland possess armies which are little more than national militias, based on a small professional cadre supplemented by annual classes of recruits training for but a few weeks; it is not by chance that in Switzerland, for example, no officer of the national forces could, until very recently, attain a rank higher than that of colonel save in time of war or great emergency. The underlying thought is to make the national defense forces a part of the nation, responsive not to the leadership of a military caste, but to the feeling and aspirations of the people generally; and allowing the young men of the country to be subjected to military control just so long, and no longer, as is necessary for them to acquire the minimum of military instruction essential for the security of the state against external aggression. In this manner the requirements of external security are balanced against those of internal security.

But while internal security can be guarded by domestic laws and institutions within the control of the state, external security, being in part dependent upon the acts or forbearances of other states, can less often be considered as assured beyond question. For a state possessing powerful and potentially dangerous neighbors, the weighing of the two demands involves the nicest judgment. Usually, the requirements of external security will prevail; especially if the foreign menace be active and readily to be perceived.

Estimation of foreign dangers involves examination of the strategical factor, which, in such estimates, is basically geographic. The questions to be asked are — who can attack us, by land, sea or air? With what force? And how quickly? When these questions are answered, some idea can be gained of the necessary defensive measures and forces required. These need not be equal in number or power to the forces which may be brought to the attack; indeed, in many cases they cannot be. But if they are to afford any measure of security, they must, in the case of a small power, be sufficient to make the cost of successful attack more than the potential enemy will feel victory worth, or, if the political situation be such as to make the arrival of help from an ally a possible factor in the situation, the defense forces must be sufficient to hold out until that help arrives. In the case of a great power, the defense forces ought to be sufficient to act offensively, paradoxical as such phraseology may sound, since the best assurance of being allowed to remain at peace is a well-founded suspicion on the part of possible disturbers of your peace that if they do disturb it, they will in the outcome be worse hurt than you will.

When the requirements of external security, weighed in the strategical scale, are thus determined, it may be found that a military establishment is imposed on a free people which not only will be a financial burden, but may be of a size disquieting to those who believe that standing armies are ever a peril to freedom. Fortunate indeed will be that state which, in its geo-strategical estimates, has found that a great part of its defense can be committed to the care of a navy; since a navy cannot conquer territory, nor over-run provinces, nor be in any other way the instrument of a *coup d'état* against the popular liberties, save insofar as on occasion (as has happened in Chile and Brazil) its guns might dominate a seacoast city, or its sailors and marines (who will always be comparatively few in number as compared with the size of an army raised by universal service) can be landed on shore.

Examining the application of these principles to the liberal nations of the Continent, aforementioned, we discover that in each case where the army is still dependent on a short-service system with small permanent effectives, there is some countervailing advantage, geographical or political, which allows the demands of external security (for a strong army) to be partially disregarded. Thus, Norway and Sweden are to all intents and purposes insular, their land frontiers being remote and almost without communications; both nations are by this accident of geography enabled to depend partly on navies for their protection, and though neither has the resources or indeed the need for an oceanic fleet, they maintain respectable coast-defense forces composed of small armored ships, torpedo craft, submarines and mine-layers which would certainly have a high defensive value in dealing with any attempt at oversea invasion of their territories, or of a blockade of their coasts. Finland, on the other hand, equally liberal in institutions, maintains an army based on full universal service (1 year or more with the colors) and has a peace establishment 50% greater than Sweden's, though she has little more than half Sweden's population. The reason is, of course, her long land frontier with a major military power — Soviet Russia. The Netherlands, which has a short-service army, has a scheme of inundations for the defense of her German frontier which gave the Germans pause during the World War, and she is moreover defended by the known and historical determination of Great Britain to allow no great Continental power to become established in the Low Countries. In the Netherlands Indies, it may be observed, the Dutch maintain a professional regular army considerably stronger than their peace establishment at home, and they are rapidly building up a sea-going fleet of cruisers and flotilla craft and a powerful air force for the defense of their rich colonial domain, which is uncomfortably close to ambitious Japan and uncomfortably far from home. The Swiss, favored by difficult terrain and still more by the rivalries of their three mighty neighbors, feel secure enough in their mountains with their native militia. But Belgium, with frontiers less naturally strong, learned in the last war the price of military unreadiness, and today has a very large military establishment compared to that of Sweden or Holland. Czechoslovakia, the one outpost of democracy in Central Europe, must bear a huge military burden in proportion to her resources.

In the case of every one of these smaller free nations, however, the best assurance of safety is from external aid in case of need. The Scandinavian nations have a mutual defense pact, and together they are sufficiently formidable to give any great power pause; France and Britain cannot permit Germany to seize Belgium any more now than in 1914, nor could Germany regard complacently a French occupation of that country; none of Switzerland's neighbors could allow that republic to be overrun by any of the others; and the international relations of Czechoslovakia are headline material at this moment and may have plunged Europe into war ere these words are in print. The military establishments of these lesser States are, then, defensive forces in the purest sense of the word; in the military term, they are delaying forces. Their mission is to hold all or part of the national territory and to delay the enemy until help can come.

With great powers, as already observed, this is not true.

A great power may of course form alliances, but it must be prepared to fight alone if need be; and it must be prepared, in the face of menace, to oppose a counter-menace of so formidable a nature as to require the most careful consideration from those who would attack it. It is not sufficient merely to await attack, leaving to the prospective enemy the choice of the most favorable time and place, and putting him under no greater apprehension than that his attack may fail. A great power which adopts such an attitude, and creates military institutions adapted and trained purely for defense, in fact invites the very calamity which it seeks to avoid, since it reduces to a minimum the element of risk for those with whom its interests may clash, and who may be tempted to advance their side of the argument by force. Such a temptation is difficult to resist precisely in proportion to the risk involved; the power which deliberately minimizes that risk must be prepared to crook the pregnant hinges of the knee in the face of arrogance and injury, or to fight, at last, under conditions of the gravest disadvantage.

This lesson France learned to her cost in 1870, when, having mistakenly ascribed the victories of Prussia in the Seven Weeks' War entirely to the breech-loading needle-gun, the French had re-armed their infantry with a better breech-loader and had taught their troops a defensive doctrine based on the belief that their superior fire-power would annihilate the Germans. But, as Moltke points out, "they ruined by that doctrine the spirit of their army." Bismarck took few risks when he maneuvered France into war, gained two provinces as a result — and consolidated the German states into a German nation which is at this moment France's most formidable rival. It is a lesson which France is unlikely to forget; the Maginot line of today must be considered as much a springboard for offensive or counter-offensive operations as it is a shield.

Of Europe's two great democracies, France, having a land frontier with two powerful neighbors and a third frontier as a source of potential danger, must ever maintain a very strong army, supported by a powerful air force; her navy must always be a secondary and auxiliary consideration. France cannot afford to give too much weight to the problem of internal security; the external danger is too pressing in a nation which has been four times invaded since first she became a republic. It has chanced, as a matter of fact, that both the First and the Second Republics were overthrown by military *coups d'état,* and the Third Republic has at least twice (in Boulanger's time and during the Dreyfus affair) been in serious danger of a similar fate. The only possible safeguards lie not in reduction of the military establishment (in face of Germany and Italy with swiftly rising, numerically superior populations while that of France has been stationary for years) but in seeking as far as possible to assure the maintenance of democratic loyalties by the personnel of the army, and especially by the officer corps. Thus in France, a very large proportion of the officers of the regular army are obtained from the ranks and from specially qualified officers of the reserve; the cadet schools (Saint Cyr and the Polytechnique) have no such practical monopoly of officer appointments as have Sandhurst and Woolwich in Britain.

But a greater factor of safety lies in the memories and traditions of freedom. The Third Republic has now endured for sixty-seven years. There are few living Frenchmen who have ever known any other form of government; none who can today take an active part in affairs. The present personnel, both officer and enlisted, of the French army, has grown to manhood under the Republic, and their fathers before them. This was not the case when Leclerc's grenadiers drove the deputies of the First Republic from the Chambers, for the First Republic had endured but a few years, and the leaders of the *coup d'état* had grown up under the Bourbon kingdom; the Second Republic had had a still shorter life when it was destroyed, and those who overthrew it were habituated to the institutions and trappings of monarchy. Liberty is a dish for which the appetite grows with eating; loyalty to a republic is a thing of the spirit in a sense which loyalty to a king can never be. And new loyalties, like all tender shoots, must be nursed and tended and given time to grow, to fasten their roots in the soil, to gather strength to resist the gusty winds of faction and treasonable ambition.

Two other weaknesses of the French military system are worthy of note; one is the present use of considerable numbers of native colonial troops in France, in an endeavor to

[29]

make up for the previously-remarked stationary French man-power, and the dependence in war upon large native drafts drawn from North Africa, the assurance of the communications for this purpose being now the primary war-mission of the French navy; the other is the French tendency to subject naval and military establishments to sudden and radical changes due to the pet ideas entertained by the various sets of politicians who enter and leave the seats of power with, at times, almost kaleidoscopic rapidity. One Navy Minister will be all for building battleships, while another thinks battleships a waste of good francs and plumps for aircraft and submarines. Continuity of policy, so essential to sound progress in military affairs, has suffered severely in France from this cause, as it has in the United States; while from such perils British conservatism largely protects Great Britain, though occasionally tending to lean too far the other way in its instinctive dislike of all change, however salutary.

Britain, the other great democratic power of Europe, has had perhaps good reason for conservatism in the larger view of military policy, since that which she has unswervingly pursued for more than a century has served her well indeed. Britain has historically enjoyed an advantage of position, due to her insularity, which has enabled her to dispense with the burden of conscript armies. By maintaining a predominant navy, adequate to the task of assuring the safety of her vital sea communications, and a small long-service professional army for defense against raids, for colonial policing, and on occasion for expeditionary operations of limited aim (such as the Crimean and Peninsular wars) of which the navy assured the communications, the British people have been enabled to indulge to the full their inborn distaste for standing armies, while creating a vast colonial empire and enjoying at home, in perfect safety, the prosperity and power epitomized in the phrase "business as usual."

British military policy is particularly worthy of extended

examination here, because, as will be seen, it presents many instructive points of analogy with American conditions. Furthermore it is certainly the most striking and successful modern example of the strictly naval policy which all insular states ought to pursue if they can, since a great navy is not so onerous a burden either upon the treasury or upon the productive life of the nation as a great army, nor is it likely to be (as previously noted) a peril to liberal institutions.

The whole enormous structure of the British Empire, extending to every continent and every ocean of the world so that it may be truly said that the sun never sets upon the British flag, rests upon seapower — upon the ability of the British navy, in peace as in war, to protect and control its far-flung maritime communication routes, which alone link together the several parts of the Empire and over which passes the vast commerce which is the foundation of British life, maintaining the industries of the British Isles with raw materials and bringing to the people of those Isles the very food by which they live. If those routes can be severed by an enemy, not only will British industry be no longer able to operate, but British folk will starve; for the industrial revolution transformed the British Isles from a self-supporting agricultural community to one almost wholly industrial in character.

The manner in which British seapower assures the safety of these thousands of miles of sea communication is not generally understood. How often does one read, in ill-informed discussions of this subject, that the British navy, strong as it is, could not act with concentrated force against an enemy "because it has to protect the colonies." One might suppose that its manner of accomplishing this purpose would be to station a battleship or two in front of every colonial port!

The actuality is quite different. To begin with, the strength of the Royal Navy is calculated upon the basis of the strength of the fleets with which it may have to deal in war. The underlying principle is that a navy must stand or fall by its strength at the time war breaks out, since the construction of battleships is a matter of two or three years and even more under certain conditions. Moreover, the construction of all types of warships is strictly limited by available building ways, drafting lofts, and machine-shop equipment of a highly specialized nature, such as gun-factories, armor-forging plants, turret shops and torpedo works. The instruments of seapower can no longer be turned out in every seaside village which is close to a good stand of timber, nor is the skilled and highly trained personnel necessary for their fabrication to be found in such abundance as were ship carpenters and riggers in the days when the building of a frigate was little different in its technical demands upon the artisan from the building of an Indiaman or a trading-brig.

So considered, and to go back no farther than the era of the modern, turreted battleship, it was decided in 1889, with the rise of Russian seapower and the coming into force of the Franco-Russian alliance, that the British navy must be at least equal to the two strongest non-British fleets combined: those of France and Russia.

The National Defense Act of that year authorized a systematic building programme and adopted the principle of constructing both capital ships and cruisers in homogeneous groups, or squadrons, capable of acting together with far greater efficiency than the "collection of samples" of which the navy then consisted, no more than two ships being alike in tactical qualities.

The Russo-Japanese war (1904-5) wiped out Russian seapower, and that of France began to decay from neglect, while about this time France began to be regarded as an ally rather than a foe; but the swift rise of the German navy and the expressed ambitions of the ruling class in Germany afforded new anxieties to the Admiralty. The appearance of the all-big-gun battleship mounting eight or more heavy turret guns instead of the traditional four made the greater part of Britain's pre-dreadnought fleet obsolescent for first-line purposes; rapid German construction of the new type imposed on Britain the need for increased construction if she would not be over-matched, and the financial burden thereby created became so formidable that the Two-Power Standard was of necessity reduced to one of 50% superiority over Germany alone. Even that was maintained with the utmost difficulty, since in Germany the British had a rival whose technical and industrial quality was equal if not superior to their own.

It is not alone by numbers, but by distribution at the moment of the outbreak of hostilities that a navy must stand or fall since, if correct principles are violated and too great peace-time dispersion has been permitted, an active enemy will exert himself to prevent the error from being corrected, will take all advantage of such central position as he may possess to prevent the junction of opposing detachments and to destroy the latter in detail. The point of greatest interest in the British naval policy of the period under examination is therefore the manner in which they disposed their navy to meet the changing exigencies of the international situation. One hears today an occasional lament by British writers for the good old days in which battleships were stationed in the Far East to care for British interests in that quarter. The truth is that, while battleships did find their way to the China Squadron, their number was kept to an absolute minimum and was accurately proportioned to the Far Eastern battleship detachments of the potential enemy, on the corollary to the principle of concentration (called by Mahan the ABC of war) that any considerable detachment is justified only insofar as it contains and neutralizes an enemy detachment of equal or superior force.

Thus in 1898, a period of considerable international stress in the Far East, the British had in those seas three battleships (two of which were a temporary loan from the Mediterranean Fleet) and seven first-class cruisers. The potential enemy then was Russia, whose Far Eastern squadron consisted of two battleships and six first-class cruisers, to which France could add a single armored ship. The strongest British concentration was in the Mediterranean, guarding the principal line of Imperial communications; here, based on Malta and Gibraltar, were ten battleships and two first-class cruisers, against an exactly equivalent Franco-Russian total. The Channel Fleet of eight battleships and two first-class cruisers offset the combined force of the French Northern Squadron and the Russian Baltic Fleet, superior by one ship in each class but greatly inferior in fighting power. Finally, there was at home a reserve force of twelve older battleships and two first-class cruisers, against which France had three and one respectively and Russia nothing of consequence. This force, coupled with the very considerable ship-for-ship superiority of the British as against the French and Russians, gave Britain a considerable margin of strength above her two-power standard. It will be observed that at Gibraltar, Malta, Suez, and Aden she possessed positions which dominated the line of communications between the Channel and Mediterranean Fleets on the one hand, and between the Mediterranean and China forces on the other; thus conferring upon her navy a strategical mobility which would have enabled it to concentrate its power in any direction that might have seemed advisable. She was able to confront every considerable detachment of the "enemy" with a force not only immediately superior (all things considered) but capable of being quickly reinforced; while it would have been quite impossible for the Franco-Russian alliance to concentrate a superior force against any of the three British detachments without at the same time insuring the simultaneous arrival of additional British forces. The apparent dispersion of power thus turns out to be a true concentration in the most acceptable military sense of the word. Meanwhile British second- and third-class cruisers were scattered over the vast trade routes on guard against possible raiders, assuming the duties of Imperial police, and in general performing the job of showing the White Ensign and upholding British prestige and authority without in any way detracting from the fighting power of the main forces, to which those distant operations would in war actually become a direct and necessary contribution of far greater value than would have been the presence with the flags of the several Admirals of a superfluity of small cruisers.

The situation in 1914, at the outbreak of the World War, was quite different, though its basic principle was the same. The "enemy" was now Germany, and under the terms of the Triple Alliance the contingency had to be considered of Germany being supported in the Mediterranean by the combined fleets of Austria-Hungary and Italy. Britain, on the other hand, could rely on the support of France. Under these circumstances, the British navy almost wholly abandoned the Mediterranean, leaving that theater to the French, reinforced by four British battle-cruisers. All remaining battle-cruisers and every all-big-gun battleship of the British navy were concentrated in home waters, giving a superiority in capital ships actually ready on August 4, 1914, of 24 to 16 over the Germans, while the Franco-British strength in the Mediterranean was on the whole a little better than equal to the combined forces of Austria-Hungary and Italy plus the one German battle-cruiser on that station. Again there was no possibility of a combination against either Allied detachment without the other being able to intervene, while the major enemy force (the German High Seas Fleet) was contained by a markedly superior force. In the Far East, at this time, there was a German squadron of which the principal ships were two very good armored cruisers. The British China Squadron had one fast pre-dreadnought battleship, one large and one small armored cruiser — a force almost double that of von Spee in fighting power, but one which (lacking first-line ships) took nothing from Jellicoe at home. Again all the British light cruisers not absolutely required with the fleet were scattered over the various distant stations — and, in the event, since the Germans had a few scattered cruisers too, proved none too many for the task of running down these menaces to seaborne trade.

Today, with the rise of Japanese hostility to British interests in the Far East, Britain is feverishly building capital ships while she employs the resources of diplomacy to calm the troubled waters of Italo-British rivalry and to limit the new German fleet to 35% of British tonnage. When the new ships are finished there will be twenty-five ships of the line wearing the White Ensign, which will permit a sizable detachment to be based on Singapore, where the base facilities for them are already waiting, while still maintaining Anglo-French superiority over the Italo-German forces in European waters. The home forces will have a central position as regards Germany and Italy, preventing junction; the Far Eastern fleet, though it probably cannot have superiority over Japan, will be of sufficient strength to make perilous any Japanese excursions into the South China Sea, and thus adequately to defend against Japanese ambitions not only Malaya, but India, Australia and the Netherlands Indies.

In this manner combining strategy with diplomacy and making each serve the ends of the other, Britain has contrived to maintain the safety of her far-flung lines of communication along which moves the trade that is her life-blood. It will be remarked, in each of the cases instanced, how the whole fabric is dependent on the security of the base, of the British Isles; whose harbors sheltered the ships of the reserve fleet; whose geographical position gave a central location as between France and Russia in 1898 and between Germany and Italy forty years later, and enabled the close blockade of the German fleet in 1914-1918; and from whose boundless industrial resources flowed out the vast stream of new ships, munitions, and supplies which maintained the whole in being and in readiness for action, from the battlefleets down to the last distant cruiser rolling in the swells of the Pacific. Bases such as Gibraltar, Malta, Aden, Singapore, and Hongkong have no resources (or very little) of their own and are wholly dependent upon renewal of their stores by sea as these are depleted by the demands of the ships the bases serve. Bases in the great Dominions are of course in a different category; but it is notable that the very bases upon which the British naval system most depends are those which are in turn most dependent upon the maintenance of open communications with the British Isles.

It follows necessarily that the British navy can maintain the security of the Empire's sea communications only while the base of the whole structure is itself secure; that is, while the island of Great Britain is safe from being directly assailed. For centuries this safety was assured by the navy itself, commanding as it did the waters across which any invading army must come. The vast combinations of Napoleon in 1805 (for which he had been preparing for two years) were intended to secure the command of the Channel for but a brief period of time, sufficient to pass across the army of invasion he had collected at Boulogne. With this army he hoped to humble the nation in which he recognized his most dangerous and implacable enemy, inexorably devoted to the principle of preventing the undue aggrandizement of any continental power. Here again we will find the principle of "controlled dispersion" actually as a concentration. The French fleet was scattered in its various naval ports, before each of which was a British blockading squadron approximately equal to the French inside. Napoleon hoped that his various detachments could escape, at favorable opportunities largely dependent upon the weather, and that while the British were hastening off in various directions to search for them, the French might concentrate, by a prearranged plan, in the West Indies, and thence return to the Channel in greatly superior force to that of Admiral Cornwallis, who, with the Channel Fleet, was blockading Brest. The British Admiralty, however, was well aware of the danger, and by a single order completely dealt with it; they directed that in case of the escape of any French squadron, the British force blockading it should promptly fall back on Cornwallis, thus assuring that officer of always having a force equal to any which the French might concentrate against him. The subsequent operations, which ended with Nelson's victory at Trafalgar, need not be recounted in order to illustrate the point: that while the French could not command the Channel with a superior force, their invading army could not pass over to England, and thus the British fleet, even while scattered before several French ports or, later, while part of it under Nelson was pursuing Villeneuve to the West Indies, was yet securing Britain against the peril of invasion; and this though not a single ship of the line was actually in the Straits of Dover in front of the concentration-point of the Grande Armée, this duty being adequately performed by lesser craft.

The close of the Napoleonic Wars inaugurated a long period of peace and prosperity for Britain, broken for just under a hundred years only by the Crimean War (fought by the navy and a comparatively small regular army, with a limited objective) and various colonial wars, in only one of which (that in South Africa) were the British people called on for anything like a major effort. During all this period their naval system preserved their peace, guarded their trade and their Empire, and relieved them from the cost and peril of maintaining the huge armies of their Continental neighbors. During all this period they were, by reason of their insular position and their command of the sea, perfectly secure against even the possibility of the invasion of their homeland by a hostile army.

In 1898, for example, the Regular Army in the British Isles numbered but 131,000 officers and men, with 51,000 more in the Colonies, exclusive of India, where both the British and native establishments were supported at the cost of the Indian budget. The second-line citizen forces (militia, volunteers and yeomanry), somewhat analogous to our National Guard, totaled 338,000. At this period the Metropolitan Army of France had a peace establishment of 570,000 and the Colonial Army of 50,000; there were trained reserves totalling 3,600,000. The peace strength of the German army was 545,000; the Italian, 216,000; the Russian, 896,000; and the Austro-Hungarian, 349,000 — with, in each case, masses of trained reserves running up into seven figures. All these Continental armies were organized on the principle of universal and compulsory service; which means that every youth who was physically fit was called up for service at the age of 20 or 21, and though there were certain exemptions, the greater part of each country's young manhood spent from two to three years with the colors, withdrawn from productive employment. It was a necessity imposed by geographical and political conditions which Britain, by geographical accident, was enabled to escape. During the hundred years of peace, the gradual transformation of the professional armies of the Napoleonic wars into the mass armies of "the nation in arms," begun during the Napoleonic period by Prussia under the spur of necessity and gradually evolving into the magnificent military machine which crushed France in 1870 and forced all Continental Europe to adopt the German model, left Britain wholly untouched, complacent in her security, guarded by her mighty fleet.

Yet with the beginning of the twentieth century, two events occurred which were to bring that seemingly eternal insular security into deadly peril; the one for a time, the other permanently, setting up an entirely new set of conditions in warfare. The first event was the passage, in 1900, of the new German Navy Bill, laying the foundations for the rise of a new naval power in Europe, and declaring that, "to protect her sea trade and colonies, Germany must have a fleet so strong that a war, even with the greatest naval power, would involve such risks as to jeopardize the position of that power." The second occurred on December 17, 1903, at Kitty Hawk, North Carolina, when the Wright brothers achieved the first successful flight in a man-made flying-machine.

The first event brought about that Anglo-German naval rivalry and diplomatic tension which directly contributed to Britain's prompt intervention when a German army marched into Belgium in August, 1914; for from the viewpoint of British security it was unthinkable that the Belgian coast-line and perhaps the French Channel ports should be permitted to fall into the hands of a strong and aggressive naval power which also possessed a powerful army. The British navy contained the German Fleet behind its minefields; and the small British regular army was despatched to the mainland to assist the French and Belgians in rolling back the tide of invasion. But it quickly became apparent that the regular army was not going to be enough; and for the first time Britain found herself compelled to raise a great citizen army for operations on the continent, to put forth the whole of her power and resources to defend herself from a peril more menacing than even Napoleon's threat at Boulogne. The outcome of the titanic struggle which followed is of course well known to the reader; and it is perhaps natural, though scarcely the part of wisdom, that at its close the British people should have promptly returned to the system which had served them so well for a century. The terrible sacrifices which had been demanded of them, the frightful price of blood which they had been compelled to pay for victory, engendered a psychological recoil from the very idea of having to repeat the experience. "Never again!" was the cry which rose from the tormented and bereaved hearts of millions of Britons.

Yet during the war there had blossomed into early, but not yet full flower the seed which the Wright brothers had sown in 1903. The airplane had become a recognized and increasingly dangerous weapon of war; German airplanes had in fact raided London on more than one occasion, doing considerable damage and taking a toll of some hundreds of lives; French and British airplanes had likewise raided the Rhine cities of Germany. The Channel had been bridged; and as aeronautical progress moved forward by leaps and bounds during the years following the war, the nature and extent of the direct menace to Britain began slowly to be understood. The rise of Mussolini in Italy and Hitler in Germany, the vast expansion of their respective air forces, and the increase in the speed, range and carrying power of bombing planes combined political and technical factors which in sum total sounded the death-knell of Britain's comfortable motto: "In war or peace, business as usual!"

The base and foundation stone of the Empire, the island of Great Britain, is no longer untouchable by enemy assaults. But two hours of flight separate London and the German airdromes along the North Sea coast. Nor can the reply be to create an air force superior to that of Germany, as the Britain of 1900-1914 created a superior navy; for the vast theater in which air forces operate, the illimitable reaches of the sky, being cubic rather than plane, offers infinite opportunities for evasion. Ground defenses against air attacks, while far more efficient than in World War days, still afford no absolute assurance of safety to so great an area as London, or to the many tempting industrial targets of the Midlands. Probably the best deterrent against air attacks are offensive air operations of one's own; yet in the case of Britain and

Germany, Britain is in such a duel at a grave disadvantage. Not only are the German targets much more widely dispersed, Germany possessing no single center comparable in proportional importance to London, but the distances from British dromes to many points in Germany (Berlin for instance) are much greater than the distance from the most westerly German air bases to London. German planes attacking London would have to fly but a few moments over British soil before reaching their bomb-release points, coming in from the sea in unpredictable directions with all the advantage of surprise; while this advantage could not be possessed by British planes attacking targets anywhere in the interior of Germany, though they took off (as very likely they would) from French bases.

It comes down to this; that if there is no war for a year or two — if Germany avoids conflict until she is ready, until she has made up, at least in part, for the lag in the training of annual conscript classes and of officers imposed upon her by the now defunct Treaty of Versailles, and until she has re-equipped her military forces with such items as heavy artillery and tanks — the day will come, is, in fact, now within sight, when Britain will have to build up an army capable of acting swiftly in support of the French in another great Continental war. For the only way she can secure herself against the air menace is to attack and conquer the bases from which it proceeds. This, of course, is setting aside the possibility of surprise air attacks at the very outset having a decisive effect, as the Italian General Douhet prophesied and as some people still believe possible; the weight of considered military opinion is against this possibility, on the evidence of Madrid, Barcelona, Hankow and Canton.

The reader will of course ask himself why, if the air weapon was unable to obtain a decisive effect in these instances, it should be so serious a menace to Great Britain. The answer is that while air attacks will probably not be decisive against the British any more than against others, they can so disrupt the industrial life of the nation, its communications, its consolidated electric-power system; they can inflict so much injury upon its dockyards, arsenals, and harbored shipping, that if allowed to continue they might in the end reduce the nation to impotence. Of course it would take time to do this; and equally of course, before such a result was attained, there would be large numbers of armed and furious Britons on the Continent striving to get at the source of all the slaughtering and destroying. Which is precisely the point: that the security of Britain today depends on her ability to act offensively against a Continental enemy, not only by naval blockade and intermittent and limited attacks, but with her full strength, land, sea and air; she is in this respect no longer in a privileged position, but is in little better case than the Continental nations themselves, and the sooner a realization of this fact seeps into the British consciousness, the safer the British nation will be. For a Britain able instantly to throw her full weight into a Continental war, and a Britain able to do so only after a considerable period of time spent in training citizen armies, present two very different types of risk to an aggressively-minded power which may be weighing the chances of peace or war.

Thus the coming of air power has taken from Britain the security which her navy once gave her, and will soon present her with the necessity of organizing her military institutions on the same basis as those of her neighbors; while her distant communications still impose upon her the necessity of keeping up her navy on the old, though fluctuating standards required by the seapower at the disposal of other states with which she may come into conflict.

Some mention ought to be made of other maritime states which have pursued a naval policy. Portugal, in the days of her greatness, built up a huge colonial empire in Africa,

Asia and South America, an empire which drained her small resources of men and material and left her too weak at home to defend her land frontier against Spain. The result was the sixty years' captivity (1580-1640) and the loss of the greater part of her colonial domain, and of her prestige and influence in world affairs. Holland, similarly, sent her ships and traders into the four corners of the world, establishing herself at various times at the Cape of Good Hope, in Brazil, the West Indies, Java, India and Malaya. Yet at home her rulers must forever be dabbling in the military and political troubles of the Continent, not always with good reason, and in the end it was the drain of these continental wars which exhausted the finances of the nation and toppled it from its position among the great powers of Europe.

The principle which all this discussion seeks to illustrate is not the oft-stated but historically inaccurate premise that no nation can support a naval and a military (army) policy simultaneously; but that no nation can depend, for its chief defense, upon a predominantly naval policy while it has a vulnerable land frontier across which enemy land forces can assail it. Nowadays, this applies as well to air power; the homeland, the base upon which all naval operations depend, must be out of reach of direct attack by any means whatever save those with which the navy can adequately deal. Otherwise, there must be maintained land military establishments sufficient to insure the safety of the country, and the navy either becomes auxiliary thereto (as in the case of France) or must be maintained at high strength in addition thereto (as in the case of Britain).

It will by this time be clear to the discerning reader that the strategical position of the United States is in many ways strikingly like that of Britain prior to the rise of the German navy and to the development of air power.

It is not identical, of course; situations of such complexity cannot be. Thus, the United States is not dependent on external communications for its food, nor for any save a few (though some of these are quite important) of its industrial raw materials. Yet if it were deprived of the use of the sea, if not only its foreign trade but its coastal and inter-coastal maritime traffic were interrupted, great hardships would be imposed on its people and the result, while not as immediately drastic as would be a similar calamity to the British Isles, would assuredly in the end be disastrous. The United States has no world-girdling colonial empire; yet it does possess outlying positions, the safe-keeping of one of which (the Panama Canal Zone) is absolutely vital to its military security, and of certain of the others scarcely less than that. Moreover, it has interests and responsibilities in connection with its sister republics of Latin America which (while disclaiming all political control therein) are still essential to its interests and safety, and can be adequately maintained only by seapower. Its military position as compared with that of 19th century Britain is, in the words of Thucydides, "if not exactly the same, yet very similar."

The fundamental fact stands clearly out, that today the United States is the only one of the great powers of the world which is in a position to pursue the old British policy, that is, a naval policy, in matters of national defense. Japan, whose insular position has often been compared with that of Britain, has seen fit to indulge continental ambitions which have provided her with land frontiers and involved her in continental warfare; her position in this respect is more like that of the Britain of the Hundred Years' War, during which the nation was constantly involved in bloody struggles to maintain her position in France, than the Britain of modern times, which has rigorously eschewed the acquisition of positions on the mainland of Europe (save Gibraltar) despite the fact that her armies have been fighting there intermittently throughout all her history. Moreover, as the range of aircraft increases, Japan is just now coming within bombing range of the Russian positions at Vladivostok and elsewhere.

The United States alone is out of reach of the air weapon as proceeding from any land base in the possession of a conceivably hostile power; and she possesses no land frontiers across which could come armies of sufficient strength to menace her security.

These priceless privileges, the gifts of her geographical and (in the military sense) insular position, enable the United States to depend upon her navy, primarily, for her defense and for the maintenance of her rights and vital interests; and since a navy can rarely be a menace to free political institutions, the United States may thus pursue a military policy consonant with her internal security in this respect, at no sacrifice of external security.

Moreover, our American institutions have now been sanctified by a hundred and seventy-three years of existence under one form or another — a hundred and fifty-one under our present Constitution, more than twice the life of the Third Republic of France; and in that time have but once been seriously disturbed by armed internal revolt, an occurrence which itself antedates the establishment of the Third Republic. A free people whose democracy has so bravely and firmly endured the vicissitudes of time and fortune, upheld by the devoted loyalty of their military services, may well feel confident in the endurance of that loyalty; while they would be ill-advised indeed to fundamentally alter the nature and intrinsic character of those tried-and-true services unless compelled thereto — as Britain is today — by external apprehensions of the gravest sort.

Similar apprehensions, as we have said, the United States need not entertain. There is no necessity for drastic reorganization, change, and realignment in our military policy; our military institutions can be, and should be, built on the secure foundations of the past — natural and gradual growths rather than rash and dangerous experiments.

Every effort should in fact be made, by wise provision and thoughtful foresight, to insure such a continuity of military policy as has distinguished the past policy of Great Britain, and to protect that continuity against the vicissitudes of politics, as well as against the national predilection for attractive novelties; while avoiding so far as possible that intense British conservatism and resistance to all change, however beneficial, which manifested itself in stout opposition to the successive introduction of explosive shells, steam propulsion, armor and the breech-loading gun into the Royal Navy, and today makes thorny the path of British naval aviation.

Foresight in military policy is even more essential for a naval power than for any other, since the instruments of naval power take longer to create and can rarely be improvised after the outbreak of hostilities, while they must be adequate in military qualities to deal with the instruments of similar purpose possessed by others. Some sort of defense can be made against a hostile army even by the men of a *levée en masse,* hastily embodied and armed when the approach of danger is perceived; especially if the defense is aided by the terrain. Madrid was thus successfully defended against Franco in 1936, and time was gained for bettering the Loyalist military institutions. A modern navy, however, cannot be thus conjured up out of merchant ships and yachts; it must (as previously remarked) stand or fall on its constitution and state of readiness when war begins.

The size, the disposition and the armament of our military establishments, of course, must be subject to the exigencies of our foreign policy and the requirements of sound strategical principles; and it is these considerations, as conditioned by our geographical position and by the existing international situation, which must now be examined in detail.

[47]

Chapter IV

THE RELATIONS OF OUR FOREIGN AND MILITARY POLICIES

"Our country! In her intercourse with foreign nations, may she always be in the right; but, right or wrong, our country!"

STEPHEN DECATUR,
COMMODORE, UNITED STATES NAVY.
Toast given at Norfolk, Virginia, April, 1816.

As ANTECEDENT to any discussion of national strategy, the foreign policy of which that strategy is or may become the instrument must be determined. No general could estimate the size of the force he required for a given mission until he knew what the mission was; when a new warship is to be designed, the first question to be asked is, "What is this ship meant to do?" Just so must a Government decide upon the questions of the military policy and the military institutions of the State. They must first know what they want to do; and they must, like the general just mentioned, also know what forces, and how strong forces, may be brought into opposition to them: not necessarily in actual war, but in the course of that interplay of interests which we call international relations, and which is in the last analysis dependent upon actual or potential force. Finally, they must — also like the general — calculate the element of risk.

[48]

In examining the relations of our foreign and military policies, it is primarily necessary to know what the foreign policy is, to answer questions such as the following:

(1) What external policies do we have, and what external interests, which may run counter to the policies or interests of foreign states?

(2) For which, if any, of these policies and these interests do we propose to fight if they cannot be otherwise conserved?

(3) With what nation, or nations, may we thus become involved in war?

(4) If we adopt such and such a policy, and we come into conflict with a given nation or nations, can we accept the risk of war? Or can we make that risk so great for our opponent that he will let us pursue our ends in peace?

It is thus seen that foreign and military policy are interdependent, foreign policy being under the necessity of keeping within the bounds of military adequacy while military policy is under the necessity of providing a sufficient support for foreign policy and of anticipating its requirements.

The exigencies of such interdependence, as has been pointed out, are more easily arranged in an authoritarian state than in a democracy.

In considering those questions affecting the external policy of a democratic country, which in turn must shape the size and character of its military institutions, the first consideration to be given weight must be that of the popular feeling with regard to such of those questions as have been the subject of any perceptible crystallization of opinion. It will be, as a practical matter, impossible for those charged with the immediate handling of foreign relations to run a course very far counter to well-established popular wishes. Such a course would lack that internal support upon which all continuity of policy depends, a state of affairs which, in a nation where free speech and a free press are among the pillars of the state, could not long remain unknown to the foreign governments upon whose interests the unpopular policy might have incidence.

At the very beginning of our discussion of American foreign policy, therefore, arises the difficulty of determining just what the weight of popular opinion on this matter and that may be. It is not always possible to say with any certainty. Like any other free people, ours are concerned with their daily affairs as individuals, to the considerable, though not entire exclusion of matters concerning distant folk of whom they have little real knowledge. And in foreign as in military affairs, there is a tendency to substitute easily remembered clichés for actual thought. There are a thousand Americans who could today offer a questioner a reasoned and informed discussion of the probable course of the pennant race in either of the great baseball leagues next season, to one who could similarly discuss the future of Pan-American relations, though the latter subject is one which may in years to come much more weightily affect the lives, incomes and fortunes of a far greater number of our people than the former. There are a thousand who when Japan is mentioned will say: "Yeah! We gotta lick those Japs one o' these days!" to one who can appreciate the tremendous strategical difficulties of such a war.

Yet there are certain points upon which there is an apparent agreement among us which approaches unanimity. This is evidenced either in continued adherence by our Government to a given viewpoint, with continued popular support therein, or by means no less tangible, but requiring more careful evaluation on the part of the observer, afforded in the columns of the press (not neglecting the "Letters to the Editor"), in magazine articles and radio speeches, and in various other forms of public discussion which, while of course giving representation to extremes of opinion on either hand, also afford some clue to the settled mean between those extremes which represents the view of the majority of citizens.

Where a firm popular support can be determined, as to any point of foreign policy, it is quite futile to waste time in considering, in connection with the coordination of foreign policy with military policy, a different and perhaps more nearly ideal state of affairs. The practical soldier deals with facts as they are; he does not, in preparing an estimate of the situation based on the enemy's known presence at a certain place, confuse the issue by long discussions of how much nicer and easier it would be for his side if the enemy were not, as he is, intrenched on Line A-B, but were instead on the march from C to D. Just so must the statesman, who is responsible for the foundation work of military policy, avoid the treacherous pitfalls of wishful thinking. It is useless for American public men, for example, to consider what the situation might be if the United States were to join the League of Nations, because it is perfectly apparent that the trend of public sentiment in the country is definitely away from such a proposal; we are much farther from such participation than we were fifteen years ago. The incidence of foreign upon military policy can be here clearly exemplified, if consideration be given to the responsibilities imposed by the League Convenant and the very considerable difference between the military force required to execute such responsibilities and that required if our military commitments be freed of such artificial burdens.

What, then, are the determinable points of foreign policy upon which we may say that there is any fixity of opinion in this country?

First, that already mentioned — a disinclination, growing stronger year by year as experience proves it sound, to commit the United States in advance to active participation in the quarrels of the Old World, by joining in any collective agreement whatever which may lead to that end. Whatever opinions may be entertained by individual Americans on this subject, the unshakable fact is that such opinions cannot be translated into policy unless and until popular opinion in this country undergoes a radical change with respect thereto; a change of which there is not the least sign at the moment. The country-wide reaction to President Roosevelt's "quarantine" speech at Chicago affords ample proof of the present views of our people on this point.

Second, that European and Asiatic territorial expansion in the Western Hemisphere shall not be countenanced. This is, of course, a part of the much-discussed Monroe Doctrine, which made the United States the guarantor of the self-determination of the peoples of Latin America as against European powers. This guaranty is still in force, though the method of its application has undergone considerable alteration as the political and military stability of Latin-American nations has developed. There are also to be considered in this connection the problems to be anticipated from new methods of aggression, less flagrant than outright conquest but tending to the accomplishment of the same purpose. Without examining in detail the very complex possibilities which may thus be envisaged, it may be suggested, by way of example, that at the moment there can be little doubt that American public opinion would be vigorously stirred by, let us say, an attempt (inspired and supported from Germany) by the German population of the Brazilian state of Rio Grande do Sul to secede from the Brazilian union and place itself under the protection of the German Reich, as the American inhabitants of Texas seceded from Mexico a hundred years ago and came within a few years into our own Union. It would be somewhat less likely that our people would support the Government in taking a strong line, involving the possible use of force as a final arbiter, toward the development of political movements within the Brazilian nation which might result in the eventual emplacement of

German influence as the "power behind the throne" without any public and concrete acknowledgment of that fact. Yet such a situation might at a crucial moment be quite as productive of unfortunate military conditions for us in the South Atlantic as the establishment there of an outright German colony. (It should be understood that this is an example merely, designed to show how what is called the new technique of conquest has altered the conditions of Monroe's time, and is in no way intended as a commentary upon current affairs in the territory of a great and friendly neighbor state.)

In our attitude toward these matters, it is probable that time will produce a gradual development in harmony with the trend of events and of a growing public realization of new types of international procedure.

This attitude ought to be conditioned by an element of responsibility toward our neighbors for their safety against Old World aggression. Resentment against our somewhat paternalistic attitude in regard to this matter in the past, and especially to the remarks thereupon by certain of our less tactful statesmen, is gradually giving place among thoughtful Latin Americans to a realization of the new dangers — as yet, perhaps, remote, but growing more threatening with every passing day — which are springing up beyond the seas. Not in such times can they confidently demand, as Lord Bryce phrased it in the days before the World War, "Since there are no longer rain clouds coming up from the east, why should our friend, however well-intentioned, insist on holding an umbrella over us?" Despite irritation born of Latin pride, it is plain that today the dangers of the situation, and our relation thereto, are well enough recognized in Latin America. None of the southern republics (with the exception of Argentina) has sought to create military institutions adequate for its own defense, nor has a desire to be independent of our help caused any practical combined military policy to receive implementation. Improvements in the Brazilian and Chilian navies have again and again been postponed, during the last twenty years, doubtless for adequate internal and especially financial reasons; but that these would weigh in the balance against the exigent demands of external security, if there were not a comfortable feeling that that security is already assured by our historic policy, seems little likely. Indeed, even the comparatively modern and powerful Argentine fleet, reinforced by the whole effective naval strength of Brazil and Chile, could not without help assure (as against either Germany or Italy, for example) control of the sea-approaches to South American ports. It is our fleet upon which, in the last resort, the peoples and the governments of Latin American tacitly depend for that assurance.

The third, and sole remaining angle of foreign policy toward which is directed the attention of a crystallized public opinion in this country, is the matter of foreign immigration. Strictly speaking, this is a domestic affair; but its bearing upon our relations with other states is so considerable that it must be considered under the head of foreign policy. Few impartial observers would disagree with the statement that the majority of our people are unalterably determined to impose the most severe restrictions upon foreign immigration unless and until our domestic labor market becomes inadequate to our requirements — a condition which now seems highly unlikely to arise. The tendency will probably be to impose even further checks upon immigration than now exist. Furthermore, the *total* exclusion of Oriental immigration seems likely to continue to command popular support.

These three fixed points of popular determination can hardly be the subjects of official discretion and must be considered for the present as immutable, not only by foreign nations, but by those who may from time to time occupy the seats of executive authority in this country; and by both executive and legislative officials these points must be taken into account in the formulation of that military policy which must support them if need be.

The writer expresses no opinion as to the virtues, or otherwise, of these several points; he merely calls attention to their existence and to the practical necessity of conforming thereto in the interests of national security. An example, not directly connected with foreign policy, may here serve the purpose of emphasizing the need for the practical acceptance of facts as facts.

A generation of effort and compromise and patching-up on the part of some of our greatest statesmen of the past could not overcome the basic determination of the majority of the inhabitants of the Northern states that slavery should be extinguished, or at least not be permitted further extension; nor the basic determination of a majority of the people of the South that they would not submit to what they termed coercion in a matter which they considered bound up with their economic security. The matter had at length to be resolved by a great civil war, when it came to involve, as it did, the integrity of the Union. A more realistic policy which took into account the fundamentals of public feeling in the two sections of the country and, eschewing the vapors of sentiment and the pressure of extraneous details, sought with wisdom and courage for some method, not of immediate compromise but of permanent solution in the interests of the entire nation, might have spared us the horrors of internecine conflict. As contributory to the success of such a solution, a military policy which would have provided the National Government with a force of 30,000 regular troops immediately available for action and suitably distributed would have rendered the appeal to arms much less attractive, because far more risky, while if that appeal had nevertheless been made such a force would, in the considered judgment of most military students, have quickly suppressed it and returned the question at issue to the status of peaceful negotiation and adjustment.

The three fixed points of foreign policy which we have so far determined upon may be briefly restated:

(1) The people of this country will not stand behind any league or covenant with foreign nations which may automatically involve us in a war not of our making, and in which we have no direct and vital interest.

(2) They will not permit any territory in the Western Hemisphere to become the field of forcible exploitation and colonization by any non-American nation.

(3) They are resolved to continue at least the existing measures of restriction upon foreign immigration.

The military factors involved in the first of these are negative rather than positive, tending to permit us to devote our military attention to our own requirements rather than to the possibility of having to contribute to an international force for the suppression of an "aggressor state." The second point will be dependent first of all upon naval power and, since it is a fixed and definite policy, will be further considered in the chapters having to do with our national strategy. Military assurance of the third point is implicit in the whole question of the defense of our home country from aggression or force however and wherever applied, and involves no military considerations peculiar to itself.

As to the nations with which these three points might bring us into conflict, the first is unlikely to do so with any, tending rather the other way; its influence is in any case indirect, since if it involves us in war it will do so because of the fact that there may break out a war into which we shall eventually be drawn but which might have been prevented had we been members of some group for collective security — a rather vague and uncertain speculation.

The second point may bring us into collision with any European or Asiatic power which has or may later acquire

interests or ambitions in Latin America. As a practical matter this means any of the other six naval powers of the world,
or a combination of two or more of them. But the number
may be reduced as the factor of probability is examined. Our
principal commercial rival in Latin America is Great Britain,
which also has possessions in the West Indies, Guiana and
the Falkland Islands, and on the African coast, enabling her
to operate in the Caribbean and South Atlantic. It may however be doubted that Great Britain has the smallest desire to
increase her already unwieldy empire by acquisitions in
Latin America which could only be secured at the price of
war with the United States — the one naval power whose
fleet would be a serious threat to British naval security in the
Atlantic. Nor does France, also a Caribbean colonial power,
seem a likely aggressor in the Western Hemisphere, having
also all the colonies she well can manage and — like Britain
— having pressing difficulties at home. Soviet Russia has at
present no navy capable of carrying on overseas operations.
There is a remote possibility that she might be a source of
difficulty in case of Communist disorders in Mexico, or perhaps elsewhere, by seeking to supply arms and ammunition
to partisan groups as she did in Spain. But such an eventuality would be easily dealt with if we decided to intervene,
since we command the seas over which the munitions must
come. There remain the other three naval powers, Germany,
Italy and Japan. All have Latin American interests, all have
been industriously propagandizing among our southern
neighbors, all are pushing their trade and financial interests
there very hard, all are aggressive, authoritarian states, all
have very recently extended their dominions by the use of
force. They are therefore proper subjects for suspicious examination, especially when it be considered that they have a
tri-partite agreement among themselves, nominally against
"international Bolshevism," but which is said to contain
secret military clauses. Who knows but tomorrow or the next

day the government of some South American republic might be discovered to be a very hot-bed of "Bolshevism" if it suited ambitious purpose so to define it? According to the Nazi press, the government of Czechoslovakia is "Communist"; according to the *Giornale d'Italia,* all Spaniards who are supporting the Loyalist cause are creatures of the Moscow Comintern. There are many Germans and Italians (by blood) now living in South America, who might turn out some day to be in need of aid against "ruthless Communist oppression." There is an Italian police mission in Peru; there are Italian air missions in Venezuela and Chile. German officers trained the Bolivian army; German military ideas are influential in army circles in Argentina and Mexico. Japanese influence is particularly strong in Peru and in Salvador, which latter country was the first foreign power to recognize the independence of Manchukuo. Germany, Italy and Japan are all trying to get some of Mexico's expropriated oil, and having little cash (especially the first two) are making all sorts of barter offers and, no doubt, offers of other sorts.

Possible antagonists under point two are therefore quite clearly indicated.

Point three, if it brings us into trouble at all, seems most likely to be a contributory cause to a conflict with Japan, with whose sensitive people our Asiatic exclusion laws have been a sore point. The only other nation with whom we could conceivably have any serious trouble over immigration might be Mexico.

Beyond our three fixed points, of course, lies a wide field in which may arise many difficulties, as to which there exists no determinative degree of fixity in American public opinion. Such fixity may in future take form under the pressure of events, but remains a matter for immediate speculation and therefore cannot be the subject of a firm orientation of policy, either diplomatic or military.

Without attempting unduly to foresee future events, examination may be given to some of the possibilities in this field which may engage the present or future attention of our government, and which bear upon our military policy in greater or less degree.

The determination of the future status of the Philippine Islands is perhaps the most important and pressing, as it is the most dangerous question in the field referred to. At the moment, their status is something like that of one of the Dominions of the British Commonwealth of Nations; but it is a temporary status, to be transformed, under existing legislation, into complete independence in 1946. There is a noticeable trend, however, in Philippine opinion — reinforced by some American opinion — toward a modification of this prospect, toward some sort of political adjustment which would retain the islands under the American flag, while allowing the Filipino people autonomy in matters of local government. In the military sense, the Philippines are our one indefensible outpost, being beyond the radius of action of a fleet based on any of our securely fortified naval stations. Their geographical position is unfortunate in another sense, in that they lie within easy reach of the Japanese fleet, which can command, without undue effort, all their maritime communications; their possession would not only give the Japanese a more secure grip, in turn, upon the maritime communications of China, but would greatly advantage the Japanese in any future struggle in the Orient with either Great Britain or France, since from Philippine bases the Japanese could conduct operations against Singapore or Saigon with far greater facility and far less risk than would be the case if Formosa were — as it is now — their southernmost outpost. Furthermore, if established in the Philippines the Japanese would be able to make direct contact with the Dutch East Indies, their nearest source of fuel-oil, and one which is yearly increasing in proportionate importance to them. One cannot suppose the Japanese military and naval leaders, who in that country exercise so great an influence upon external policy, to be blind to these very great strategical advantages; advantages which, unless the nation exhaust her resources in continental wars, should go far to make her absolute mistress of the Western Pacific and the economic ruler of all East Asia.

The attainment of an absolutely independent status by the Philippines would leave those islands, in the military sense, at the mercy of Japan. For, despite much brave talk, it is inconceivable that the Philippine budget, burdened with the weight of maintaining government services now possessed at the charge of the American taxpayer and harassed by the inevitable loss of revenue incident to the gradual application of American tariffs to Philippine sugar and other products, could support a military establishment large enough to constitute a risk which would outweigh, in Japanese calculations, the very great advantages to be derived from acquisition of full control of the Philippines.

Present Japanese assurances of good intentions may be accepted at face value, without in any way affecting the action to be taken by some future Japanese government confronted with conditions now unforeseeable and impelled by that instinct of self-preservation which is the first law of nature in international as in individual affairs.

American policy must therefore determine whether it is willing to envisage an eventual acquirement by Japan of the Philippine Islands either by force of arms or by the no less inexorable, though slower, processes of economic pressure and exploitation. It is not a question which can be answered, off-hand, in the hearty affirmative which some American discussions have given it; an affirmative in which the writer admits having joined, on occasion, but which sober second thought has led him to re-examine.

Quite aside from the eventual results to our foreign trade,

to our strategic position in the Pacific and to our general status in world affairs which might accrue from such Japanese aggrandizement, there must be considered the immediate impact upon American public opinion of forcible action by Japan to the subversion of Philippine independence. Our flag has waved over those islands for forty years. Hundreds of American soldiers have died, and many more have suffered the effects of wounds and tropical disease, in the course of their acquisition and policing. Millions of American dollars have been spent there. The Philippines came into our possession, originally, as a result of one of the most boldly and capably directed naval operations in our history, and one which still holds a high place in the imagination of our people, as does the memory of its author in their affections. Many an American to whom the names of Porter, of Macdonough, of Truxtun would mean nothing will react proudly and instantly to any mention of Dewey and Manila Bay. Many others amongst that smaller group who have given more extended and informed consideration to the subject of the Philippines and have therefore to do with the molding of less-informed opinion, take the gravest view of the responsibilities which we have assumed toward the Filipinos — responsibilities not lightly to be cast aside by a people with any sense of duty, or any feelings of national honor.

The practical question which must be answered, therefore, by those who advocate complete washing of American hands of responsibility for the future of the islands, is whether our people would acquiesce, not in the policy itself, but in the accomplishment of its possible result — the hoisting of the Japanese flag over territory where the Stars and Stripes have flown for a generation, have always flown within the memory of the majority of our living citizens.

Here we are dealing with intangibles; but, examining our history, weighing the past reactions of our people under circumstances far less dramatic and exigent (as in the Oregon dispute — "Fifty-Four-Forty or Fight!"), the balance of probability seems to incline toward their refusal to stand by while Japanese ambitions in the Philippines were accomplished *vi et armis*.

But there must also be considered the cold, hard military fact that we possess neither a fleet of sufficient strength to dominate the sea-communications between Japan and the Philippines in the face of the Japanese navy — having due regard to the factor of distance — nor any adequate base in those distant seas from which our fleet could operate. Hence, if Philippine independence is achieved, as will be the case unless there occurs a Congressional *volte-face* on the subject, and if, subsequently, that independence is endangered by Japanese action, which is a very strong possibility and one not to be ignored in the formulation of a foresighted policy by ourselves, we face the further possibility of being compelled, suddenly and without adequate preparation, to fight a war to preserve that independence under the most unfavorable military conditions.

There are two possible courses of action which we might adopt to discount this unhappy contingency: the one military, the other diplomatic. We might proceed to such measures as shall enable us to defend the Philippines under any conceivable circumstances. But this would require so very large an addition to our military and naval establishments, both at home and in the Western Pacific, and would be so certain to be regarded as a challenging menace by Japan, that we ought not to consider it if there is another way out of the difficulty. The other way may be found in some international arrangement for neutralizing the Philippines and guaranteeing that neutrality. It is to the very definite advantage of Great Britain, France and the Netherlands that this neutrality be maintained. Where self-interest is so clearly involved, some arrangement should be possible. Of course we ought to participate — would have to participate — as co-

guarantors in such a treaty. We could not simply divest ourselves of our responsibilities and hand them over to others.
But those responsibilities would, if we had to fulfil them by
action, be greatly lessened in cost if we were assured of the
support at least of the British, French and Dutch squadrons
now in the Far East, and of the admirable bases of Singapore and Soerabaya. These factors would make all the difference in the world in the amount of effort we should have
to put forth in a war for the defense of Philippine independence. They would also make a great difference in the
quality of the risk which Japan would have to calculate before making an attack upon that independence.

There have been suggestions in the past that Great Britain
might find the acquisition of a Philippine Dominion advantageous. If so, there ought to be a *quid pro quo* in the
matter of British West Indian possessions. This however is
a rather remote possibility. There is no present discernible
sentiment in the Philippines for such a change.

The Philippine problem is certainly one which is, for us,
most menacing in its possibilities of foreign embroilment,
and steps for its solution must be taken without undue delay,
lest we be caught unprepared to meet difficulties which can
now be foreseen and prepared against.

But there are other problems in which the relationships of
our military and foreign policies require examination.

That of Pan-American relations is perhaps the most important of these, may be even more pressing in certain aspects
than that of the Philippines. The relations to be here considered are those which do not involve the matter of defense
against foreign territorial conquest — our second "fixed point"
of policy, already discussed — nor the complementary question of a mutual defense pact.

There remain however certain other Pan-American questions which may be briefly examined at this point. We cannot, of course, isolate the nations of the Western Hemisphere

[63]

from all contact with the nations of the Old World. We have wisely foregone all political ambitions at their expense, and are endeavoring, by our present attitude and conduct, to allay suspicions of our imperialistic intentions born of a century of sad experience.

Beyond question it is our true policy to seek the cordial friendship and to study to deserve the confidence of our neighbors, rather than to adopt toward them that attitude of superiority and tutelage which they have in the past so seriously and justly resented. To this end, to the healing of old wounds and the introduction of an era of better feeling toward "the Colossus of the North," President Roosevelt's good neighbor policy has greatly contributed.

But it would be foolish of us to assume, as some public utterances on the subject of this policy have set forth, that we have to do with democracies of like character and aspirations to our own. With notable exceptions, such as Costa Rica and Colombia, we have rather to do with more or less complete dictatorships, in some of which individual rights are subjected to as grievous a tyranny, and liberal political institutions are quite as non-existent, as in any authoritarian state of Europe: the *forms* of republican government are generally maintained, but the substance is lacking.

There is therefore always a danger of irresponsible action to our injury, or to that of some European power, by the ruler of one of these countries; and there are recurrent disorders in certain of them, incident to personal rivalries for power or to popular resentment against misrule.

As sovereign states, these neighbors of ours have diplomatic, commercial and financial relations with the powers of Europe and Asia, which in many cases involve interests and nationals of the latter, cause foreign money to be invested in Latin America, bringing foreign citizens into situations of personal peril arising from politically unstable conditions, and excite, on occasion, foreign ambitions looking toward the extension of commercial and financial interests into the political field.

It must also be remembered that many of our Latin American neighbors have no reason to love us; and that Europe and Asia afford them a market for their products (this is notably the case with Argentina) which we, for reasons not within our control, cannot hope to equal.

On the other hand, some experienced observers of Latin American affairs are arriving at the conclusion that there is a growing realization of the menacing character of certain European political trends among Latin American public men; the successive withdrawal from the League of Nations of one American state after another is perhaps one evidence of the fact that our neighbors are realizing the inadvisability of becoming tied in any way to a trans-Atlantic political institution.

We have of course our own financial and commercial enterprises in Latin America, and must realize that whatever soothing words may be uttered in Pan-American conferences, and whatever noble sentiments may burn in the hearts of our public men, nevertheless those Americans who have a financial stake in Latin America will continue to be with us, and to exercise pressure at opportune moments to obtain political action from our Government in support of their interests. This has in the past had some unhappy results; it has given rise to the term "dollar diplomacy," with which we are still reproached in Latin American circles. But there is little validity in an attitude which assumes that we shall never make the old mistakes again; nor in one which starts out from the position that a man who invests a dollar in a foreign country becomes *ipso facto* an international outlaw, deserving neither the consideration nor the support of his government, whatever injustices may be done him. In our differences with our neighbors we have not always been in the wrong — nor always in the right. What is needed is a closer approach to reality in these matters, as in others, a realization that governments composed of imperfect human beings are still and will continue to be liable to error and injustice; that in all relations between a great power and a lesser one (and, for the life of the present generation at least, we shall continue to be far more powerful than any Latin American nation) the temptation to associate justice with might for the achievement of a desired end may not always prove resistible.

This very brief general survey of the Pan-American situation in no way pretends to be a complete examination of its innumerable ramifications, nor a brief for any particular form of solution of the problems presented. It is rather offered as a general background against which the reader may consider the incidence of those problems upon the military policy of our country, and as a preface to an examination of certain particular situations which may affect that policy.

Mexico, one of our two continental neighbors, demands our first attention in this respect. Since the termination of the Mexican war of 1846-48 our relations with that nation have been good or bad almost in precise proportion to the degree of public order and stability of government prevailing south of the Rio Grande. When there has existed a Mexican government capable of keeping peace in its own house, the two powers have in general been able to adjust by the usual processes of diplomacy such differences as arose between them. When, as has happened, Mexico has been torn by disorder and revolution, we have had difficulties which at times have involved the use of armed force on our part; these difficulties have not always arisen with the recognized Government of Mexico, or with the faction holding Mexico City, but more generally with more or less irresponsible "governments" or military leaders operating in, or for the moment controlling, the border States of the Mexican Republic. Our border has at times been raided by guerrilla bands, our citizens murdered and their property carried off; one such attack, that on Columbus, New Mexico, in 1916, by the followers of Francisco Villa, resulted in a punitive American military expedition into Mexico which eventually reached a strength of 12,000 men. Subsequently it was thought necessary to call out almost the entire National Guard for border service. The Villa raid on Columbus is said to have been motivated by Villa's desire to involve the recognized (Carranza) Government of Mexico, which he opposed, in difficulties with the United States, and is mentioned as an instance of the sort of problem which Mexican disorder may require us to meet. It is worthy of note, as indicating Mexican feeling, that when General Pershing's column moved into Mexico it met with armed opposition from Carranza's forces, despite Carranza's violent antipathy to Villa, just as the operations of the Mexican War for the moment consolidated Mexican factions of an earlier generation behind the President, Santa Anna, who was supported in his resistance to the United States troops by men who were, before and afterward, his deadly and implacable enemies.

One military aspect of the need for preparing against future disturbed conditions along the Mexican frontier is the need thereby imposed upon us for maintaining considerable forces of horse mounted cavalry; since, on both sides of the border, but especially on the Mexican side, there is a dearth of communications and of local sources of gasoline supply which would gravely impede the operations of troops wholly dependent on motor transportation. In such a terrain, horsed cavalry alone is adequate to the more extended duties of the service of security and information, insofar as these cannot be performed by the Air Corps or by armored cars operating directly on the roads.

Our present relations with the Govenment of Mexico have developed a serious difference of view relating to the expropriation by that Government of American-owned or leased properties, both mineral and agricultural, and subsequent failure to compensate the owners. Any expression of opinion as to the rights and wrongs of this matter would be inappropriate to these pages; the point to be considered is the possibility that American acceptance of the Mexican viewpoint might lead to similar confiscatory action on the part of other Latin American states, and still further and more embarrassing difficulties. Moreover, American property has by no means been singled out for expropriation; the same action has been taken against British holdings, and in consequence diplomatic relations between London and Mexico City have been severed.

While perhaps inapplicable to the present situation as it exists, it may not be unprofitable to recall that in 1861 a clearly analogous set of circumstances — based on Mexican debts, in part at least acknowledged but conditioned in value by Mexican inability or refusal to pay — resulted in joint military action by Great Britain, France and Spain against the port of Veracruz, and eventually in a French military occupation of the country and the establishment of a monarchical regime, headed by a foreign Emperor whose throne was supported by French bayonets. This state of affairs, unacceptable as it was to the United States, came about while we were engaged in the Civil War and was only terminated when, at the conclusion of that conflict, General Sheridan with a considerable army was despatched to the Rio Grande frontier and an ultimatum couched in no gentle terms was delivered to Napoleon III.

Prudence will suggest taking thought against a similar situation, arising at some future moment of preoccupation on our part, perhaps not to be so happily resolved in the outcome.

The quite evident domestic difficulties of the present Mexican government are disquieting to contemplate; and Mexican endeavors to sell the products of the expropriated properties to foreign powers, notably to the "have-not" group who are hungry for oil and other raw materials but unable to pay save by barter, are enmeshing that government in still further external complications, the end of which is obviously not yet; nor can its nature be accurately predicted. Meanwhile our own attitude toward Mexico is conditioned not only by the protests of those citizens who have suffered losses, but also by the support of the Cardenas government, "right-or-wrong," by a section of our so-called liberal press and opinion. This opinion, identifying the character of the Mexican government with the political parties of Europe commonly grouped under the denomination "Popular Front," sees in all Mexican-American differences only a struggle between Mexican "liberalism" and American "entrenched greed," concerning itself thus with its ideological sympathies rather than with truth.

It is, however, not only Mexico which by reason of geographical location has a direct and immediate interest for the framers of our military policy. This applies also to all the independent nations of the West Indies, and all those of Central and South America which have Caribbean littorals; for the Caribbean is the antechamber of the Panama Canal, the vital link in our interoceanic communications. This strategical fact is one of the bases of the now-repudiated policy of "non-recognition" of revolutionary governments, so much criticized at home and abroad, by which we did in practise raise up and cast down governments in the various republics in question. The difference in stability between a government granted American recognition and thereby able to obtain loans, arms and supplies, and one suffering under not only the lack of these privileges but the moral damper of our opposition and occasionally our application of force in addition, was frequently decisive. By this policy, and by the use of force, we have at one time or another since the turn of the century interfered in the affairs of almost every one of the Caribbean nations, with greater or less effect according to circumstances. In certain of them (Haiti, the Dominican Republic, Cuba, and Nicaragua) we have temporarily effected military occupation of the country and exercised direct control. Our motives cannot always be dissociated from "dollar diplomacy," though we have on the whole greatly benefited the countries under temporary occupation in the way of sanitation, roads, public works, and the establishment of order and justice. We have acted sometimes under the pressure of extreme provocation, sometimes under motives of policy amounting to practical necessity. We are accused by some critics of having granted the aegis of our recognition to regimes of a dictatorial and indeed bloodily tyrannical nature (as in the Dominican Republic today). Such criticisms do not always give due consideration to the fact that we are primarily interested in the maintenance of order in a region so definitely associated with our military security, and that we have neither the right nor any colorable reason to dictate to sovereign states what form of government they shall adopt or to assure the maintenance therein of the democratic institutions which we prefer for ourselves, but which we ought not to assume the responsibility of imposing on others; save as such a foreign government may by its acts or omissions menace our own security. It is then that the supervening right of self-preservation and military necessity becomes paramount: military necessity being in such a case none the less exigent because it is sometimes concerned with an anticipated future menace rather than an immediately existing one.

Despite our repudiation of the policy of "non-recognition," therefore, and of unilateral intervention by force, we cannot wisely assume that there will not arise future occasions compromising our security and the peace of the Caribbean which will require some action on our part in the defense of our vital interests. Our new attitude has been most helpful in improving our relations with the Latin

American states as a whole, and allaying their suspicions of our motives. It is a wise attitude, in the long view, and one which ought to be the keystone of our conduct. But there must be worked out, probably by the painful process of trial and error, some method for dealing with such dangerous situations as we have had to face in the past; in default whereof, the demands of military necessity are quite likely to assert themselves to the detriment of our friendly relations with all our Latin neighbors.

In the affairs of Cuba we are directly and vitally interested, in a military sense, not only because of her nearness to our shores and her commanding position as regards the Gulf of Mexico, but because we hold by lease from the Cuban government the harbor of Guantanamo, which, in a war of which the Caribbean was the theater, would be our principal naval base in those waters. The two republics of the island of Haiti have only less military interest for us; Panama is of course all-important. Another Central American republic, Nicaragua, may be the site of a future second interoceanic canal, for which surveys have already been made and the construction of which is now receiving public attention in this country. This possibility also involves Costa Rica, which borders part of the proposed canal route on the south and intervenes geographically between the two canals, and Honduras and Salvador, each of which owns a part of the shores of the Gulf of Fonseca (the principal indentation of the west coast of Central America) on the Nicaraguan shore of which Gulf we have, by treaty with the latter country, acquired future rights for a naval base which would be essential to the defense of the new waterway.

As exemplary of the foreign complications in any enterprise of such far-reaching consequences, must be considered the situation which might arise as between the United States and Great Britain, incident to the proposed Nicaraguan canal. Under the old Clayton-Bulwer Treaty, the rights and interests of the British and ourselves in an interoceanic canal were recognized as equal, and the canal was to be neutralized and unfortified; under the later Hay-Pauncefote Treaty, Britain gave up her equal rights as to control and participation, permitted fortification by us, but retained equality of treatment in the use of the canal, which is supposed to be open to the vessels of all nations, on equal terms, in peace and war. (Few governments, one imagines, least of all the British, will however be naïve enough to suppose that we would permit such use by a nation with whom we were at war.) But in this matter of a Nicaraguan canal, we might with some justice take the attitude that our inter-coastal traffic or, very likely, *all* American traffic should be exempt from the payment of tolls. This would as a practical matter amount to a subsidy to our merchant marine. Great Britain, on the other hand, unwilling to see American shipping gain such an advantage over her own, would undoubtedly enter a spirited protest and claim the application of the Hay-Pauncefote Treaty (whose terms lack something of complete precision on the point) to Nicaragua as well as Panama. It is to be noted that when the treaty was signed, the Nicaragua route was being considered as well as the Panama route and indeed was then more highly favored.

In leaving the Pan-American question, one further remark may be apposite. There is now taking place in Spain a bloody civil war, which has engaged the attention and the sympathies of many of our own people on one side or the other; and to a far greater extent, an extent indeed little realized here, has engaged an attention and a sympathy passing on to passionate partisanship among the peoples of Spanish language and culture to the south of us. In general, Mexican sympathy is with the Loyalists; the rest of Spanish America inclines on the whole to Franco. The Franco government has been recognized as the legal government of Spain by some American republics. If Franco wins, the feelings thus aroused by the war will unquestionably be exploited by the new government of Spain and by those foreign powers (Germany and Italy) who will then be in a position to influence it. The tendencies now evident are epitomized by a radio address delivered at Salamanca on September 15, 1937, by Dr. Julio Urrutia, Guatemalan Ambassador to the Spanish Nationalist Government, who said, in part: "My greeting is intended not only for Guatemala, but also for all the other Republics that make up the Spanish American countries, in whose names I take the liberty of speaking. . . . The friendship that the American Republics have for Spain through the ties of custom, religion and language grows closer and closer as time marches on. For this reason *I believe in a future and common destiny* [1] for all Spanish speaking countries. . . . May my closing words be a respectful greeting to the glorious, Supreme Heads of our countries, General Jorge Ubico, President of Guatemala, and Generalissimo Francisco Franco, Head of the Spanish Nation."

One may dismiss this as Latin rhodomontade; or one may see in it the indication of a trend which, continuing and burgeoning into fuller life, may have unpleasant implications indeed for the future of our Latin American relations. The new racial nationalism which is the basis of both Fascist and Nazi doctrine is a growing force in the world today. A "common destiny," on this basis, in which a puppet Spain controlled from Rome and Berlin marched side by side with Spanish-American nations, would assuredly direct its march toward ends hardly conducive to the peace of the Western Hemisphere.

Our relations with other states, outside of Latin America, are perhaps in no case so important as with the several countries which go to make up the British Commonwealth of Nations. In considering British policy as a whole, and especially in those matters which may involve the issues of

---

[1] Italics are the author's.

peace or war, it is well to remember that Empire policy is no longer "made in England." London, before any grave commitment, must consult Ottawa, Canberra, Wellington, and Cape Town.

Just at present our Government shows a tendency toward what is called "parallel action" with Britain in certain instances; but in relating military to foreign policy, it becomes immediately necessary to remember how closely — in the military sense — the British Isles are now tied to the Continental system, by the bridging of the Channel by the airplane. Dreams of an Anglo-American alliance, policing the world by an overwhelming seapower backed by financial power, and controlling vast resources of raw materials, all in the interests of peace, had once a very attractive ring. But the airplane has changed all that. The British Isles are vulnerable to direct attack; Britain will be compelled to act with all her strength to preserve her home security against the enemies that are already rising up against her.

This makes it dangerous for us to consider anything resembling a hard-and-fast alliance with Britain, since such an alliance may at any time involve us in a European war, in which Britain alone might have any direct interest.

It is necessary to speak quite plainly about this matter. The ties of blood and language are strong; but the security of a great nation is not based on sentiment, it is based on what some may think a cold and unfeeling appraisal of selfish interest. It is precisely on these lines that British policy toward ourselves has ever been conducted, and, from the British viewpoint, quite rightly. It is on these lines that our future policy as affects Britain and all other nations must, if it is to contribute to the national security, be likewise conducted.

This is stated in no spirit of hostility to Great Britain. With that nation we have many common interests and aims. Where such common interests exist, a policy of "parallel action" is frequently wise and proper. It may even extend itself, on occasion, into the field of common military action, or at least of military pressure reinforcing a common diplomatic effort. The United States cannot, of course, as some so-called American "isolationists" advocate, cut herself off from all such international processes, as is evidenced by the need of doing something about the future status of the Philippines. Frequently our influence in the diplomatic scale may serve the cause of peace, and in the preservation of peace we are directly and vitally concerned. But our influence in this direction will be proportionate not only to our military power, but to our disinterestedness in causes of local dispute, exterior to the sphere of our proper interests and security.

For our own security we do not need, and we ought not to create, instruments of military power capable of immediate action on land in Europe or in Asia. It is not needful that we should bear such burdens, nor deliberately propose to assume such dangers to our free institutions as might accrue from a great overseas war, requiring as it would the regimentation of every aspect of our national life. We cannot therefore offer any immediate military threat to a continental power such as Germany, in reinforcement of British policy, because we could at best but add somewhat to a British naval superiority already overwhelming, and supply a certain amount of additional air power which would take some time to make itself felt in the decisive theater of operations. By the time our resources could really be thrown into the scale, the issue of the war would have been decided, in all probability; decided in favor of Germany by land power reinforced by air power, on the battlefield and amidst the ruins of blazing cities: or against Germany, by the failure of her land and air power to obtain such a decision in the opening stages of the conflict. In fact, Germany is not, under present conditions, going to engage in any war, if she can help it, which she does not feel morally certain can be decided thus swiftly. Her resources in trained reserves and raw materials are wholly unequal to a long-drawn-out contest. If it becomes a question of resources, as between Britain and France on one side and Germany and Italy, let us say, on the other, the latter are automatic losers.

We could certainly help to make their defeat inevitable, in default of a quick and overwhelming victory on land. But that defeat is inevitable anyway, in such default. And they know it. If they gamble, they will gamble on a quick victory; and a quick victory is precisely the goal which we can do little to hinder them from achieving.

Therefore our support of Britain will not appreciably increase the element of risk to be weighed by the authoritarian powers as antecedent to a further appeal to force in Europe.

If they fail to achieve victory quickly, they are beaten, whatever we do. If they succeed, on the other hand, France and Britain will be compelled to make peace at the dictators' terms, and where will we be, if we have hastily intruded ourselves into the European mess? We will be at war with a victorious alliance, compelled to engage at long range in a struggle of attrition at sea from which we can gain little advantage, or else compelled to make peace under rather humiliating circumstances, with naught gained and much (in the way of prestige if nothing else) lost.

This is the present-day picture, as conditioned by existing military factors. In time to come, the picture may change. When it does, we may have to consider new orientations of policy. Which is precisely the reason why that policy should in its larger aspects be flexible and independent, adapted and directed solely to one end: the interests, the advantage and the safe-keeping of the United States of America.

When we come to consider the various great Dominions which make up, with the United Kingdom, the British Commonwealth of Nations, we find as to each of them (except perhaps Eire) a special situation of military interest to ourselves, in some cases quite unrelated to our general policy as regards the United Kingdom and Imperial interests as a whole. The tendency for each Dominion to assume more and more the attributes of sovereignty, including a foreign policy distinct from that of Downing Street, is becoming more marked. With three of them — Canada, South Africa and Eire — the United States maintains separate diplomatic relations. American influence in the Dominions is growing, is indeed the subject of jealous scrutiny by some Britons who regard it as a danger to the unity of the Empire.

With Canada, for geographical and historical reasons, our communion is particularly close. Canada today relies in large measure for her defense — especially in the Pacific — upon the United States navy. We are indeed, for reasons of our own security, irrevocably committed to the defense of our Canadian neighbors against external aggression. We are likewise so committed to the defense — in default of British ability to take care of the matter — of the British West Indies and all the other British possessions in North America and the Caribbean area; not in Britain's interests, but in our own, which cannot suffer the emplacement in any of these positions of the forces of an aggressive European or Asiatic power.

Across the Pacific lies the great island-continent of Australia, and close by, another British Dominion, New Zealand. Australia in particular presents tempting possibilities to an overcrowded nation such as Japan. Here is an enormous and almost empty continent, large portions of which are suitable for Japanese colonization under climatic conditions acceptable to the Japanese peasant — as Manchukuo is not, while the fertile regions of China and Korea are already overcrowded with a peasantry of even lower living standards than the Japanese. Today, Japan cannot think of Australia. It is beyond her reach, and beyond her power to absorb even

[77]

if she could reach it. But tomorrow, Australia may be face to face with a Japan which, victorious on the Asiatic mainland, may have behind her Imperial resources of the most tremendous nature and which may, in New Guinea, have acquired a position on Australia's very threshold. Then it would need only the day of Britain's weakness, or inescapable engagement in Europe, to bring to Australians the end of their dream of isolation, of detachment from the cares of a warring world. Historically, no nation has ever been able to retain, save by force of arms, a vast territory which her people would neither develop and use themselves nor permit others to use. There is in this matter the working of an economic law which has brought all Africa under European flags, which has created in the southern part of that once negro continent a great Anglo-Dutch commonwealth, which has destroyed the feeble civilization of the North American Indian, which brought Spain and Portugal and their successors to South America, which indeed has been exemplified in the creation of the Australian nation itself in territory where once the blackfellow ranged free and undisturbed from Cape York to Port Philip and from the shores of the Pacific to those of the Indian Ocean.

In the event of any Japanese threat to Australian security, the interests of the United States would, in the judgment of the writer, be very definitely and clearly involved. We could hardly afford to sit quietly by and watch the growth, across the Pacific, of an Oriental empire of such grandiose proportions as would result from the acquisition by Japan of the Australian continent. Such growths, such vaulting ambitions do not stop at shore-lines. Japan today is one thing; a Japan so aggrandized would be quite another, would presently dispose of resources superior to our own, directed by a single control to the accomplishment of ends which would inevitably reach across even the vast Pacific and become our immediate concern and peril. It is a far-away prospect; it is not an eventuality of the morrow, yet it is one which, even now, it is well not to ignore in the orientation of our external policies.

It is to be noted that Canada, Australia and New Zealand are all in the same strategical position as ourselves in one respect: that is, they have no threatening land frontiers,[1] they have our privilege of defending themselves first upon the sea. But they all lack the essential complement of their geographical security, an adequate navy. Australia does have a certain naval establishment, to which additions are being made; it will consist, when complete, of five modern cruisers and a destroyer flotilla. But it could not hope to resist for long, even consulting the factor of distance, the fleet of a great naval power with its core of armored battleships. New Zealand has two cruisers, lent from the Royal Navy; Canada has six destroyers. The ultimate dependence, in all three cases, is upon the British navy or — to an extent considerably acknowledged in Canada, to an extent less openly acknowledged but nevertheless present in Australia — upon the United States navy. All three Dominions have small air forces. All three depend almost entirely, as to land forces, upon a citizen army resembling our National Guard.

The Union of South Africa has extensive land frontiers with the colonies of Portugal and Belgium. There is moreover some anxiety there lest at some future date Germany be in a position to demand return of the former German colony of Southwest Africa, now under Union mandate. The Union maintains no navy, but has contributed to the cost of refitting the Royal Navy base at Simonstown. In other respects its defense organization resembles those of the other Dominions. Its security is of interest, but not vital impor-

---

[1] An exception might be made as to Canada, in case of an Anglo-American war. In this unlikely event her exposed position would almost assure a policy of neutrality on her part.

tance, to the United States because of its position in the South Atlantic.

Our other relations of military consequence with the several nations of the world may be very briefly treated.

With France we have few if any conflicting interests, and a long tradition of friendship. France is an American power, possessing several islands in the West Indies, a foothold on the coast of South America, and two small islands to the south of Newfoundland. Our attitude toward any attacks upon these French possessions would be similar to our attitude in respect to the British West Indian islands. In the Pacific, France also possesses a number of islands which might have future interest for us, notably the Society, Tuamotu and Marquesas groups which lie on the route between Panama and our own South-Sea outpost of Samoa. One small French island, Clipperton, lies off the coast of Mexico not far from the track of our important shipping lane from Panama to West Coast ports. It is now deserted and is dangerous to approach, but the flying-boat gives all such isolated specks of land a certain military importance.

The Netherlands is also an American power, in respect to the Dutch West Indies and Surinam; in the Far East her large and rich island possessions adjoin the Philippines to the southward. Our relations with the Netherlands government have been, and seem likely to continue, cordial and friendly. We should of course adopt the same attitude in regard to attacks on Dutch possessions in this hemisphere as in regard to those of France and Great Britain. The possibility of a future conquest of Holland by an expanding Germany is perhaps remote, but should it take place it would certainly be our policy that these possessions should not pass under the German flag. This is in strict accordance with the Monroe Doctrine, which is well understood by all concerned.

It is perhaps less generally realized that Denmark is also

an American power, by virtue of her settlements in ice-capped Greenland. From Europe toward Greenland, the Danish-owned Faroe Islands, and Iceland (a sovereign state, but politically connected to Denmark by certain dynastic and constitutional ties) form stepping stones for air power which were used by Air-Marshal Balbo in his massed flight to the United States. European occurrences which brought Denmark within the orbit of any large and aggressive power would therefore be of concern to this country.

With Germany it must be at once admitted that our relations are not good, and are likely to grow worse. To begin with, our people resent the various manifestations of Naziism in its treatment of racial minorities, in its subversion of all individual liberties, and in its general truculent attitude toward foreign powers, peoples and especially those democratic institutions which Americans are accustomed to regard as sacred. The forcible annexation of Austria, and the present attitude of Germany toward democratic Czechoslovakia, are regarded with grave disquiet, not to say antagonism, in the United States. Most Americans feel that Hitler's Reich is a disturber of the peace, a dangerous member of the family of nations whose conduct requires careful watching. German conduct in this country has done nothing to allay such feelings. The arrest of a number of German spy suspects in New York, the proceedings of the German-American "bund" with its uniformed storm-troopers and Nazi camps, the testimony given before a Congressional committee as to a carefully planned German spy net and sabotage campaign in this country, have all added to American dislike of Nazi methods. If Hitler's professed Continental aspirations should be realized, if "Great Germany" were to realize the old dream of Mitteleuropa, expanding down the Danube to the Black Sea, there would be created in Europe a new and mighty power of very great resources and intrinsic strength, whose ambitions would certainly soon be directed

[81]

toward colonial expansion; and, in so doing, would shortly come into opposition to our own.

Indeed, there are already straws showing a wind blowing in this direction. Not only has the German demand for the return of her old colonies been kept alive, but recent press reports have set forth a German plan by which Portugal is, in the event of a Franco victory in Spain, to become the next Nazi objective, to be conquered, if need be, by force of arms. This would mean (in default of armed intervention to prevent it by Britain and France) the acquisition by Germany (perhaps with Italian participation) not only of Portugal, but of the Portuguese Atlantic Islands and the Portuguese colonies. The Azores Islands, particularly, lie out in the Atlantic Ocean only 2000 miles from New York and 1700 from Bermuda; to Newfoundland they are even nearer; they constitute an important link in the southern route of all proposed trans-Atlantic flying services. For these islands to pass into German control, either directly or by means of a Portuguese puppet government dominated by Nazi and Fascist influence, would be a matter of such grave concern to this country that it is a question whether we ought not to resist it by force, should it appear imminent. Farther south, the Cape Verde Islands, and the colony of Portuguese Guinea on the African mainland, lie opposite the narrowest part of the Atlantic, distant only some 1600 miles from the coast of Brazil. German trans-Atlantic air services have been operating to Brazil for some time. These Portuguese outposts, in German possession, might become foci for German efforts to assume a more important and dominant status in Brazilian affairs; or be a menace to our Caribbean security. From the Cape Verdes to Barbados in the British West Indies is a little over 2000 miles.

Toward Italy we have much less present antagonism than toward Germany; for one reason because Italy has largely refrained from active propaganda in this country, for another because, curiously enough, the average American seems to take Mussolini far less seriously than he does Hitler. It is as a supporter and possible partner-in-conquest of Germany that Italy appears most likely to be of concern to us. An Italo-German naval combination would confront us, in the Atlantic, with a fleet (counting ships under construction) of about two-thirds the strength of our own; which, considering our Pacific necessities, might prove embarrassing under easily imaginable conditions. It may of course be objected that Great Britain and France would be doing something meanwhile; but we ought not to depend on others for our defense. It is all very well to take a realistic view of the situation as it exists; and just at present it is impossible to imagine Germany and Italy undertaking any naval campaign outside European waters. However, if war comes in Europe, the two axis powers may win it, and will then be free, at least for a time, of those local restraints on their ambitions which now exist in the form of the British and French navies. As already pointed out, if they do win they will win quickly, and we can do little to prevent such a victory. Or they may, without war, continue to grow and wax powerful at the expense of lesser States, until they are so strong as to make interference with them too dangerous for close neighbors to undertake; whereupon again they may seek to expand beyond the seas.

Our relations with Soviet Russia just at present seem likely to be exacerbated only by resentment against Communist propaganda and Communist-inspired disorders in this country; dangers which are perhaps exaggerated by the more lurid sections of our press, but which certainly exist and cannot be ignored. Indeed, the whole question of propaganda and internal disorders fomented from without is a serious one for a nation such as ours, among whose inhabitants are included large blocs of diverse foreign origin. What might happen in this respect in case of a European war may easily be imagined; it suffices to say, in connection with Soviet-American relations, that the connection between the Soviet Government, via the Comintern, with the American Communist party is not conducive to cordiality between the two Governments; and however the existence of such connection may be denied, and whatever protestations of complete independence from Moscow may be made by American Communists, the American people as a whole seem firmly to believe that the connection not only exists but is an active one.

In the case (not by any means beyond possibility) of a Soviet war with Japan, a considerable degree of pro-Russian feeling might temporarily be aroused in this country, because of a very general desire to see Japanese ambitions receive a severe set-back. Indeed, if we ourselves went to war with Japan we should very likely have Soviet Russia as an ally, since no more appropriate moment could possibly be discovered by Moscow for setting a term to the Japanese menace to their Far Eastern possessions. But if in the end, with or without our participation, Russia were to defeat Japan so decisively as to eject Japan from the Continent of Asia, Soviet influence in China might well become paramount; and the state of affairs which would then arise in East Asia might present aspects which would be less pleasing to us than the present conditions.

The possibility of difficulties with Japan over the Philippines has already been examined. Just at present Japan is fully engaged on the Asian continent. She may succeed in making herself master of China, in which case we may expect a policy of commercial exclusion in that vast market, operated for her benefit. This will necessitate our remembering that Japan is a better customer of ours than China; but the aggrandizement, power and swelling ambition of a victorious Japan might bring about an attitude on the part of her ruling military clique which would be difficult to endure with patience, and eventually build up so overweening a power as to constitute a peril of which we would have to take note. There might well arrive, in the course of such a process, a moment when the making of "preventive war" — such as Britain waged against Denmark in 1807, or as was proposed in France at the time of the re-militarization of the Rhineland by Germany in 1936 — would be our safest policy. Whether, as a practical matter, any Administration would assume the appalling responsibility of deliberately preparing for such action, not only in a military way but in the building up of the indispensable popular support, is however extremely doubtful. The need may, in any case, never arise. Today, even were she free of Chinese troubles, Japan is unable — as the chapter on the strategy of the Pacific will amply demonstrate — to do us any serious injury. Tomorrow may or may not tell another story.

Japan may fail completely in China, even without Russian interference; and in that case any one of several things may happen. There may be a moral, financial and industrial collapse in Japan, accompanied perhaps by revolution, which may bring about the elimination of Japan as a factor in Pacific affairs for a period of years, or may bring to the places of power in that country either a conservative government which will seek better relations with foreign nations, or a group of fanatics which will seek new fields to conquer: as defeat in the World War threw Germany into the excesses of Nazi-ism. Japanese attention may turn in such case from the continental objectives favored by the army, which she is now striving to obtain, to the insular objectives (the Philippines, the Netherlands Indies and even Australia) favored by the navy, which has gained little glory and "face" out of the Chinese war to date save in river operations and the participation of its landing parties at Shanghai. The bitter army-navy rivalry is a factor in Japanese affairs which must not be forgotten.

Finally, Japan may achieve only a partial success in China,

[85]

holding perhaps North China and certain coastal areas; in which case she would still be subjected to the drain of continual military vigilance on a continental frontier, to the fear of Russian action at Russia's selected moment, to the possibilities of a Chinese campaign of restoration; against which she would have to strive to bolster herself by a commercial policy of ruthless exploitation of the Chinese areas she held. Out of such a situation almost any sort of foreign complication might arise; and Japan's power to deal with it would be proportionate to her ability actually to capitalize on her Chinese gains, to convert into real assets the fruits of her conquest.

So far, our survey of American foreign policy has been concerned with what might be called the political field, that is, with matters in which our State Department would be primarily concerned. There is, however, another phase of our external contacts which has to do with commercial matters, with the supply of the nation in war, the maintenance of our foreign trade and the upbuilding of our merchant marine. It is not pretended that an exhaustive survey of this subject can be given in a single chapter, but the principal relationships which it has with military policy may be briefly examined.

Chapter V

THE RELATIONS OF OUR ECONOMIC
AND MILITARY POLICIES

"The important bearing, economic, political and strategic, which the disparity of foodstuffs and essential raw materials among nations has upon their peace and war relations, is becoming universally recognized."

BROOKS EMENY,
The Strategy of Raw Materials.

WE SHALL SEE, when we come to consider the fundamental principles of war, that there are two ways in which a great nation, and especially such an insular nation as our own, may be attacked: assault and investment. Assault seeks to penetrate, to act against internal communications and, by seizing or destroying these, to paralyze the national will and power to resist. Investment acts against external communications, and its principal weapon is blockade.

It is therefore pertinent to inquire just how far the United States is vulnerable externally, a matter which concerns not only strategy but the extent of the nation's interests overseas, its dependence or lack of dependence in war upon supplies from foreign sources and in peace upon the uninterrupted continuance of its seaborne trade.

In the Report of the Temporary Mixed Commission on

[87]

Armaments of the League of Nations, in 1921, the following were recited as being among the fundamental factors upon which "the strength of a country in wartime essentially depends":

"The extent to which it is self-supporting (for instance, as regards fuel, foodstuffs, raw materials and manufactured goods), and the extent to which, as a result of its means of transport and the freedom of its communications, especially its communications by sea, and of its financial strength, it can obtain the commodities of every kind in which it is deficient from abroad."

This problem of self-sufficiency in war and peace is among the most immediately pressing causes of international discord, dividing the "haves" from the "have-nots," driving the latter to seek a greater degree of security by the use of armed force. The United States is a "have" power. We can still feed ourselves, indeed we are an exporter of most staple foodstuffs. Our supplies of the basic minerals and most other essential raw materials are sufficient for our needs. Thus stated in general terms, our position in this respect is better than that of any other great power with the possible exception of the Soviet Union; better even than hers, because of the far greater facility with which we can transport and distribute our supplies to every part of the nation.

Yet there are rifts in the lute; rifts which, unless forethought is taken, may cause us grave anxiety in war.

These rifts are classified under two headings: *Strategic* raw materials, for which we are completely dependent, or almost so, on foreign sources of supply; and *critical* raw materials, of which we produce an amount sufficient to take care of our needs for a considerable period of time, but which would require careful rationing and control if external sources were shut off.

Military policy is therefore directly concerned with the location and potentialities of the sources of such materials,

[88]

upon which, to a greater or less extent, the ability of the nation to wage successful war may depend.

For the sake of brevity and clarity, the various strategic and critical raw materials will be shown in tabular form, grouped by classes, and with the external sources of supply likewise grouped under two headings: those in the Western Hemisphere, with which our supply lines could not easily be cut, and those outside the Western Hemisphere, which it might require an extensive effort to maintain. The figures shown are percentages of domestic consumption for the five-year period ending with 1929:

FOODSTUFFS

Commodity	Domestic Production	Western Hemisphere Sources (%)	All Other Sources (%)
Bananas	0	Central America, Mexico, Cuba and Jamaica	None
Cocoa Beans .	0	Brazil, Trinidad, Venezuela, Dom. Republic	British W. Africa, 41.5
Coffee	0	Brazil, Colombia, Venezuela	Negligible
Sugar	17.5	Cuba, Puerto Rico, Hawaii, 74.6	Philippines, 7.9
Tea	0	0	Japan, Ceylon, China, Great Britain, India, Netherlands Indies

In the matter of food, therefore, the United States would be completely self-sufficient in war, save that we might not be able to get tea at all, and might have to cut down on our

[89]

cocoa. The place of Philippine sugar could easily be supplied. In all other items of foodstuffs our own supplies are ample.

There is but one disquieting thought in this connection: will those supplies continue to be ample? Our population is rapidly becoming urban and industrial. In 1860 but 16.1% of our people lived in cities of 8000 or more population, while in 1930, 49.1% were so domiciled. As late as 1890, 41.2% of the persons gainfully employed in the United States were farmers or agricultural laborers; in 1930 the figure was 21.3%. The perils of drought and soil erosion have but recently been vividly impressed on our minds. We must take thought for the future, remembering the history of Britain, the present problems of Italy and Japan. We are fortunate in having the vast storehouse of Canada at our doors, but we must remember that Canada has her responsibilities as a member of the British Empire.

Metallic Minerals

Commodity	Domestic Production (%)	Western Hemisphere Sources (%)	All Other Sources (%)
Manganese	8	Brazil, 25; Cuba, 3; Canada, 5	Russia, 33; India, 10; British West Africa, 8; Others, 8
Chromite	0	Cuba, 15	South Africa, 62; New Caledonia, 6; India, 7; Others, 10
Mercury	40	Mexico, 4	Spain, 30; Italy, 22; Others, 4
Nickel	2	Canada, 89	Great Britain, 9
Platinum	5	Colombia, 42	Great Britain, 42; Germany, 11

Tin	0	Bolivia, 4	British Malaya, 65; Great Britain, 22; Netherlands, 9
Tungsten	24	Bolivia, 4	China, 45; Great Britain, 14; Germany, 8; Others, 5
Antimony	0	Mexico, 9; Bolivia, 6	China, 70; Others, 15
Vanadium	37	Peru, 62	Others, 1

Manganese is listed first in the foregoing list, because it is by all odds our most serious metallic deficiency. It is absolutely essential to the manufacture of steel; during the World War, when imports from Russia were cut off, there was a time when a complete shut-down of our steel industry within seven months was foreseen unless additional sources of manganese could be tapped. War reserves of this item are now being maintained, but our principal war reliance will be on Brazil.

The incidence of this situation on military policy may be exemplified by the loss during the World War of the U.S.S. *Cyclops,* carrying 12,000 tons of Brazilian manganese. The cause of her loss has never been discovered; enemy action cannot be ruled out. Certainly our shortage of manganese is well known abroad, and in another war our enemy would do all in his power to keep us from obtaining Brazilian supplies. This might very well require us to provide naval convoy for manganese ships; and since the Brazilian mines are in the state of Minas Geraes, which has no railway outlet to any port north of Victoria, we would have to keep open a trade route extending 3700 miles beyond our outermost base at Saint Thomas; possibly a serious strain on our naval resources in a war with an Atlantic enemy.

[91]

The United States possesses large deposits of low-grade manganese ores; if metallurgical science could discover a reasonably satisfactory means of reducing these, our position would be greatly strengthened.

The other minerals in this list (except tin) either are not required in great bulk, and can be the subject of reserve accumulation, or are easily available in the Western Hemisphere. Bolivian tin deposits are ample for all our needs, provided we resurrect our smelting industry.

We have certain non-metallic mineral deficiencies, notably in iodine and nitrates, of which Chile is our chief source of supply, and in sheet mica, principally imported from India, but with domestic and Canadian production caring for more than a third of our needs.

In this field, special note should be taken of petroleum. The possible exhaustion of our petroleum reserves is a subject which has received much study on the part of governmental and industrial research bodies. Next to steel and coal, it is the most essential of all minerals for war purposes. Fortunately we have at hand, in Mexico and Venezuela, two neighbors who are very large producers; so that we need not be seriously disquieted as to the chance of a war shortage.

Of other materials (aside from certain medicinal products, which are not needed in great quantities) our most notable shortages are in rubber, wool, silk and manila fiber. Of these rubber is by far the most important.

We have no domestic production. Of our imports, 66% come from British Malaya, 18.5% from the Netherlands Indies, 9% from Ceylon, and the rest from other sources. Imports of Brazilian rubber are however beginning to increase, as are those from other Latin American sources. No better foreign investment, in the strategic sense, could be found for American capital than in helping to resurrect the Latin American rubber industry.

It must however be remembered that we keep very large industrial stocks on hand in this country at all times, and that secondary recovery will take care of a good many needs. Substitutes have been developed, but are expensive.

For silk our sources are chiefly Asiatic — Japan and China. Military requirements are for cartridge cases and parachutes; no satisfactory substitute has been found. The only recourse is the accumulation of war reserves, which has been done on the basis of about 3 months' supply. Certainly in case of a Pacific war the silk stocking would presently vanish from the feminine leg.

Our domestic production of wool is large, but insufficient. Our largest external sources are Argentina, Australia, Great Britain and China.

Our manila fiber comes almost entirely from the Philippine Islands. Sisal, used for binder twine, is principally supplied from Mexico.

In the commercial sense, our self-sufficiency is conditioned by our very considerable dependence for many items on Latin-American or Canadian sources of supply. But in the military sense, while we maintain our present good relations with those nations, and while we have a navy capable under all conditions of keeping open our trade routes with Latin America *and especially of commanding the Caribbean Sea,* which insures our access to all the Caribbean countries and, via Panama, to the west coast of South America, our self-sufficiency is very much greater; is indeed almost complete. No other great power can match us in this respect. Great Britain is dependent on sea communications for her very food, as well as every other essential raw material save coal, iron and nitrates. Germany is self-sufficient or nearly so as to food, but must import large quantities of the other essentials, except coal, nitrates and potash. Japan, with her continental empire, can feed herself, but is otherwise adequately supplied only with coal, copper, sulphur, chromite, tungsten, mica and silk. Italy can feed herself only in good harvest years, and is so badly deficient in other items that she must import great quantities of every one of the great essentials except sulphur and zinc. Soviet Russia is much better off, but lacks transportation facilities to distribute her scattered riches, and is short of rubber, nickel, tungsten, tin and some other items.

The answer to our question, "Is the United States self-sufficient?" must therefore be, "No, not as to all the necessary commodities; but far better off proportionately than is any other nation."

This has two military bearings; first, the necessity of keeping open our sea communications with the sources of supply for those things that we require; second, the very grave injury which our seapower, if strong enough, can inflict on an enemy whose routes of maritime communications it can reach, in whole or in part. Soviet Russia excepted, there is not one of the great powers which (granting sufficiency of naval strength) we could not deprive of several vital sources of raw materials; nor need we do this by direct blockade, but only by stopping their commerce at focal points more easily within our reach. Germany, for example, could be cut off from her chief sources of rubber, cotton, and copper by cruiser patrols operating in the western approaches to the British Isles. Of course Germany could obtain some supplies through the Mediterranean, by transshipment to continental railways; but as against sea transport, rail transport is slow, expensive and lacking in capacity.

More serious, however, would be the cumulative effect of our captures of enemy-flag shipping. This would gradually force the blockaded power to a dependence on neutral shipping; and neutral shipping may in war prove a broken reed. It may be withdrawn by a neutral anxious to avoid embroilment, or under pressure of necessities of its own. It may be reduced by reluctance of neutral owners to incur risks, especially if other profitable and safe ventures are available for it.

We must, however, examine the reverse of this shield. If war breaks out elsewhere in the world we may find ourselves dependent, not only for our military needs but for our normal foreign trade, on American-flag ships; especially if the greatest carrier of world trade, Great Britain, be a belligerent. In the World War, prior to our entry into the conflict, we were driven to the most extraordinary expedients to keep up our trade with other neutral nations.

Our merchant marine is now the second in the world, giving place only to that of Great Britain. Our position in this respect, as of December 31, 1936, in ocean-going iron and steel vessels of 2000 gross tons and over, is shown by the following table (lake shipping excluded):

Ocean-going Iron and Steel Vessels of 2000 Gross Tons and Over [1]

Nation	No. of Ships	Gross Tonnage	% of Tonnage Over 15 Years Old
Great Britain	2511	15,717,828	37.2
United States	1444	8,461,603	87.3
Japan	637	3,268,490	63.4
Germany	498	2,943,297	32.6
Italy	433	2,611,259	59.5
France	410	2,407,361	47.9

It is clear from an examination of the last column that, in default of rapid replacement of aging vessels, our present high status as an ocean carrier is bound to grow progressively worse as the years go by. But our actual position as a carrier of foreign trade is much less than an examination of the table might lead one to suppose. Many of our older ships

[1] Table prepared by National Council of American Shipbuilders, January, 1938.

are now laid up; and about 60% of our active merchant fleet is engaged in coastwise trade (including intercoastal services via Panama). Our actual average participation in the ocean carrying trade (other than coastal) for the four years 1933-1936 inclusive has been about 5½% of the world total, while American foreign trade has represented about 13.2% of the world total during that time; meaning that about 1½ times as much of our foreign trade is carried in foreign bottoms as in American.

Our construction of merchant vessels has greatly fallen off since the hectic days of the World War. For the fifteen years 1922-1936, inclusive, we built only a little over 1,000,000 tons of new ships, while in the same period Great Britain built almost 10,000,000 tons, Germany about 2,000,-000, and Japan 1,200,000. Our active merchant fleet engaged in foreign trade in 1936 was 2,700,000 gross tons. In order to maintain our trade at a time when foreign-flag shipping might be withdrawn we should, without injuring our coastwise trade, require at least 4,000,000 tons more, plus necessary replacements within the next fifteen years of about 6,000,000 tons (inclusive of vessels now in the coastwise trade). This means that our average shipbuilding should be raised, for the next fifteen years, to an annual increment of 660,000 tons, about ten times the average of the period 1922-1936. There are many problems to be solved in this connection, problems of labor, of operation, of subsidy, to all of which the new Maritime Commission is giving the closest attention. It is to be hoped that they will find means to immediate progress.

An American-flag merchant marine is not only an insurance against the loss by reason of a foreign war of our external trade but forms an essential reserve of ships and seamen for our navy if we ourselves are involved in war. In examining our Pacific strategy, for instance, we shall see what tremendous demands would be made by the navy for

cargo and tank ships in the course of offensive operations
against Japan. In any naval war, the demands on our merchant marine would be very great; not only for supply
service, but for armed merchant cruisers, converted aircraft
carriers, patrol vessels, tugs, and naval auxiliaries of various
types.

There is another phase of this matter to be considered.
The expansion of our merchant marine brings us an increased number of daily foreign contacts all over the world.
Already American ships travel all the trade routes of the
seven seas.

Our exports of domestic products in 1936 amounted to
$2,417,939,000. This figure has been steadily increasing
since the "depression low" of $1,611,016,000 in 1932; it
must be remembered that the average for the period 1922-
1929 was almost $5,000,000,000. The exponents of a "closed
economy" do not like to think of a return to this figure,
but it represents prosperity for many an American worker;
and while we are under the necessity of importing many
products from abroad, we must likewise export American
products to maintain our trade balances.

American commercial and shipping firms maintain offices
and establishments in many foreign countries, and American funds are invested in many foreign enterprises. The
value of these "direct investments" was estimated by the
Brookings Institution, at the end of 1935, to be $7,219,-
200,000, of which $4,953,600,000 was in Canada, Newfound-
land and Latin America.

Our investments in foreign securities at the same period
(less repatriations and repudiations) was $5,621,500,000, plus
$853,000,000 of short-term credits.

This in sum total is an enormous stake, even for so rich
a nation as the United States. Its loss would be disastrous,
and its existence is perhaps the best answer to the hard-and-
fast "isolationists." Innumerable occasions have arisen dur-

[97]

ing our history in which our shipping, our citizens and our property in foreign lands have required protection at the hands of our naval forces; not only in war, but on occasions of public disorders, of floods, earthquakes, fires and other disasters. That protection must continue. It will from time to time require the presence of our naval vessels in situations of grave danger; but the navy has never flinched from the missions exacted of it at the call of duty, and may be expected to continue in the same splendid tradition.

The complications which may arise from the presence of our vessels of war, engaged in protecting our citizens and property in foreign parts, in zones where political conditions of stress or actual conflict prevail, are all too frequently overestimated; this point will be more fully examined a little farther on. Here need only be noted, as affecting our foreign policy and its relations to military policy, the extent of our interests and the necessity of their protection insofar as protection can be given: which is generally proportionate to distance from our shores, to ease of access from the sea, and to the degree of political influence which we are able to exercise and the prestige we possess in the region where the danger arises. This influence and prestige will most certainly be in turn proportionate to our military strength and the facility with which we may bring it to bear at the threatened point—a factor which of course will have less to do with great natural disasters than with those arising from human causes but is not to be disregarded even in case of the former.

One thing should be clear, even to those whose terror of being drawn into war takes precedence of all other fears: and that is, that the proper and reasonable protection of those Americans who are engaged in the various activities of American enterprise abroad is in a very real sense protection also of the welfare and livelihood of millions of Americans at home, who, in one fashion or another, participate in the benefits of such enterprise. It is not only the rich capitalist and manufacturer and ship-owner whose interests are served when the world is made safer for American ships and investments; it is also the farmer whose products go to the export market, the artisan in the factory which draws its profits from foreign trade, the railroad worker who assists in transporting goods to our seaports, the truck driver, the longshoreman and the sailor who handle them in other phases of their journey. And beyond these are the thousands of small investors of savings earned from years of hard work who have put their little capital into the securities of firms dependent in whole or in part upon export profits.

There is a tendency today to regard as something approaching the traitor and the criminal the American who, by the incidence of events wholly beyond his control, chances to be caught in a zone of foreign disorder and shows reluctance to withdraw therefrom instantly, leaving perhaps his life's work and savings in ruins behind him. There is a tendency to regard as a ruthless war-monger, reckless of the blood of his fellow-citizens, the American who invests money in an enterprise beyond the boundaries of his country and who, in time of trouble, seeks protection at the hands of that country. It was not always so. Time was when the American who risked his money and in some cases his life in foreign trade, of which the profits were spent in the United States, was regarded as a public benefactor, well worthy of protection and aid from his government. Time was when the prosperity derived from that foreign trade and enterprise was recognized as a national asset, to be conserved and cared for like any other asset. Time was when a suspicion of moral obliquity did not attach to the seeking of an honest profit, at home or abroad; when it was held that enterprise and "Yankee push" were among the pillars of the nation.

Time was, indeed, when the work of the navy in the

protection of our citizens abroad "upon their lawful occasions" was thought well worth the cost, and reckoned as an ample return upon our investment in the upkeep of ships and officers and men.

And the time has come — is presently at hand — for a revival of straight thinking on this subject, with which the fortunes of millions of our citizens are so intimately bound up. Are they, too, not part of our country? Do they not participate in the paying of the taxes which support our navy and our foreign service? What have they done that they should be a class apart, pariahs among their fellow-countrymen, doomed to economic destruction because, disregarding in their blind fears all the lessons of experience, all the examples of the past, certain others among us have fixed their narrow minds upon the idiotic theory that foreign trade is somehow pernicious and dangerous and a breeder of foreign war?

Unless we do arrive at a clear understanding of this matter, it will be futile to build up our merchant marine, to conclude trade agreements beneficial to our commerce abroad, to seek new markets for American goods and new fields for American enterprise. We might as well cease these activities today, if we are not going to afford protection — armed protection, if need be — to the American men and women and goods which are thereby scattered over the globe, beyond our boundaries.

The protection to be given cannot of course always be complete, nor of immediate effect, as in the case of the Mexican expropriations. It is necessary in these matters as in others to preserve a sense of proportion. To the favorite question of the unthinking isolationist, "Would you go to war to save dear old Standard Oil?" it is possible to return an unqualified negative without acceding to the idea that American employees of that company on foreign service should be abandoned to slaughter while American naval vessels withdraw in haste at the first hint of burnt powder. As a matter of fact, wars do not commonly arise from the employment of force under such conditions, nor from unfortunate "incidents," such as the sinking of the *Panay,* which are occasioned by the presence of naval vessels in zones of disorder. The sinking of the *Maine* in Havana harbor is customarily quoted as having led directly to war, to which it certainly contributed, though there were other and more deeply-seated causes; but this is an isolated instance of a peculiarly dramatic and violent nature, while on the other side can be quoted from our history literally scores of occasions on which force in one form or another has been used by our naval forces in protection of Americans abroad without war having resulted.

The extent and amount of protection to be furnished to American interests may sometimes be decided by the Government at home; sometimes (though less often in these days of radio) it has to be decided by the naval officer on the spot, whose recommendations, in any case, usually are given due weight. It is the glory of our navy that its officers have acted in these difficult cases with so much courage, good judgment, fairness and success. Few officers and few diplomats have been placed in a more difficult and trying position than that now occupied by Admiral Harry E. Yarnell, Commander-in-Chief of the Asiatic Fleet, whose duties are being so capably and firmly discharged—and are contributing, let it be noted, to the safety of Americans far out of reach of the guns of his ships. He is heir to a tradition which began with Truxtun's frigate actions against the French in the West Indies and the roar of Preble's guns before the castle of Tripoli, and which has in a century and a third of development saved the lives and livelihoods of many American citizens. It is a tradition which we can do worse than to preserve.

Protection does not necessarily consist in the bombardment of foreign seaports and the landing of our marines on foreign shores, though both these things have been necessary as a last resort in the past, and may be so again. It rests, rather, on a firm basis of mutual respect as between ourselves and other nations: a respect which will have its origin in the knowledge of others that, if need be, it can and will have the backing of force.

One has but to compare conditions the world over, as regards this matter of respect, during the decade or two following the War of 1812, in which our seamen and our frigates had again and again so gallantly and successfully upheld in distant waters the honor of our flag against the greatest naval power of the world, with those in the decade immediately succeeding the Civil War, when our navy was allowed to fall into decay and our foreign policy was perhaps at its nadir of weakness and futility.

Such respect, born of a firm, just and resolute policy, supported by instruments of national power adequate to their purpose and their responsibilities, is no breeder of wars; it is the best assurance of peace.

The preservation of peace, so necessary for our prosperity, so essential to our undistracted labors in solving our pressing domestic problems, is in fact itself a principal aim of American policy. Toward this end, our influence in world affairs ought ever to be turned, so long as we keep our feet on the firm ground of reality and do not stray into the quicksands of fantasy; so long as some impossible ideal, or some unworthy and unfounded fearfulness is not allowed to subordinate greater and definite national interests. If we do not look after these interests ourselves, we may be quite sure that no one else is going to do so. In fact, we may be equally sure that others will eagerly seize the benefits we relinquish through cowardice or mistaken altruism.

Nor should we arrogate to ourselves a superior moral position in these issues of peace and war, thanking God that we are not as other men. We have our record of aggressions and conquests, and that we are now full-glutted with territory and possessions gives us no title to an attitude of ethical preeminence. War may come to us again, and may come through our own seeking; we ought not to indulge what Mauritz Hallgren justly terms "the naïve impression that America will fight only if dragged into somebody else's war." [1] We entertain no present purpose of aggression against anyone; we are unlikely to engage in a war of conquest within the immediate future. But we are human beings and not angels; we are as susceptible as any other people to bursts of popular fury, we are perhaps more susceptible than some to the insidious influence of propaganda. These things are matters wholly divorced from any state of preparedness, or otherwise, as is testified to by our military condition at the outbreak of the wars with Mexico in 1846 and with Spain in 1898. It is to be hoped that such impulses do not seize upon us again; but it is also to be hoped that, if they do, we shall be prepared to face the consequences with less of needless waste of life and treasure than was the case in former times.

We ought not, to repeat, to thank God that we are not as other men, for we are, with much the same weaknesses and powers, hopes and fears, appetites and ambitions. But we *should* thank God that today we can pursue our national way, secure as yet from the fear of invasion by land and from the horror of bombs from the skies above us, unique among the great powers of the earth in possession of our priceless privilege of defending ourselves first upon the sea.

We have now examined the various aspects of our relations with other nations and of our own policies, tendencies and needs which may bring us to situations requiring not necessarily the employment, but certainly the possession, of the instruments of force. We have seen how our geographical security must be reinforced by military security; how our

---

[1] Mauritz Hallgren, *The Tragic Fallacy*.

foreign policy, in its inevitable clashes with the interests of other peoples, must likewise have the support of military policy; and how each must be proportioned to the needs and powers of the other.

This brings us to the more definite examination of the methods by which military power must act to defend us against attacks and to support our rights and our possessions against what challenge may arise. These considerations come under the heading of national strategy.

Chapter VI

THE ELEMENTS OF
AMERICAN STRATEGY

There must be a national strategy — a national tactics.

GENERAL KARL VON CLAUSEWITZ,
On War.

THE WORD *strategy* is derived from the ancient Greek term
(strategos) for a commander-in-chief in war, whether by
land or sea, and means literally "the art of the commander."
It is generally defined by modern writers as the art of maneuvering land or sea forces within the theater of operations,
as distinguished from the handling of such forces in actual
contact with the enemy on a particular field of action, which
is called *tactics.*

In the national sense, it may be said that strategy begins
where military policy leaves off; military policy provides the
instruments for the situations with which strategy has to
deal. Military policy must therefore take heed of strategical
considerations, while strategy need concern itself with military policy only as the latter sets it an impossible task, or
provides it with means inadequate to the accomplishment
of its mission.

Strategy, like any other art, is based on broad general

principles rather than a long catalogue of fixed rules. In execution, it consists in the application of these principles to varying situations, conditioned by the action of the enemy, the terrain, the weather, the forces available, the state of their armament, morale, discipline, training and general condition, the like considerations as to the enemy forces, the object to be achieved, the instructions of superior authority, and even political affairs. While the principles of the art are few, their application presents an infinite variety of complexities which require on the part of the successful commander a combination of personal qualities far above the average. Of these qualities, imagination, resourcefulness and on occasion the moral courage to throw cut-and-dried methods to the winds and act as the immediate situation seems to require, are not the least. Reflecting that precisely these characteristics have frequently been displayed by American commanders in the past, we begin to see the underlying wisdom of Clausewitz's insistence on a "national strategy."

It is the modern fashion, especially amongst the newer school of military writers, to deride principle (on no better basis than that, on occasion, it has been ignored with successful results) and to see in the development of new weapons far-reaching changes in the art of war which render the principles of the past of no avail. A like contempt for principle as applied to the art of painting presented the world with the fantasies of the cubist and sur-realist, which seem little likely to assume in the affections of puzzled generations to come the place we give today to the work of a Raphael, a Titian or a Corot.

But weapons, the instruments of war, do not alter its principles, any more than the invention of the air-brush altered the principles of painting. On the other hand, nothing could be more deadening to all initiative, to every hope of victory founded on leadership, than a book-thumbing attitude of seeking a rule to apply to every new situation. In acquiring the ability to take appropriate action to fit the continually emergent exigencies of war, action which, based on correct principle, shall yet be adapted to the needs of the moment and the means at hand, the value of actual experience of war is of supreme importance. Indeed, nothing can wholly take its place, though in its absence that place is best supplied by a study of the experience of others, of military history. "The happiest inspiration on the battle-field," once remarked Napoleon, "is often only a recollection."

We are fortunate today in that almost all our general and flag officers have had war experience. Yet we must also take thought for the morrow when these leaders will be gone.

Likewise, in determining a scheme of national strategy, with all the leisure and opportunity for mature reflection afforded by the absence of immediate emergency, this matter of experience conditioned by a basic adherence to principle is the only sure guide to proper dispositions; as we have already seen in examining the similarity between the strategical problems of the United States and those of Great Britain before the invention of flying-machines.

The principles of war have been variously listed and defined. They may be boiled down to three which are of controlling importance: Concentration, Offensive Action, and Security.[1]

Concentration (Mahan's "ABC of war") consists in the bringing together against an enemy of a superior force — of the greatest possible force — at the decisive point and time. It presupposes the keeping of detachments down to the minimum of absolute necessity, and the selection of an objective or a direction of attack which will bring our strength to bear against the enemy's weakness. This is simple to state, but difficult to achieve in practice, since the enemy will be contriving counter-moves.

---

[1] For a full general discussion of the principles of war, see *If War Comes*, by Majors R. Ernest Dupuy and George Fielding Eliot. (Macmillan, 1937).

In American strategy, the principle of concentration applies first of all to our naval distribution in time of peace. We have seen how Britain disposed her fleet at various periods of her history, in accordance with the dispositions of others who might threaten her maritime supremacy. Our problem is no less difficult than hers. We have two great maritime frontiers, on the Atlantic and the Pacific, connected by a narrow defile which is in our possession—the Panama Canal. The steaming distance between our principal naval arsenal on the Atlantic Coast—Norfolk—and that on the Pacific—Puget Sound—is about 5800 nautical miles, or approximately sixteen days' steaming at a made-good average speed of fifteen knots, which is about the best fleet speed that can be calculated on. Add time for passage of the Canal and re-fueling of destroyers, and we find that it will take three weeks to transfer the fleet from one ocean to the other. In the strategical sense, there could be a certain reduction in these figures, since the arrival of the fleet either in the Guantanamo area in the Atlantic or the San Diego area in the Pacific would begin to exercise an immediate effect upon the military situation in the respective oceans. It is not probable that any serious injury could be done us in either ocean, by way of attacks on our coast or outlying possessions, or by an attempt to seize a base for operations against us, in the time which would be at the disposal of an enemy from the moment when we were first apprised of his intentions until the arrival in the theater of proposed operations of the bulk of our fleet.

The reason for this is that such injury could not be accomplished by naval forces alone, since the seizure of territory requires the use of troops, while air attacks of major importance not only require large numbers of planes (far more than can be operated from the existing aircraft-carriers of any naval power) but also must involve troops to seize and fortify a land base for the planes. Naval landing-parties might occupy some undefended island of the West Indies or the Aleutians, but could not hold it in such strength as to make dislodgement difficult after our fleet had restored maritime command of the adjacent waters. In consequence, we need not fear a surprise attack of more formidable nature than a raid. The preparations for a great overseas expedition involving the use of a considerable body of troops, a large air force, and all the impedimenta required for the purpose must necessarily involve the assembling of transports and cargo vessels in the ports from which the expedition is to set sail and the concentration there of vast quantities of material and supplies. Such preparations could not possibly be kept secret in time of peace, not even with the advantages possessed in this respect by authoritarian powers; it need not be supposed for a moment that the United States is so ill-served by its diplomatic and consular services and by the sources of intelligence at the disposal of the War, Navy, Commerce and Treasury Departments. The same considerations apply to an attack against any Latin American state.

Therefore, so long as we keep the main battle-line strength of our fleet together in either ocean, and so long as we maintain our grip on the Panama Canal, the "short-line" of communications between the oceans, we may be well assured that as against an enemy unable to fight in our waters the full power of our fleet, we are certain of being able to present that full power in opposition to his efforts before he can do us any great or irreparable damage; whether, at the outset, the fleet be in the wrong ocean or not.

But if we divide the battle-line strength of our fleet between the oceans, the situation is quite different. We might then be subject to a sudden appearance in our waters of an enemy force of superior strength to the fraction of our fleet there present. Our commander would then be faced with the problem either of evading battle and falling back on his line of communications with Panama, which he might not be able to do if the enemy force succeeded in getting between him and Panama; or of delivering battle against a superior force, which might result in his destruction; or of allowing himself to be cooped up in a defended port, which would automatically separate the two fractions of our fleet and leave between them an enemy force superior not to the whole, but to either fraction separately — a position of commanding advantage, enabling the fractions of our fleet to be dealt with in detail. Thus the policy of dividing the fleet lays us open to the possibility of being surprised — since the movements of purely naval forces can be effected with great secrecy and swiftness — and of subsequent loss of control of our maritime communications. If in the event, as would be quite likely, one fraction of our fleet were badly beaten or even wiped out, the enemy could contain the other fraction and would, in respect to his further operations against us, have attained comparative freedom of action.

It is assumed in this exposition that our fleet as a whole possesses a safe margin of superiority over any enemy or combination of enemies likely to concentrate against us in either ocean; at which level of strength it is of course our proper policy to maintain it.

Another bearing of the principle of concentration upon American military policy is seen in the creation of the General Headquarters Air Force, which permits the rapid assembling, under a single command, of the full striking power of our combat squadrons at any threatened point on either coast. The necessary dispersion of these squadrons at various bases for peace-time maintenance, training and administration does no violence to the principle, when compensated for by high speed and the efficiency of control provided by a unified command.

Offensive Action, which draws its strength from and is achieved by concentration, bases its title to be called a principle of war on the fundamental truth that decisive results in war are to be gained only by equally decisive acts. The simple defensive is foredoomed to failure. Such an attitude abandons all initiative to the enemy, allowing him to attack at his chosen place and time, under conditions selected by him as the most advantageous. It imposes on the defender the necessity of guarding himself everywhere, of being ready to meet the enemy's attack wherever it may fall. Thus it compels him either to depart from the principle of concentration by dispersing his force over the whole area, or line, or coast to be defended, condemning himself to be equally weak everywhere; or it requires him to await the enemy's attack before making his own dispositions, allowing what may prove a fatal initial advantage to be seized without resistance. This is not to say that the defensive is always the wrong form of war. Defensive and offensive are instruments in the hand of the skilled commander, to be employed as circumstances may require; it will almost always be the case that attack in one place must be based on defense elsewhere.

Whatever the immediate solution accepted for immediate ends, a finally decisive result will be attained only by the offensive, whether it come soon or late.

There is a great deal of confusion of thought on this point, as applied to our own military problem. The use of the term "National Defense" implies to many minds the very sort of static defensive attitude which is the inevitable prelude to military disaster. There is an apparent impression among some students of the matter that all we have to do is to insure ourselves against actual invasion. This is very far from being the case. We have many external interests by land and sea, the destruction or interruption of which would cause profound distress in this country, distress amounting in sum total to a national disaster comparable with actual invasion by an enemy army, distress far more serious in evil effects than the effort necessary to protect these external interests in the first place. Moreover, a purely defensive attitude even if successful for the time being admits of enemy advances into our vital sphere of interest which will gravely compromise our present admirable military position and eventually bring us to ruin.

"On the highest plane," writes an English naval officer,[1] whose words apply as aptly to America's policy as to Britain's, "all our operations are defensive, for our aim in war is to protect our territory and defend our right to whatever form of government and type of economic conditions we consider best. . . . But when it comes to fighting, the best way to safeguard your possessions is to bring such pressure to bear on the enemy that he will be unable, or will not think it worth while, to continue his efforts to deprive you of them. In other words it is best to *act* offensively."

Offensive action is the all-important principle of American strategy; for it is normally to our advantage to preserve those peaceful conditions under which we carry on our trade and solve our domestic problems undisturbed by the harassments of war. This being the case, as will be generally admitted, it is obviously also to our advantage to make the waging of war against us an unlikely contingency.

It will be unlikely in precise ratio to the element of risk involved. To have a truly deterrent effect, however, the risk must not be merely that of possible failure; it must be a risk to the vital interests of the nation which is weighing it against the possible advantages to be derived from a belligerent policy. A risk which involves no more than the losses to be anticipated in case an attack is beaten back by a stout defense is of a very different nature from one which must take into account the possibility of being vigorously and relentlessly attacked oneself, one's fleet destroyed or driven to take ignominious refuge in its home waters, one's commerce swept from the seas, and one's vital interests and

---

[1] Commander John Creswell, R.N., *Naval Warfare.*

enterprises insofar as they are within reach of the enemy's seapower wiped out; to say nothing of the privations and domestic distress to be expected from the subsequent maintenance of a distant blockade and cruiser operations, if nothing worse befalls. Nor is this all; for any maritime nation so dealt with must lose, in prestige and position, assets of intangible nature but transcendent importance, difficult to set forth in detail but of consequential value sufficient to weaken and hamper it in all its foreign contacts, in the execution of every department of its policy. It will find itself unable to maintain itself and support its interests against rivals which formerly it overawed; nor can the domestic consequences of such a defeat be overlooked by governments whose tenure of power is dependent on maintaining their prestige with their own people, and who have deliberately for that purpose created the legend of their own invincibility.

Such a government might find plausible explanation for mere failure to achieve victory on some distant scene of action; there can be none for a state of affairs in which the grass grows in the streets of once busy seaports, in which ships which once plied the oceans of the world lie rotting at silent wharves, in which factories dependent on the export trade or on raw materials obtainable only from distant lands are shut down while their employees find themselves and their families dependent on dwindling doles of government or private charity, in which the relatives and friends of men who went forth amid the thunderous acclaim of the nation to bring new glories and new power to a people confident in the infallibility of their leadership, now wait anxiously, week after week and month after month, for the victorious return of their dear ones — and realize at last that they wait in vain.

All these ills it should be within our power to visit upon any great nation which might, conceivably, become our enemy in war. All these ills it ought to be our relentless purpose to inflict upon any such power as chooses to attack us; until, at last, wearying of so hopeless and wearing a struggle, our enemy shall sue for peace on the terms we see fit to dictate, in the interests of our subsequent security. The effort required of us to do these things may be in some cases more, in others less; but once the appeal to arms is made there must be no half-measures, no holding of the hand, until the enemy realizes, and admits, that he is beaten. Then, and not before, comes the hour in which mercy and forbearance may have their say.

Such a strategic policy, defensive in principle, offensive in execution, does not require of us the maintenance of large armies, nor the fighting of land campaigns on distant continents. Seapower in sufficient strength, with an adequate air arm, and reinforced by a small, highly trained, completely equipped regular army sufficient to provide expeditionary forces for operations of limited extent and objective such as the seizure of advance bases for the fleet or the occupation of some outlying possession of an enemy, will be quite adequate to our purposes.

While we possess these instruments of offensive war, and while we make it clear that behind them lies the determination to use them offensively against any foe, we shall be as safe as human foresight can make us from the actual challenge that will compel us to employ them.

If, however, we continue to talk of a mere defensive policy, eschewing aggressive action and perhaps depriving ourselves of its instruments in favor of those — such as the airplane — of limited range and effect, we shall be constantly exposed to the possibility of aggression, our foreign policies will be in that measure rendered futile, our interests laid open to attack.

It was a favorite maxim of Napoleon that war is not made without taking risks. All war, all contemplation of war is indeed based upon the weighing of risk against advantage. It should be the maxim of modern America, compelled to live in a world where force is the basic factor in international relations, that the balance of contemplated war against her, peace-loving though she may be, should ever incline heavily on the side of dire and immediate risk to an aggressor. To repeat Guibert's maxim, "We must make our arms to be feared, though never our ambition."

In such a policy lies the best hope of remaining at peace. In such a policy lies the only hope that if, despite it, we are compelled to make war, we shall do so victoriously. To such a policy, the principle of offensive action is fundamental.

Security, as a principle of war, is concerned with a due regard for the safety of one's own forces and vital interests against enemy offensive action, and the establishment of a firm foundation for our own action. In trying to bring about that concentration of force against the enemy's weakness which in turn leads to offensive action, care has to be taken, not only that the enemy does not effect a concentration of his own and fall upon some exposed or detached portion of one's forces before one's concentration is complete, but that, in concentrating, no vital interest or position is uncovered to enemy attack. This will frequently require local defensive measures to be taken to assure at least for a time the security of such interests or positions until the main fleet or army has accomplished its primary mission.

It is not for a moment suggested that our naval policy ought to be one of headlong, reckless attack. The time for such an attack may not arrive coincidentally with the opening of hostilities. Meanwhile we must maintain the security of our vital positions; either by fixed defenses, or by the location with respect thereto of mobile forces, land, air or naval. In a war with Japan, for example, with our lack of bases in the Western Pacific, a very long and trying period of minor operations would probably ensue while we were feeling our way westward, fighting for a series of island stepping-stones which would extend the arm of our seapower until it could begin exerting pressure on Japanese sea-communications. All this time the anxiety of our admiral would be chiefly fixed upon the question of security; the security of his heavy ships from submarine, air and mine attack, the security of his ever-lengthening line of communications from raiding cruisers, the security of his series of advance bases from more serious raids bent on their destruction. Our high command at home would be likewise greatly concerned with the security of our coastal cities against tip-and-run air raids, of our shipping against the operations of surface raiders and long-range submarines, and in particular the security of the Panama Canal against any sort of desperate enterprise set on foot by either secret or open means.

In the unlikely, but possible event of our being simultaneously attacked in both oceans, the principle of security would become paramount in one ocean, that of offensive action in the other. In the one, we should have to stand on the defensive; in the other, our fleet would operate offensively in order to bring about a decision as quickly as possible, or at least a state of affairs which would permit it to remove itself to the other ocean and restore the situation there in our favor.

Fortunately we possess in the Panama Canal an interior line of operations which permits us to transfer our fleet quickly from ocean to ocean, while denying a like privilege to any enemy. As against two fleets, each inferior to our own in fighting power, our navy (while Panama is securely ours) occupies the same position strategically as that already considered in the matter of an enemy fleet which might interpose between the two fractions of our own were we foolish enough to divide it. There is a difference, but it is one of degree and not of principle, in the fact that, the distances being so much greater, the problems to be met so much more complex and the size of the whole theater of operations (embracing both oceans and their connecting waters) so enormous, much time would doubtless elapse before the fruit of our advantage of position could be entirely realized.

The enemy fleets can hardly effect a concentration of their total force against our own, for to do so one of them must go around South America, a journey of many thousands of miles during which, from our central position, we would assuredly be able to arrange to interrupt the route of one of the fractions with our full force; or else one of them must proceed, east or west, via the Suez Canal and the Mediterranean, leaving its home waters completely uncovered to our operations for a considerable period during which we should be under no immediate threat — an unthinkable procedure which might well result in the downfall of the government which thus abandoned its people to foreign attack.

But we must also remember that in executing such a strategy, based on the correct use of our interior position, our Government will be in like case as to popular reaction along the seaboard which is temporarily uncovered by the fleet. It will be very hard to make people who are being raided, even sporadically, by enemy cruisers and aircraft, understand that thousands of miles away, against another enemy, their fleet is giving them the best protection in its power. We ought not to forget the panic which spread along our Atlantic coast during the war with Spain, when the news came that Cervera's squadron was at sea, and which not only detained half our fighting strength at Hampton Roads when it ought to have been in the Caribbean, but compelled our Government to man with naval reservists (who could have been usefully employed elsewhere) a scratch lot of old Civil War ironclads armed with muzzle-loading guns and station them solemnly in front of a few of the more vociferous seaside communities in order to let the inhabitants have some visual assurance of naval protection. It was impossible to make them understand that the real protection was being given them by Sampson and his fleet, far away to the southward, engaged in the masterly series of combinations which in the end brought the Spanish squadron to its ruin.

In this sense it is perhaps fortunate that American imaginations have been so fired by aircraft, since there will always be naval aircraft operating on the "refused" sea-frontier. Submarines and flotilla craft should also be available in considerable numbers. The chief responsibility of the defense will however be the army's, holding as it will the fixed defenses of the great harbors, and controlling the mobile land forces and the General Headquarters Air Force which will furnish the striking power to deal with any attack in force. Here again we see the relation between defense and offense; since our attitude and purpose on this frontier will be purely though temporarily defensive, while the action of the mobile forces will be offensive as against any enemy which comes within their reach. It is not suggested that any permanent success can be thus obtained, but that is not necessary; what is essential is that the refused frontier be stoutly defended until the fleet can make opportunity to arrive and upset the whole of the enemy's dispositions by threatening his control of his sea-communications.

That such a two-ocean attack would place us in a situation of the greatest danger and impose upon us the most serious difficulties, is beyond question. It is not desired to minimize the gravity of the problems which would in such a case confront those responsible for our defense. It might well be that diplomacy would here be called to the aid of military power and that we should seek (probably as the danger became apparent rather than after it had transformed itself into actuality) a suitable alliance which would in some measure offset it. Such an alliance would of course have to afford an attractive advantage to our proposed ally as well as to ourselves, and its future implications would have to be carefully examined. We ought therefore not to depend on it, while on the other hand not disregarding the possibility of such measures. Our own strength, at least, we have always at hand; the strength of others may fail us in our hour of need, as Italy failed her former Allies in 1914.

A greater degree of security would of course be ours if we were to create two fleets, each superior or at least fully equal to any which could be brought against it. But enough, it is thought, has been already said to make it clear that so vast an expenditure for construction and maintenance is hardly necessary at present. If ever the future becomes so charged with menace that the American people must bear such burdens, they will doubtless be assumed and borne. At the moment our advantage of position is so great and the likelihood of a two-ocean combination against us so remote that, considering further the extreme difficulty of coordinating with efficiency the operations of the forces of a great alliance as against a single determined power (to which all the history of such efforts bears witness) we may well rest content with a degree of naval strength which enables us to be superior to any one enemy or possible coalition which may menace us on either side.

The keystone of our arch of security is however the Panama Canal. From Norfolk to Puget Sound via Panama is, as we have said, 5800 sea-miles or about three weeks of time in terms of fleet transfer. From Norfolk to Puget Sound (or vice versa) via the Strait of Magellan is 13,600 miles,[1] or at least seven or eight weeks for the fleet with all the luck in the world as to re-fueling and every cooperation in that respect from South American nations, and assuming no interruptions en route from enemy action of any kind. Even four extra

---

[1] All sea distances in this book are stated in nautical miles; all land distances, including all references to the flying range of land-based aircraft, are stated in statute miles.

weeks might make all the difference in the outcome of whatever operations an enemy was meanwhile attempting, and would very greatly diminish the risk to be weighed by him in advance of attempting them at all.

It is not, one must admit, very likely that the safe transit of the Panama Canal can be interrupted by enemy action, fiction thrillers to the contrary notwithstanding. But the possibility of its being done, however remote, ought to be provided against, since the consequences might be so far-reaching and so calamitous; and it is upon consideration of these consequences that the writer feels that we ought at once to proceed with the construction of the Nicaragua Canal as a second means of transit between the two oceans. The chance of both canals being simultaneously put out of action is so trifling as to be negligible. It is now estimated that the Nicaragua Canal could be built for about half a billion dollars; a considerable sum, it is true, and much more than would be needed for increasing the capacity of the Panama Canal. But the latter measure would not appreciably reduce the risk of interruption by some means; nor would it give us those commercial advantages which we might expect from a new canal whose use by American ships would, we may hope, have no treaty strings to it. The cost would be but a fraction of what it would cost us, for ship construction alone, to build a second fleet. Finally, the Nicaragua route shortens the distance between our east and west coast ports by about 700 miles, a notable gain from both the military and commercial viewpoints. Such a canal would be an asset in peace and war. It is better to be safe than sorry.

Having now related to American strategic problems certain of the basic principles of war, it seems appropriate to examine the general conditions of overseas warfare, the various methods by which an insular nation such as ours may be attacked, and by which it may defend itself.

A nation, considered from the defensive point of view, is

much like a fortress; it may be attacked either by assault or by investment. Naval power can invest, but it cannot assault, save in the limited sense of its ability to bombard seacoast positions. Air power cannot invest, since it lacks range and endurance of flight and is too dependent on the weather; it can however contribute by its peculiar qualities to the efficiency of a naval investment, i.e., blockade. Its powers of assault are also limited by its range, flight endurance, and lifting power; it can do great damage within the enemy country, but it cannot bring about a decision unaided because it cannot hold territory, nor is it capable of a long-sustained destructive effort. Land power cannot invest a sea-girt nation, but it can assault; and land power alone is capable of bringing about a decision by assault, by driving within our fortress and overpowering the garrison, that is, the army of the defender, and thereafter taking possession of the vital centers and means of communication of the country invaded, bringing such pressure to bear upon the citizens thereof that they will yield what is demanded of them rather than continue to endure the exactions and sacrifices of further resistance. A like situation may be brought about by investment alone, that is, by naval blockade, but it usually takes much longer for this to achieve its purpose unless reinforced by assault, for which it requires the aid of land forces or of very considerable air forces.

In general it may be said that investment seeks to attack the exterior communications of a country, cutting it off from its foreign sources of supply and imposing such consequent hardships upon its inhabitants that they will submit, while also impairing their ability to continue to resist. Assault seeks to attack the internal communications and the means of production and distribution, gaining the same end by more arduous and costly, but at the same time more immediately decisive means.

Investment will be successful — aside from the question of

military resistance — in direct proportion to the dependence of the invested nation on external sources of supply, either of foodstuffs for its population, or of raw materials for its industries, or of any other necessary which it cannot itself produce.

Assault will be successful — with the same exception — in proportion to its ability to reach and hold a sufficient number of the vital centers of communication and industry upon which the invaded country depends for the carrying on of the various processes of its national life; and therefore, in proportion to the vulnerability of these centers to attack from without, or to the ability of the attacker to arrange for cooperation from within by disaffected elements of the population. Air assault unsupported by land forces will be able to have a decisive effect only as it reinforces and makes finally unbearable the exactions of naval blockade; it acts in this respect as the last straw to break the back of the national will to go on fighting.

Attacks need not be directly launched against the homeland of a country but may be directed against some outlying possession, either for the purpose of getting hold of it for its intrinsic worth, or as a preliminary to further operations which it will facilitate.

Troops cannot be transported overseas in any number save when naval command of the waters over which they are to pass has previously been assured, since a troop convoy is a large, slow and vulnerable target, and will assuredly suffer heavily if its escort be attacked by anything like an equal force.

Nor can troops land on a hostile shore, against resistance, save with a powerful air support sufficient to establish temporary air superiority at the point and time of landing, since transports at anchor and troops crowded in small boats or scattered in detachments along a beach are the most attractive targets imaginable for the defender's aviation. A sufficiently powerful air support for this purpose cannot be attained by carrier-borne aircraft, which must necessarily be inferior in numbers to aircraft based on the infinitely more numerous and larger airdromes afforded by the wide expanse of the land, and less efficient in the details of their operation. Hence, as a preliminary to any landing, a shore air base must be obtained within easy flying distance of the selected point of disembarkation; and this will frequently entail a minor combined expedition for the purpose.

Large armies, accompanied as modern armies must be by artillery of various calibers, tanks, and other heavy equipment, as well as vast quantities of munitions and supplies, cannot usually be landed over an open beach; but must first obtain possession of a secure harbor with the necessary piers, cranes and other accessories for getting ashore their impedimenta. Since such harbors are customarily defended by heavy guns and controlled minefields, a landing on an open coast will usually be an operation of limited objective and extent, directed to the end of taking the fixed defenses of a selected harbor in the rear and thus enabling a more considerable force to effect invasion.

Just as aircraft cannot operate save from a base within their radius of action, making due allowance for the fuel expenditure incident to fighting and maneuvering, so ships are likewise limited by the same considerations. Nor is the radius of the battleship or the heavy cruiser here determinative, since these must be accompanied by large numbers of destroyers to screen them against torpedo attack by enemy destroyers or submarines. A fleet, therefore, considered as a whole, is limited to maritime areas within the radius of action of its destroyers, or about 2500 sea-miles at best, probably nearer 2000 under war conditions.

Hence it cannot undertake any operation, either of its own or in support of other instrumentalities of war, at a distance much greater than 2000 miles from a secure base, adequate to supply its needs for fuel, stores and munitions and secured against raids by fixed defenses and local mobile forces. The base must likewise be able to effect repairs to damaged ships, which otherwise will be likely to fall prey to enemy submarines while steaming at slow speeds or being towed.

In an attack on the external communications of a country, two methods are open to a naval force; it may send cruisers to patrol the trade routes and pick up individually the ships carrying the enemy commerce, or it may blockade the ports to which the commerce is bound. In exceptional cases it may watch constricted waterways through which commerce is compelled to pass. Cruiser operations are therefore said to strike at the branches of the tree of commerce, while block-ade strikes at the roots. Cruiser operations, however, may be conducted at long distances from any base, since they may be carried on by large ships of great fuel-capacity; while blockade, if it be a close blockade, will demand large num-bers of small craft of various types (there will never be enough big ones to watch all the ports of a great country) and thus possesses the same requirement as to a nearby base as do fleet operations. Distant blockade, effected by watching focal points or constricted waterways, is a special type of operation whose requirements as to bases are propor-tioned to circumstances; but may easily be deduced in any particular case from the principles above set forth.

But, like the overseas transport of troops, blockade cannot be made effective without antecedent command of the wa-ters in which the blockading force must operate; without the assurance, either by the defeat of the enemy fleet or its con-finement by superior force in a defended harbor, that it will not be able to interfere with the blockading detachments, which will, by reason of their wide dispersion, be particu-larly vulnerable to the action of concentrated force.

Hence no attack of a serious nature can be made upon a

truly insular country, save on the condition of obtaining a sufficient degree of naval command of the waters which wash its shores to enable troops and air forces to be brought within striking distance for assault, or to enable blockading forces to operate effectively against its external communications.

Hence also the true defense of such an insular country is principally, indeed almost wholly, dependent upon preserving such command to its own possession, which it can do only by maintaining a fleet adequate for the purpose and supported by the necessary bases from which to operate.

So long as it possesses such a fleet, and such bases, the chance of success in an attack upon it will be small indeed. The fleet must first be disposed of either by battle, or by being contained by a superior fleet. In either case the fleet of an assailant must have an appropriate base; and if such a base must first be fought for, the same set of conditions applies to the operations necessary to obtain it. It cannot be had if command of the waters leading to it cannot be assured; if it is closer to the bases of the defending fleet than to those of the assailant, the risks, in default of great disparity of numbers, mount up very rapidly. The same considerations attach to an assault on any outlying possession or colony.

Distant blockade is attended with a less degree of risk, and may have the advantage of bringing the defending fleet out to fight under unfavorable conditions. However, it too must depend on the protection of a sufficient battle-force to guard from concentrated attack the vessels engaged in it.

As distinguished from distant blockade, mere raids against commercial shipping have never been successful in bringing about a decision in war; they can only be minor incidents in the great drama, incidents of sporadic and annoying, but not decisive nature. The same is true of "tip-and-run" raids by warships or aircraft against an enemy coast, in the absence of a force able to command the sea. They can annoy, but they cannot seriously injure; they may however have their effect if undertaken as part of a more ambitious scheme, in that they may produce an undue dispersion of force to deal with them.

By this exposition, we have arrived at the great fundamental truth which conditions all sea-warfare:

The ultimate object of all naval operations in war is the control of maritime communications: the denial of them to the enemy, the assurance of them for one's own use, whether for military or commercial purposes.

To this ultimate purpose the destruction or neutralization of the enemy's fleet is a means, a necessary means, but not in itself an end.

Destruction will serve the end better than neutralization, since a fleet destroyed or disabled in battle is wiped off the board and ceases to be a source of concern; while one cooped up in harbor may always emerge at a favorable moment, to disturb that control of sea-communications which has been established by its enemy. Moreover — as was evidenced in the last war — the containing of an enemy fleet imposes a condition of continual strain and anxiety, and a series of minor operations and activities, which are not only trying to the nerves of officers and men but may result in the loss by torpedo, mine, bomb or accident of one or more battleships, perhaps reducing the battle-strength of the containing fleet below the limit of safety.

The control of maritime communications, however, rests on the firm foundation of a superior battle-fleet adequate either to destroy or to contain the battle-fleet of the enemy.

It cannot be achieved by air forces, since these can closely watch only inshore waters. When they are required to fly great distances, they cannot exercise any continuity of control. This is not to say that the airplane is not a menace to the battleship under certain conditions, for it may well be so; although as yet there has been no demonstration of the ability of airplane bombs to sink a modern battleship under war conditions, the experiments conducted respectively by the American and British navies on the *Washington* and *Emperor of India* tending rather to the contrary conclusion. But in any case the airplane is strictly limited as to range and carrying power; when a bomber has discharged its load of bombs it must return to its base for more before it can effect any further damage. A battleship, on the other hand, having fired a salvo, merely requires to reload its guns to fire another. The airplane has a single chance or perhaps two or three, and must then leave the field of action; the battleship can stay there and go on fighting. The airplane is dependent to a great extent on the weather; the battleship can fight in almost any sort of weather, subject to the factor of visibility. The radius of action of a fleet is more than double that of an air force for large-scale operations; moreover cruisers engaged in the actual work of controlling and guarding maritime communications can operate over extended areas and long periods of time quite impossible to the airplane. Thus the control of maritime communications exercised by the airplane is intermittent, precarious and limited in space, while that exercised by surface ships may be continuous, dependable and adequate to all reasonable purposes.

The only method by which these disabilities of the airplane may be even partially overcome, as to a particular area of sea within their range, is to employ enormous numbers of them. This, when calculated on a practical basis, leads at once into a maze of absurdities and impossibilities. Take the matter of continuity of effort. The number of airplanes required to keep one airplane continually in flight over a vital position or sea-route is very large. It is affected by a number of considerations. First the time in coming and going, dependent on the distance from the airdrome to the perimeter of the area to be controlled. Next, the matter of endurance of personnel; it was considered in the last war that active missions should be limited to two hours, beyond which point the pilots and other flying personnel tended to "go stale"; even though this may now be increased, due to technical improvements which lessen the strain, it is obvious that there is a point beyond which it is not safe to go. Next is the question of fuel capacity; a given plane has so much total lift, and for every gallon of gasoline the military load (on which is dependent its ability to damage an enemy) must be correspondingly reduced. When to these is added the necessity for making up losses due to accident, to the operations of the enemy and to mechanical defect, and the imperative requirement of periodical and frequent overhaul, and when there is considered the enormous ground organization necessitated by the operation of modern air forces, it begins to be apparent that the alleged economy of an air force as against a navy is not likely to be realized in fact.

The Chief of the Bureau of Aeronautics of the Navy Department, Rear Admiral Cook, in testifying before the House Naval Affairs Committee last February, pointed out that, in comparing the ability of airplanes to destroy a hostile fleet approaching our shores with the ability of a battleship force to produce the same effect, it would, by calculation, require 6750 bombing-planes to produce within one hour the same volume of destructive fire as could be produced by fifteen battleships of the type of the new U.S.S. *North Carolina*. The fifteen battleships would cost roughly $70,000,000 each, or a total of a little over a billion dollars in all. The 6750 bombers (each capable of carrying two 2000-pound bombs) would cost $350,000 each, or two-and-a-third billion dollars. The battleships would have a useful life of at least twenty-six years, the airplanes of not more than eight years. On this basis, in twenty-six years the airplane policy would have cost more than seven times as much as the battleship policy for new construction alone.

Considered from another angle, the fifteen battleships will

require complements of about 1500 officers and men each, or a total of 22,500. It is calculated that a modern air force, for the strictly military duties connected with the operation of its units, requires about fifteen officers and men per airplane; the fleet of 6750 bombers would therefore require a total personnel of about 100,000.

Of course this does not include on the naval side the complements of the cruisers, destroyers, submarines, and auxiliaries which the fleet must have; but neither does it include on the air side the enormous number of scouting, pursuit and observation planes which the bombing force must have.

This is perhaps a *reductio ad absurdum,* in that it would as a practical matter be quite impossible to operate or control any such enormous mass of airplanes, while fifteen battleships may be easily handled as a fleet unit; but it will serve to indicate how a tendency to depend on one weapon leads to impossible conclusions when the claims of theory are examined in the light of war requirements. The favorite comparison of the air enthusiast of the cost of one plane against that of one battleship disappears from such practical calculations and is replaced by the far more important factor of comparative fire effect, of actual ability to inflict damage on an enemy. When the cost of such fire effect produced in one way is compared with the cost of the same fire effect produced in another, the interests of the taxpayer are seen to be directly concerned in the maintenance of intelligent military policy, quite aside from the matter of his basic interest in national security.

But this is not, by any means, the whole story. The limitations of the airplane as to radius of action (500 miles for large formations of average planes carrying medium bomb loads, 600-750 for very large planes carrying half their normal bomb loads) tie air power to its bases as a bird may be tied by the leg to its perch. Thus the operations of air forces are limited to coastal waters, or to circumscribed areas around our outlying possessions.

Getting back to the necessity of maintaining control of sea-communications in the execution of a naval policy of national defense, it is immediately apparent that air power cannot alone prevent an enemy from establishing a base of operations in this hemisphere, while naval power can do so. Air power cannot go far out to sea to seek for and destroy the enemy fleet, the destruction or neutralization of which is a necessary means for obtaining sea-command; cannot in fact injure it at all unless the fleet is considerate enough to come within flying radius. The operations incident to the establishment of bases and to distant blockade could be carried on by enemy forces, naval, air and land, without serious interruption by our air power, or at the best, disturbed only by sporadic raids of indecisive character. Air power could not protect our use of the Panama Canal, the vital link in our most important line of sea-communications, since the operations necessary to stop the greater part of the traffic through the Canal could be carried on by cruisers operating beyond the reach of Zone-based planes. If ships cannot use it, the Canal might as well not exist. Air power could not prevent a Pacific enemy from establishing himself in one of the harbors of the Aleutian Islands and thence conducting cruiser and submarine operations against our shipping on the Pacific coast.

Finally—air power as our sole military reliance must stand or fall on this: that by its limited range it is committed to the strategical defensive, since it can attack the enemy only when he comes within reach of it. It can therefore do him no harm unless he so permits; whereas it leaves him free to work his will anywhere within the Western Hemisphere outside of its reach. It therefore allows the enemy to wage war against us at a minimum of risk to himself. It does not imperil his fleet. It does not imperil his sea-communications. It does not imperil his overseas operations unless directed against our own shores, the seat of our industrial and military power. It leaves him in the position of being able to hurt us, while we are deprived of the ability to hurt him.

It is not desired in any way to impugn the truly remarkable military qualities possessed by modern air forces, or the contribution which air power may make to our defense. It possesses, by reason of its speed and range, a quality of strategic concentration, appreciation of which is the key to its employment, and which renders it formidable indeed to an enemy attempting a landing on the shore of a great country possessed of ample air resources. It is an essential arm of the fleet both in defensive and offensive operations, as it is of the army in the execution of various war missions. Its flexibility enables it to be quickly adapted to changing conditions of enemy action, and goes far to offset a surprise effected by more slowly moving forces. In reconnaissance, whether by land or sea, it has a great role to play; and it is an essential adjunct to the fire-control of heavy guns, whether of a battleship or a land battery. There is a danger in undue lack of understanding of its qualities, leading to failure to make full use of them, just as there is danger in placing entire reliance upon it for missions and duties for which it is not fitted. Within its limitations of range, carrying power and endurance, it is an inherently offensive weapon and must be so employed by the high command which would get the ultimate return for its cost. Nowhere will a defensive policy or a defensive spirit be so damaging to morale as in an air force, dependent as it is upon the qualities of audacity and determination usually associated with youth — and flying, especially war flying, is still a young man's job. The scope of its offensive opportunities will be immensely enhanced when it is used, as it ought to be, as part of the whole military team, in cooperation with the other agencies of national war effort; while in such measure as it becomes the chief reliance, it is in that measure reduced by its limitations to a defensive policy.

Fortunately there is no present sign of any all-air policy being adopted by our Government, well advised as it is and has been by competent naval and military staffs. The discussion of the subject is nevertheless worthwhile in a work directed not so much to the professional military man as to the average citizen, who is so continually bombarded with exaggerated statements and outlandish predictions.

We return, then, to our original conception of the control of maritime communications by a battle-fleet, whose means to that end is the destruction or neutralization of the battle-fleet of the enemy. Upon this foundation rest all the far-flung minor operations incident to the actual service and use of such control. And upon the security of its bases rests in turn the ability of the battle-fleet to perform its missions.

The qualities to be considered in a naval base, as indeed in any military position, are three: Strength, Location, and Resources.

Strength may be partly natural and partly artificial. Natural strength, in a naval base, implies a secure harbor with sufficient depth at the entrance and sufficient anchorage to provide shelter for all the ships which may use it; hydrographic conditions permitting freedom of entrance and exit, the latter in face of a possible enemy blockading force; a topography facilitating the defense by fixed batteries or mobile guns of the entrance and approaches. Too great depth in the entrance channel is not desirable as it impedes the laying of controlled mines. Two or more entrances, while requiring additional artificial defenses, are in other respects a decided advantage, especially if their *débouchements* into the deep be too far apart to enable them to be watched by the same enemy force. New York affords a striking example of such a situation, or will when the new Hell Gate project is completed. A modern naval base should have facilities for one or more air bases in the immediate vicinity; that is, for aircraft other than those which alight on water surfaces. The lack of this is one of the great weaknesses of Gibraltar. Strength is contributed to by a lack of nearby beaches suitable for landing, and by shoals and reefs (elsewhere than within the sweep of the fixed batteries) which impede the operations of ships covering a landing and compel a long journey in small boats before one may be effected. Such hydrographic conditions often afford excellent opportunities for local naval forces of small submarines, motor torpedo-boats and the like, familiar with the local conditions as the enemy is likely not to be. The strength of a base in home territory will of course be greatly enhanced by the immediate backing of the various armed forces available in the vicinity, and by its ample communications with the rest of the country. That of an outlying base should be sufficient to protect it against enemy attack in the measure to which that attack may be considered probable. If the base be of very great strategic importance (as Hawaii) it must be strong enough to resist an attack in full force for the period of time (usually calculable quite closely) which must elapse before reinforcements can reach it, with an allowance for unforeseen contingencies. This will usually demand not only fixed defenses but a considerable garrison of mobile troops, an air force, and local naval defense units. If the base be of lesser importance, perhaps an outpost covering the approaches to a more vital position and within the radius of action of a fleet based on the latter, it need have only sufficient defensive strength to insure it against raids by enemy detachments, since it is hardly an objective likely to attract the enemy's main effort. Whatever the nature of the defenses, they must be such as to relieve the commander of the main fleet of any anxiety as to the security of his base; his freedom of action will otherwise be seriously and perhaps fatally compromised. The base exists for the fleet and not the fleet for the base.

Location is a quality to which artifice can contribute nothing. A base designed to afford control of maritime communications within a certain area of sea must be so placed that from it a fleet may comfortably operate in every part of that area, or may at least cover all the approaches to it. The base itself commands nothing beyond the reach of its own weapons. In case of a very narrow approach, such as the Strait of Gibraltar, the weapons of the base may themselves directly contribute to maritime control; otherwise the base controls only as it gives support and mobility to the fleet. Location may make a contribution to strength insofar as it renders the base difficult of approach and attack by an enemy.

Resources, again, may be natural or artificial. They consist of two elements: permanent resources, largely concerned with repair and refitting and including drydocks, machine-shops and the like; and fluid resources, concerned with the supply of fuel, stores, munitions and food. Permanent resources may however be improvised to a certain extent by the use of repair ships, floating drydocks and coffer-dam equipment. In a base located in home territory there will usually be no difficulty about fluid resources; an outlying base will be dependent to a greater or less extent upon its sea-communications with home. To the extent that local resources can fill any of its needs, including not only the various sorts of supplies, but skilled and unskilled labor, a base possessing such local facilities will be more valuable than a base which has none. In any case the communications of an outlying base with its home country will be of the greatest importance. It is one of the chief factors of strength in our position at Panama that if it be attacked from either side, it may be reinforced from the other; and its shortest line of communications with a home port, that via the Yucatan Channel to New Orleans, is also by far the best protected from exterior attack.

All bases do not have to be of this character with respect to every category of resources. There may be advance bases, carrying forward to a fleet operating at a distance the support of a main base; these may have no repair facilities, or only sufficient to handle destroyers and submarines. When active operations by large ships are being conducted from such a base, temporary repair facilities may be established there. Smaller bases, adapted only to the supply and shelter of flotilla craft or aircraft, may also be found useful, especially in such an area as the Pacific Ocean with its great distances and numerous small, scattered islands.

In all oceanic warfare the difficulties imposed on a fleet operating at a long distance from its base must be kept in mind. In a very real sense, bases mean ships. The farther a fleet is operating from its base, the more ships it must have to produce a certain mean of fighting power ever at the command of the admiral. Time spent in coming and going for repairs and replenishment, details for convoy escorts if the line of communications is open to enemy raiders, and the difficulties to be encountered in taking care of crippled ships, are all a drain on the available strength. The care necessary to conserve fuel will frequently impose severe restrictions on operations. The use of fuel-ships and other auxiliaries — the so-called "train" — may give the admiral a sort of floating, movable base; but it imposes upon him continual anxiety for its protection, since vessels of this type are usually slow and comparatively helpless against enemy destroyers or aircraft.

The fleet cannot, of course, assure against raids such long coast lines as those which we possess to east and west while the enemy's fleet occupies its attention. Raids will not, as observed, have any decisive military effect, but may produce considerable loss and suffering. Raids may be carried out by ships using their guns to bombard coastal towns; or by ship-borne aircraft which may penetrate farther inland; or by a combination of these methods. Small landing parties may occasionally be used to effect more complete destruction of some work of military value such as a railway bridge or a canal lock. Defense against raids is a function of local forces, air, land and naval. For this purpose, careful coordination and planning are needed to insure full cooperation between the army and navy, especially as to the employment of their respective air arms. When raids are considered possible, a certain number of destroyers and submarines may be made available; defensive mining may be carried out in defined areas; air forces will usually undertake a fixed system of oversea patrolling, holding the bulk of their offensive (bombing) planes in reserve at central points. Large seacoast cities, of commercial importance sufficient to make an enemy attempt to destroy them worth the risk, ought to have fixed defenses whether or not they are naval bases. Mobile artillery may be used to supplement such defenses. For the air defense of large cities and important industrial and military centers, anti-aircraft artillery will be required. A properly coordinated system of this sort should make coast raiding an expensive luxury for the enemy; it cannot, however, provide an absolute assurance against a few bombs from ship-borne aircraft falling on our territory, or a few shells being fired into some seacoast town. The only assurance of that sort which can be given is by the fleet, after it has destroyed or contained the enemy fleet; whereafter the matter of raiders can be dealt with at their sources, or in the waters of transit or approach, by the customary methods of blockade and patrol. The offensive form of war is thus again seen to be our only sure defense.

Quite different from the matter of defense against raids will be the problem presented by the defense of one of our coasts against a powerful enemy while our fleet is engaged in the other ocean, or is otherwise prevented from immediate arrival in the theater of operations: say by the destruction of the Panama Canal. In this case the responsibilities of the army and local naval forces for coast defense operations will become very heavy, and are fully examined in the chapter dealing with that subject. But unless our fleet is defeated in battle, its eventual arrival on the scene is certain, to the complete upsetting of all the enemy's plans until he has disposed of it. Since he cannot, in default of greatly superior strength, feel any confidence in his ability to do this, he must consider very gravely the risks of any large overseas expedition which rests on such merely temporary command of sea-communications. Our object must be to prevent the enemy's getting such a foothold in the time available to him that he cannot thereafter be dislodged without great loss and trouble, even though his sea-communications be severed.

In view of all the foregoing considerations, it is now possible for us to lay down certain principles upon which our national defense should be based—the elements, we might say, of American strategy:

(1) To maintain a properly constituted fleet superior in fighting power to any fleet or combination of fleets which can be assumed as our possible antagonists in either ocean.

(2) To keep that fleet, as to its main battle elements, concentrated in one ocean or the other and not divided between them.

(3) To maintain an army adequate to the defense of the bases (both continental and outlying) from which the fleet operates, and of all other harbors of commercial importance, and further capable of providing anti-aircraft defense for our cities, a General Headquarters Air Force of suitable size for dealing with any conceivable attack, and mobile troops sufficient to provide for small expeditionary forces in offensive warfare, or to deal with any possible landing-force in defensive warfare.

(4) To give particular thought and attention to the matter of the local defense of the Panama Canal and its approaches; and to supplement it by the construction at an early date of the Nicaragua Canal.

(5) To maintain a just and carefully coordinated balance between all the elements of our military establishments, neither placing entire dependence on any one arm, nor neglecting to give each its due and proportionate place; and to make coordinated plans for the cooperation of army and navy, with their respective air arms, in the missions they may be called upon to execute.

(6) While our purpose in maintaining military establishments is the defense of our territory, rights and vital interests, we must be prepared to *act* offensively against any enemy which threatens or attacks them. The element of risk to be weighed by such an enemy must extend not only to the possibility of failure, but to immediate danger to himself and his own vital interests.

It remains to examine the details of the forces and dispositions required to implement this strategy, and the theaters in which those forces may be called upon to operate; and as geography is the basis of all strategy, the geographical factors may well be given precedence.

Chapter VII

OUR STRATEGICAL POSITION IN THE ATLANTIC

One thing is sure — in the Caribbean Sea is the strategical key to two great oceans, the Atlantic and the Pacific; our own chief maritime frontiers.

ALFRED THAYER MAHAN,
REAR ADMIRAL, UNITED STATES NAVY,
Naval Strategy.

A MILITARY STUDY of any region, maritime or land, with a view to examining its possibilities as a theater of war, must first of all — in the interests of clarity — define the limits of the theater to be studied, and must next examine the principal natural features which affect or control the operation within it of armed forces, either those which are to defend it, or those which may attack it. Such a study must also concern itself with whatever positions exist beyond its limits, which may serve as bases for an attacking force; the limitations of this interest must be the radius of action of the several types of mobile instruments of which an attacker may make use. The study is incidentally concerned, of course, with the nature and strength of the armed forces of powers which hold such positions and with the fixed military establishments within the area concerned which contribute to its defense. There must also be examined the respective values to the defender, values not only military but intrinsic in nature, of the interests possessed by him in its several parts, and which it is his object to protect. If the region be in whole or in part maritime, the control of sea-communications is fundamental in such a study; and these communications must be considered from not only the military but the commercial point of view. "Commercial value cannot be separated from military in sea strategy, for the greatest interest of the sea is commerce." [1]

In a strategical examination of the maritime frontier of any naval power, a further classification should be adhered to under the headings of offensive and defensive qualities. The offensive qualities are those which support and aid the operations of a fleet, including its air force, enabling it to act freely throughout the limits of the region to be controlled. The defensive qualities are those which affect the defense of the frontier, in the absence of its fleet, by the action of land-based aircraft, fixed defenses, mobile troops and such small naval forces as may be apportioned to the duties of local defense. In this and the succeeding chapter, the strategical elements only will be considered under these headings, that is, those which have to do with the operations of the various types of forces in the theater as a whole. The details of the attack or defense of a particular position are tactical rather than strategical in nature, and insofar as such details come within the scope of this book they are considered in the chapters having to do with the details of our armed forces and their several tasks. To make this distinction clear: it is, for example, of *strategical* importance in the defense of our Atlantic frontier that Key West should be a fortified post. The amount and disposition of the armament and garrison required to give it the degree of security it ought to have are *tactical* considerations.

---

[1] Mahan, *Naval Strategy.*

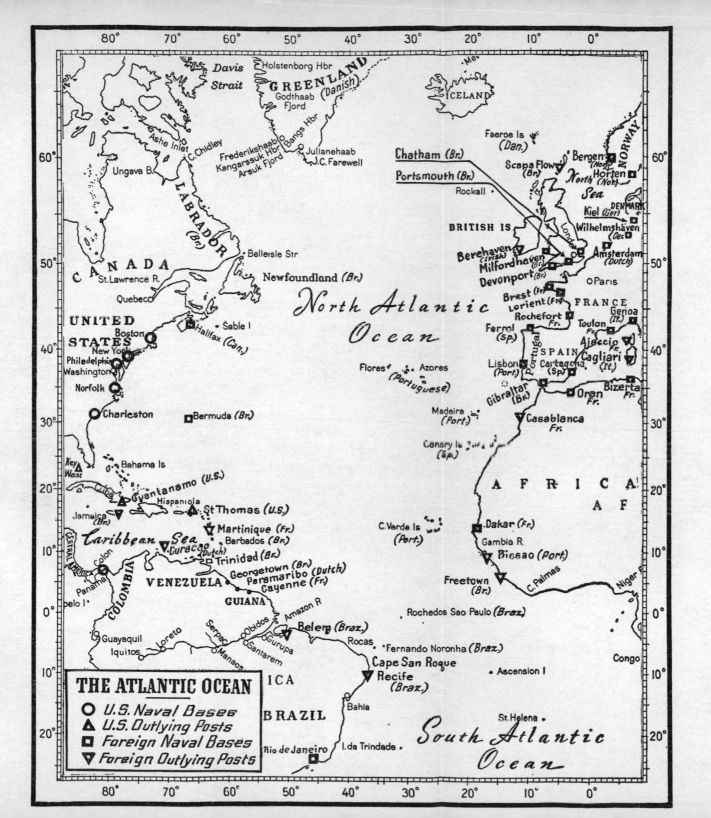

THE ATLANTIC OCEAN

○ U.S. Naval Bases
△ U.S. Outlying Posts
▢ Foreign Naval Bases
▽ Foreign Outlying Posts

The maritime frontier of the United States in the Atlantic Ocean may be described as the coast-line from Maine to Florida, and a projection from the tip of Florida to Puerto Rico and the Virgin Islands. The Gulf Coast, sheltered by command of the Strait of Florida, no longer forms a true part of the frontier, as in a military sense the Gulf of Mexico is now an American lake.

From the tip of Florida a chain of islands stretches a thousand miles to seaward, out into the Atlantic. Some of these islands are in our possession and some are not; the two chief of them are controlled by independent governments whose territorial integrity is of particular importance to us. Beyond these West Indian islands is another great enclosed sea, the Caribbean, which is the antechamber to the Panama Canal and in which, therefore, we must maintain naval dominance at all times in order to secure our most vital line of maritime communications, that via Panama between our east and west coasts.

The region to be examined may be divided into two general sectors:

(1) The coast-line from Maine to Florida, inclusive.
(2) The Caribbean Sea and the Gulf of Mexico.

The Coast-Line from Maine to Florida

Behind the northern part of this sea-frontier lies our most thickly populated and most industrially important region, the dwelling place of one-third of our population and the heart of our industrial, commercial, financial and political power. The defense of this region is of supreme importance to us, and must, if it be threatened, take precedence over every other military consideration.

To the southward we find areas of a more generally agricultural characters, but growing also in industrial consequence.

[141]

There are four important naval bases and arsenals of the
first rank on this coast — Boston, New York, Philadelphia
and Norfolk. There are lesser Navy Yards at Washington,
D. C., Portsmouth, New Hampshire, and Charleston, South
Carolina.

Of the first four, Norfolk is by all odds the most important
as a point of support for the fleet. It has in its vicinity not
only a Navy Yard but a large naval operating base, a naval
air station, a mine depot and an ammunition depot. One of
the three principal civilian ship-building yards of the coast
is located in this area (the others are in the Philadelphia and
Boston areas). Behind Norfolk lies the long estuary of Chesapeake Bay, giving protected access to the great commercial
city of Baltimore and, via the Potomac River, to the national
capital. In this area are the Naval Gun Factory, the Naval
Powder Factory, an air station, and the station of the eastern
portion of the Fleet Marine Force. The entrance to Chesapeake Bay is fortified, and is within easy range of the large
army air base at Langley Field. Norfolk enjoys excellent rail
and road communications with the interior, and with other
coastal cities.

New York, the principal commercial seaport and maritime
center of the Atlantic coast, has a Navy Yard and several
supply and ammunition establishments. Within its strategical area are located the submarine base at New London and
the torpedo factory and naval fuel depot near Newport, R. I.,
on Narragansett Bay, which is a large and commodious fortified harbor admirably adapted for fleet use. These three
points are connected through Long Island Sound, a fact
which will be of greater naval value when the project for
deepening and straightening the Hell Gate channel has been
carried out; this channel cannot at present be used by battleships, carriers or heavy cruisers.

Boston would be a base of great importance in any operations to the northeastward. It has a Navy Yard and an

ammunition depot. The Navy Yard at Portsmouth is available for smaller classes of ships.

Philadelphia Navy Yard is now used to a great extent as a building yard and for the care of ships out of commission. Charleston yard, much smaller, can accommodate light cruisers and destroyers. The naval station at Key West is in an inactive status.

Other seaports of commercial importance possessing some facilities for supply and repair are Portland, Maine, New Bedford, Massachusetts, and Savannah, Georgia, which are fortified; and Wilmington, North Carolina, Jacksonville and Miami, Florida, which are not.

Taken together, our four chief naval ports on the Atlantic seaboard — Norfolk, Philadelphia, New York and Boston — with their intermediate and auxiliary positions, form a secure and in most respects wholly adequate base of operations for the fleet. They are linked together by ample land communications, and have immediately behind them the chief industrial resources of the country. From this composite base the fleet can operate offensively against any enemy force approaching by the North Atlantic sea-lanes, and can reach out to meet such a threat almost, if not quite, to the shores of Europe. Cruiser and long-range submarine operations in European waters, if required, can quite well be supported.

The various bases and positions can support the fleet, or fractions of it, in a flexible and efficient manner.

From the northern end of the line — Boston — the limits of fleet radius reach as far as Cape Farewell, Greenland, and to the Azores. The southern tip of Nova Scotia is something over 200 miles away, and St. John's, Newfoundland, about 900.

From the southern end of the line — Norfolk — the most distant island of the West Indies (Barbados) and the Panama Canal are within reach (about 1800 miles each). Key West is distant about 1000 miles.

[143]

There are certain deficiencies, however, worthy of note. One is in the matter of fixed defenses, and especially the shortage of permanent Coast Artillery garrisons therefor. No harbor-defense on the Atlantic coast has today an adequate garrison, and only Long Island Sound, New York and Chesapeake Bay have anything more than maintenance detachments. This matter will be covered in greater detail in the subsequent discussion of the army. It is mentioned here because of the possible restriction imposed on the fleet's freedom of action by any anxiety as to the security of its bases. Another deficiency is the lack of any dock in the Port of New York capable of taking the larger battleships. Boston, Philadelphia and Norfolk, however, have such docks.

Finally, there is the lack of air bases at the Boston end of the line. A large naval air base and an army air base ought to be located in this vicinity, for the support of naval operations to the east and northeast.

The distances which constrain offensive operations in the Atlantic are materially less than those of the Pacific. From or to Boston, the approximate distances of the nearest bases of the principal naval powers of Europe are as follows:

Country	Nearest Base	Distance (nautical miles)
Great Britain	Devonport	2800
France	Brest	2800
Germany	Wilhelmshaven	3600
Italy	Spezia	3900
Soviet Union	Kronstadt	4000
Spain	Ferrol	2700

The distances from or to New York average about 200 miles more, and from or to Norfolk 300 upwards. A British fleet able to base on Berehaven (Eire) would cut about 200 miles from the Devonport figure.

Considering that the radius of fleet operations is 2000-2500 miles, it appears that neither American nor European fleets could conduct such operations in trans-Atlantic waters in default of a trans-Atlantic base. At least they must do so at great risk and inconvenience and under many limitations: such as are imposed, for example, by the use of a train. In either direction, however, cruiser operations against trade routes are more practicable; thus if we were at war with a Mediterranean power whose fleet we had defeated it would be possible for us to keep our heavy cruisers on station in the western approaches to Gibraltar, cutting off access to the Atlantic for enemy shipping, on a basis of about one cruiser on station for one coming and going: excluding losses, accidents and extended liberty for crews. The enemy's ability to drive the cruisers off would depend on the degree of injury we had previously inflicted on his fleet; which would, of course, be our gauge in judging the scale of blockading operations it was safe to undertake. But the operations even of long-range cruisers would be immensely facilitated if we could find a friendly port nearby to use as a base, or even a quiet anchorage where our ships could refuel from tankers. The same considerations apply when the directions are reversed.

No naval base is available to an enemy on this side of the North Atlantic, since nothing can be more certain than a common line of action against European aggression by Canada and the United States; or in the unlikely event of an Anglo-American war, at the very least Canadian neutrality. This rules out the small Canadian naval base at Halifax as a source of danger to us. There are however certain positions on the Canadian coast, and in the island of Newfoundland, of which an enemy might avail himself.

The military establishments of Canada are therefore a factor to be examined. They are wholly defensive in nature, possessing no offensive qualities worth considering. Canada has in the Atlantic a naval force of two destroyers and a few small craft such as mine-sweepers and fishery protection gun-boats. Her air force has a total of eight squadrons (established on a two-flight basis) plus nine squadrons of the Non-Permanent Air Force (resembling our National Guard squadrons) complete as to personnel, but having equipment for but one flight per squadron. The regular army (Permanent Force) has a strength of about 4000 officers and men, to which might be added the 2500 Royal Canadian Mounted Police. There is a citizen force (Non-Permanent Active Militia) with a nominal establishment of over 100,000; the actual strength as of December 31, 1936, was however but 45,000. Halifax possesses fixed defenses. Newfoundland, politically not part of Canada, has no defense forces whatever.

Canada can therefore only begin to defend herself after she is actually invaded, except for such small powers of resistance as her tiny navy and air force could effect within their exterior radii of action. Many parts of the great Dominion, and of Labrador, a dependency of Newfoundland, are quite out of reach of her land forces.

Both as to her own defense and as to its bearing on ours — as for example against a European attempt to establish an air or naval base of operations in Canadian territory for use against us — Canada is in the first instance dependent, in the absence of British ability to protect her, on the offensive powers of the American fleet and air force. To these elements her defensive strength will afford support, extending the radius of action of our ships and planes to cover thoroughly all the areas in which dangerous enemy activities might be apprehended. If our fleet were present in the Atlantic the support of Halifax would give it a valuable advanced position; if it were not, that support would be still more valuable proportionately in extending the field of operations of our light naval forces.

One more position must be mentioned before leaving the

northern sector of our study, and that is the British island of Bermuda, lying in mid-ocean 680 miles from New York. If Bermuda fell into the hands of an enemy, it would not only afford an excellent base for cruisers attacking our trade-routes, but from it large flying-boats might bomb our coastal cities, coming in from the sea with every prospect of effecting surprise. It is this ability to strike from over the sea, without warning, which has made the raids conducted from the island of Majorca against the Spanish coast so effective and so difficult to counter, though the distances are of course much smaller. If a condition of affairs ever arose, in which we might foresee a period of British impotence to defend Bermuda at a moment when there was prospect of our being involved in war with a European power, it might be necessary for us to assume the responsibility for Bermuda's defense, at least for the time being.

Bermuda has at present a small regular garrison (infantry and an Ordnance Corps maintenance party for the fixed defenses) numbering about 400; this is supplemented by local volunteers and militia (infantry, coast artillery and engineers) some 450 strong. The fortifications are armed with a battery of six-inch guns. There is no air force. The naval station, which is the headquarters of the America and West Indies Squadron, has a small permanent naval staff, and possesses a floating drydock adequate for destroyers or for the smaller types of British light cruisers; it is just too short to take any American cruiser.

In its present state the island is hardly capable of resisting an attack in force. Its hydrographic conditions, however, lend it strength; if defended by heavy guns and a system of controlled mines, supplemented by a seaplane base and a squadron of submarines, it could be rendered quite formidable. In our hands, it would for offensive warfare afford an excellent point of support for cruiser and other operations in European waters, being a stepping-stone toward the

Azores; defensively, it would enable our patrol-planes to cover a very wide area of sea and would support operations conducted by any class of ships we had available for countering enemy cruiser attacks on our commerce. Long-range submarines based here and energetically employed in conjunction with patrol-planes should be able to find opportunities for intercepting enemy ships.

Toward the tremendous "bight" of the North American coast, curving round from Nova Scotia to Florida, Bermuda bears a relationship similar in principle, though far more extensive in scope—a relationship in fact strategical rather than tactical—to that which Heligoland bore to the bight of the German coast in the World War. Held by an enemy, it would impose upon us very grievous disadvantages; held by ourselves, it would be an advanced position of the greatest defensive and offensive value.

One other feature of our Atlantic coast is the existence of a system of inland waterways, notably to the south of Norfolk. These afford excellent opportunities for light naval craft, and would enable such vessels (if daringly and skilfully handled) to afford a certain degree of protection to coastwise shipping.

As we come to the southern limit of the coast, however, we are drawn into the consideration of the second sector of our Atlantic strategical study, a sector of far greater military, though of less intrinsic, consequence than the first.

THE CARIBBEAN SEA AND THE GULF OF MEXICO

At the risk of tiresome repetition, the fact will again be pointed out that our real safety in the Atlantic as in the Pacific lies in the ability of our fleet to dominate the routes of sea-communication by which, alone, any serious threat may come within striking distance of our shores.

If, at the first arising of such a threat in the Atlantic, our

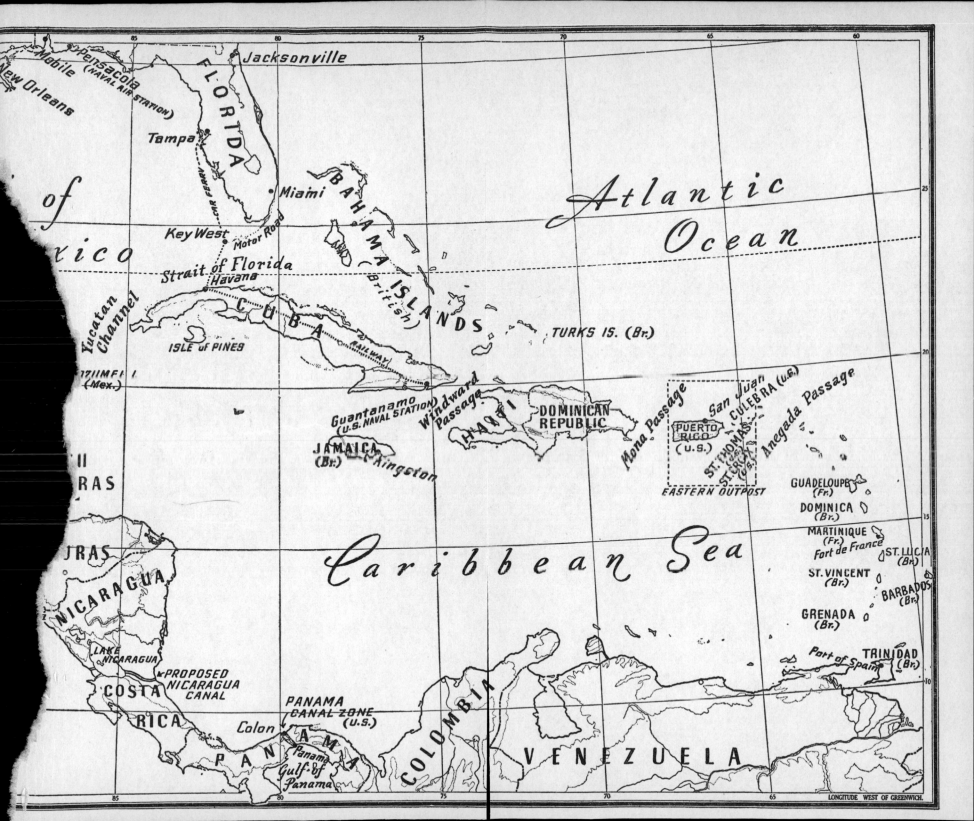

fleet is already in that ocean, it will (provided its strength has not been allowed to fall below the limit of safety imposed by the armaments of other powers) be able to exercise such dominance at once. If it be in the Pacific, our first concern in the scale of strategical importance is to assure its safe and early arrival in the threatened area. Therefore the security of the route by which it must come is the keystone of our defense plan.

This route is the Panama Canal, supplemented perhaps at some future date by an additional canal in Nicaragua.

The eastward exits of both canals debouch into the Caribbean Sea; the maintenance of complete naval control of that body of water is therefore vital to the United States. Fortunately, nature has in this as elsewhere greatly assisted our country. The islands which delimit the Caribbean to the east and north form a natural chain of defensive positions which control every Atlantic approach to that sea and, together, afford a formidable "line of control" based on which our light forces can dispute with an enemy fleet, however formidable, the inviolability of our "American Mediterranean". They thus cover the safe arrival on the east side of the Central American Isthmus of our fleet and, as it comes within their sphere of influence, in turn afford it advance bases from which it can extend that influence into the Atlantic proper.

So tremendous an advantage as we have in possessing a short line of communication between our two oceans, and in holding the only means of access from the Pacific to the Caribbean, is thus supplemented and extended, as regards the Atlantic, by a maritime position which enables us to develop the full force of our naval power without danger of attack in detail, and to employ that power in the most effective manner for accomplishing our objects in any naval war in that ocean.

[149]

The strategical study of the Caribbean area may therefore be divided into three parts:

(1) The approach from the Pacific (Panama),
(2) The approaches from the Atlantic,
(3) Points of control within the Caribbean itself.

The Panama Canal is dominated and made secure by very powerful fortifications, which cover both its Atlantic and Pacific approaches and enable a fleet proceeding in either direction to emerge and take up battle formation under their protection. There are a garrison of mobile troops, army and navy air bases, and a submarine base, also a naval ammunition depot. The heaviest ships may be docked at Balboa. Panama may be reinforced from the United States by a protected route via the Yucatan Channel, it being but 1400 miles from New Orleans to Colon. About half way, a Mexican island (Cozumel) now used as a way-station by Pan-American Airways, would greatly facilitate the air reinforcement of the Panama Canal Zone in war; arrangements for the lease of this island from Mexico might therefore be a sound contribution to our defense, as its possession would enable a steady stream of aerial reinforcements to be despatched to Panama from our air bases in Florida, Louisiana and Texas.

But, though the Pacific approach to the Caribbean is securely ours, the means of access from the Atlantic cannot be so easily controlled, because the approaches are more numerous and some of them more remote in a military sense from the center of our power.

The islands which fringe the Caribbean to the north and east diminish progressively in size and importance as one proceeds seaward from the Strait of Florida. From the Yucatan Channel and the Strait of Florida to the Windward Passage, Cuba bars the way to maritime traffic for over 500 miles; from the Windward Passage to the Mona Passage, for nearly 300 miles Haiti stands guard; and east of the Mona Passage, in turn, Puerto Rico imposes a further barrier about

100 miles long. The passages named are therefore of much greater importance proportionately than the numerous passages among the string of much smaller islands which, beyond Puerto Rico, runs east for 200 miles and then drops south another 500 to the mainland of South America. They constrain all maritime traffic into themselves, exercising an influence over its courses far beyond their own limits.

Of them all, the most important as concerns the Caribbean Sea is the Windward Passage. It is the only entrance into that sea in a line almost 1000 miles long, from Cape San Antonio at the west end of Cuba to Cape Engano at the east end of Haiti. Through it passes our most important single route of commercial sea-traffic, that from New York and other northern ports to the Panama Canal. Fifty miles wide, and too deep for mining, it cannot be controlled by fortifications, even if both shores were in our possession, as they are not. It must therefore be controlled by mobile forces—ships aided by aircraft.

For this purpose, fortunately, the United States possesses an admirably located base. Guantanamo Bay, used by us under lease from the Republic of Cuba, is a deep indentation in the south shore of that island 70 miles west of Cape Maysi, Cuba's eastern extremity on the shore of the Windward Passage. It is a commodious and well sheltered harbor, ample for the use of the fleet, and has a narrow entrance easily commanded by a few batteries of guns, and adapted for the use of controlled mines. There are no fortifications at present, but the Fleet Marine Force at Quantico, Virginia, has equipment which could be used to make Guantanamo secure in a comparatively short time. In view of the importance of this position, fixed defenses and increased repair facilities ought to be established at Guantanamo as soon as possible.

Guantanamo commands not only the Windward Passage, but the entire Caribbean, as to which it possesses a central position as well as one sheltered from direct attack from without. It is 700 miles from Panama, 600 from the Yucatan Channel, 700 from Saint Thomas and about 1200 from Trinidad, away at the southern end of the chain of the Lesser Antilles. Thus a fleet based here can operate comfortably in any part of the Caribbean, but less comfortably to the extreme eastern limits of that sea than elsewhere within it. Guantanamo, like Panama, possesses a sheltered route of supply from our Gulf ports, via the Yucatan Channel; it is about 1100 miles from New Orleans or Pensacola. But it also possesses another supply line which renders it unique among West Indian bases in the matter of resources; for it is connected by rail with Havana, which port can be reached by car-ferries from Tampa by a sea-run of only 325 miles. Thus carload freight can be delivered on the shores of Guantanamo Bay from any point in the United States without breaking bulk. This of course presumes that which may justly be presumed — the cooperation in any time of danger of the Cuban Government with our own.

Guantanamo, then, is our main base in the Caribbean and the guardian of the Windward Passage. On the Mona Passage we have Puerto Rico, a large island of considerable local resources with several good harbors, none of them, unfortunately, able comfortably to accommodate battleships. There are no fixed defenses or even mobile heavy guns here, nor is there an air base. Just east of Puerto Rico and belonging to it is the islet of Culebra, whose Great Harbor is adequate for a fleet anchorage, though difficult to defend by fortification. A few miles farther eastward, however, we possess a harbor of quite different characteristics. The island of Saint Thomas, one of the American Virgins, with its fine and easily protected port of Charlotte Amalie, is now our easternmost Caribbean possession. Together with Puerto Rico and Culebra, it forms an outpost which extends the influence of Guantanamo 700 miles to seaward and it watches the Anegada Passage, 70 miles distant, which is the principal commercial route for European traffic directed upon Panama.

Not only this, but it flanks the approaches from Europe to our eastern seaboard. It is about 700 miles south of Bermuda, and 1500 south of the southern tip of Nova Scotia. Like Puerto Rico, Saint Thomas has no fortifications, though there is a Marine Corps air base on the island, and some provision (now unused) for naval fuel storage. A fortified post, with repair facilities for small craft and a patrol-plane base, is needed in this area.

East and then south from Saint Thomas, the islands of the Lesser Antilles drop away down to the South American coast. The many passages among them afford numerous routes of access to the eastern Caribbean, and the farther one gets from Saint Thomas, the less assured becomes the control of our naval power over such access. At Trinidad, 500 miles from Saint Thomas, the control of our fleet, if present, would still be operative; but the control which might be exercised by light forces would be less certain by a good deal.

This of course is the sort of control that would have to be immediately employed in a case where the fleet was moving via Panama to an Atlantic scene of war. Entrance to the Caribbean via the Strait of Florida and the Yucatan Channel could be denied to any enemy naval force without much difficulty. From Guantanamo, aircraft and flotilla craft, to say nothing of cruisers, could operate over and in the Windward Passage; from Puerto Rico-Culebra-Saint Thomas (which for the sake of brevity we will call the Eastern Outpost area) the Mona Passage and the Anegada Passage could be watched. Penetration of the Caribbean by any of these routes would be dangerous for any enemy naval force, and a foreign admiral would think very carefully before he so risked his precious and irreplaceable battleships, which might be sunk or badly injured by torpedoes far from a friendly dockyard, or so damaged by air bombs as to reduce their speed and make them prey to submarines. In such narrow waters, indeed, submarines have their maximum of opportunity. They cannot catch a fast surface vessel after they have submerged; but when they can lie in wait, their peculiar qualities give them considerable advantages.

Through the Lesser Antilles, however, penetration of the Caribbean might be more easily achieved. There are half-a-score of channels available, and we could hardly plant a submarine division in each one and keep it there on station. The southernmost of these channels are rather beyond the range of efficient air patrol from the Eastern Outpost. To keep one patrol-plane flying over the channel between Trinidad and Grenada, for example, would require four patrol-planes and six crews at the Eastern Outpost, allowing nothing for accident and bad weather.

It would, therefore, be of great advantage to us if we could have a base at the southern end of the chain of islands, a base such as Trinidad itself or Barbados. Were we thus emplaced, we could, even in the absence of our fleet, make it extremely hazardous for any enemy fleet to try to enter the Caribbean. We could not prevent it absolutely, of course; in actual warfare nothing is as certain and clean cut as that. But we could impose such risks as to make any admiral hesitate to chance his battleships in such an enterprise.

Raiding cruisers of course could enter, and do some damage to our shipping; but these would run a double hazard, for once in, lacking a base, they would some time have to go out again.

A southeastern base would be of further advantage, in case we were compelled to carry on offensive operations in the South Atlantic to check any European enterprise directed against one of the South American powers. From Barbados, for example, a fleet can operate all the way eastward to the Cape Verdes, or south-eastward to Cape San Roque at the "corner" of Brazil. A glance at the map will show that the triangular area of sea included between straight lines joining these three points controls all access to the South Atlantic from Europe. Saint Thomas is a little too far away to give equal facility of action in this area.

The principle to be considered in this, which may well be one of the most important practical questions of American strategy in the immediate future, is that when naval power must be extended from the seat of national strength toward a distant theater of operations, it can be done only by the employment of a chain of advanced posts, adequate to carry forward to the fleet, which is the operating instrument of naval power, the supplies and support necessary to maintain it. The greater the average distance between the individual posts of such a chain, the weaker becomes the whole system; and the greater are its demands upon the fleet for mobile force to protect it, since its reliance upon stationary force is naturally proportionate to the number and strength of the points of fixed support, and to the distances between them which supply vessels, in themselves defenseless, must traverse under escort. The outer parts of such a chain, being more exposed to attack, are intrinsically weaker, and therefore require shorter intermediate distances between bases, than the parts closer home. Thus in a chain from our Gulf ports to Barbados, the first link, New Orleans-Guantanamo, of 1100 miles, is perfectly secure; the next, Guantanamo-Eastern Outpost, 700 miles, is somewhat less so; the third, Eastern Outpost-Barbados, 500 miles, is still more exposed.

As against a European power possessing a similar chain of bases on or near the coast of Africa — say the Canary and Cape Verde Islands — the outer end of our chain at Barbados would be about 500 miles farther from any South American port below Cape San Roque than would the outer end of the European chain at the Cape Verdes. The importance to us of the suggested southeastern outpost is thus emphasized, since we will be under a considerable disadvantage anyway, and cannot afford, if we can help it, to give up a further 500 miles as a hostage to the fortune of war.

We would, however, as against any European fleet or combined expedition moving into the South Atlantic for aggression against a South American state, doubtless have the support of Brazilian ports. In any case our position in the eastern Caribbean would enable us to interpose between such an aggressive force and its base, under conditions which would render it extremely hazardous for any European nation to attempt an incursion into the South Atlantic without having first disposed of our fleet. To this theater also, therefore, the Caribbean is the key, the central position from which we can act decisively and with the greatest strategical mobility.

Consideration of these questions opens up the general examination of foreign positions in the Caribbean. There are three fortified ports in that area belonging to European powers: Kingston, Jamaica (British); Fort de France, Martinique (French); and Willemstad, Curaçao (Dutch). None of these can be said to have any serious defensive strength. The British garrison at Jamaica numbers something over 600; the total French strength in the West Indies is about 400, divided between Martinique and Guadeloupe; the Dutch garrison of Curaçao and Aruba numbers 250 including marines. There are local defense forces (volunteers) on all the principal British islands, as well as armed constabulary available for military duties: total strength, about 4000 divided among 12 islands.

Nor can any of these ports be regarded as a naval base. At Kingston the British Government has a fueling station, and there is a British Government drydock at Trinidad which will take destroyers; there are private docks of similar capacity at Fort de France and Willemstad. Nowhere, however, is there any regular naval shore establishment.

Since we are unlikely to be involved in war with Britain, France or the Netherlands, these details are given merely as an indication of the weakness of these outposts, and the same principle already stated in regard to Bermuda applies: should they be threatened by a strong enemy, we might have to assume the responsibility for their defense.

The positions of some of these foreign-owned islands, however, give them great importance if the possibility of our acquiring them be envisaged. Jamaica is one of the best positions in the West Indies. It lies just within the Windward Passage, and is closer by 150 miles to Panama than is Guantanamo. Curaçao, the only other interior position held by a European power (unless Belize be so considered) has an excellent and easily defended harbor; it lies 700 miles east of Panama, controlling any approach to the Isthmus by means of the Lesser Antilles passages. The oil refineries and storage plants of Curaçao and Aruba would have military value; they handle Venezuelan oil. Trinidad has a fine, well-sheltered anchorage and a local oil production; together with the outlying island of Barbados, and Saint Lucia to the northward, it would form a splendid southeastern outpost for our fleet and air forces.

Whether it would ever be possible for us to acquire these islands or not the writer of course has little idea. The question of exchanging the Philippines for the British West Indies has already been discussed. It might also be remembered that the war-debt question with Great Britain and France is as yet unsettled. We did acquire the Virgin Islands by purchase from Denmark. The time may come when the governments now having West Indian possessions may feel that their interests would be well served in all respects by transferring possession to the United States. The Netherlands, certainly, and France and Britain under conditions easily imaginable, would be unable to protect these distant islands in war; a fact to which (as concerns Guadeloupe and Martinique) the great French naval strategist, Admiral Castex, calls definite attention in his *Théories Stratégiques*.

The western and southern shores of the Caribbean, and its two principal islands, are under the sovereignty of eleven different Latin American nations, the special nature of our relations with which has been examined in the chapter on *Military and Foreign Policies;* and, as to Cuba further emphasized above.

No discussion of the strategy of the Caribbean would be complete without some reference to the Gulf of Mexico, which lies behind it, communicating with it through the Yucatan Channel. This channel is well commanded from Key West, 300 miles distant from its center; Key West also lies directly upon the Strait of Florida, the only other entrance to the Gulf. It is therefore a post of particular importance to us, and its fortifications, which are now in charge of a mere maintenance party, ought to be placed on an active basis, as should the small naval station. The value of Key West as a point of departure for car-ferry service to Havana has been lost as a result of the hurricane which destroyed the Florida East Coast railway over the Florida keys; a motor-road, however, has now taken the place of the railway, so that Key West becomes once more a link in the communications of Guantanamo.

Directly in front of Key West, toward the Atlantic, and controlling not only access to the Strait of Florida from seaward but also access to the Windward Passage, lies the archipelago of the Bahamas, a British possession. With their extension of the Turks and Caicos Islands, this group covers a line over 600 miles long, from Florida to Haiti. There are a total of 706 islands and "cays," and 2387 rocks. Many of the islands are without any means of communication (save by boat) with the capital at Nassau. There are no defenses of any kind. The islands abound in anchorages and harbors suitable for sea-going ships. They constitute, therefore, one of the few really menacing strategical features of this region; for in isolated positions in the Bahamas, seaplane tenders could support their broods of planes, or submarines find shelter and opportunity to refuel from small tankers, under conditions which would make it very difficult to ferret them out. All traffic moving via the Windward Passage or the Strait of Florida would be menaced by such activities, and even the Mona Passage is well within their influence. In a war in which Great Britain was neutral, most embarrassing situations might arise in the course of any attempt by us to clear out such raiders; while actual violation of British neutrality by them might be difficult to prove. Our acquisition of these islands seems therefore a subject requiring serious consideration.

The American shore of the Gulf of Mexico has at present few military posts of consequence. Pensacola is our principal fortified port on the Gulf; there is a very large naval air station here, largely used for training. Tampa, Mobile, New Orleans and Galveston have harbor defenses, none of them actively garrisoned. The navy yard at New Orleans is not in operation at present. In a war in the Caribbean, the Gulf ports would unquestionably be a principal source of supply, having the advantage of a protected line of communications as against the exposure incident to the line to the northern ports. While in almost all respects this situation is ideal, it must be noted that a damaged battleship could not enter any of our Gulf ports for docking, (both because of lack of docks and insufficient depths at harbor entrances) but would have to be taken either to Norfolk or Balboa. There is indeed (except at Balboa) no dock fit even for cruisers in the whole Caribbean-Gulf area; destroyers may be docked at New Orleans or Cristobal. At least one first-class naval base ought therefore to be provided somewhere on the Gulf coast, even at the expense of dredging an entrance channel.

In this discussion of the Caribbean Sea and the Gulf of Mexico, our point of view has been toward the Atlantic. Our naval supremacy in this area is however quite as vital to our maritime position in the Pacific, to which the Caribbean is equally the gateway for our naval power; possessing, as between the two great oceans, all those advantages already abundantly illustrated, of central position and security of tenure. It is assuredly "the strategical key" to our two chief sea-frontiers, and within it our country can tolerate no foreign intrusion.

Chapter VIII

OUR STRATEGICAL POSITION
IN THE PACIFIC

The Pacific Ocean is the longest, widest and deepest ocean in the world. . . . It is no longer isolated, but has become a region of intimate contacts and conflicting interests, round which is grouped almost half the world's population.

MAJOR D. H. COLE, M.B.E., LITT.D.
Imperial Military Geography.

OUR MARITIME frontier in the Pacific, considered from the military point of view, may be likened to a defensive position on land, of which our Pacific coast forms the base, Hawaii the main advanced position, and the chain of islands beyond Hawaii the outposts.

Our principal line of sea-communications in this ocean is, like that in the Atlantic, the one connecting our home ports with Panama.

The chief factor affecting all Pacific strategy is distance; a fact which will be amply emphasized before the reader has finished this chapter, and which is first set forth in reflecting that while from our southernmost Atlantic coast naval base, Norfolk, to Panama is about 1800 miles, it is over 2800 miles from Panama to our southernmost Pacific coast base — San Diego. The Norfolk-Panama line has moreover intermediate points of support at Charleston, Key West and Guantanamo, being continuously either within the influence of our own coast positions or in enclosed waters where we are paramount. The San Diego-Panama line has no intermediate support, running as it does entirely along foreign coasts. It is, however, far more remote from the bases of any large foreign naval power than is the Atlantic line.

On our Pacific coast we have three naval bases. That at Puget Sound possesses a Navy Yard which can dock battleships, a torpedo station, a naval air station and an ammunition depot. The narrow entrance to the Sound is defended by a group of forts.

At Mare Island, a few miles up the Sacramento River from San Francisco Bay, is a Navy Yard which can dock cruisers, and an ammunition depot; on San Francisco Bay itself is a naval operating base, and there are two leased docks, one large enough for battleships. A new naval air base is under construction. The harbor is well fortified.

San Diego is the principal naval operating base on the West Coast. It has no Navy Yard; the floating drydock is suitable only for destroyers. There is a large naval air station, a supply depot, a destroyer base, and the western station of the Fleet Marine Force. It is a defended port.

Other fortified commercial ports on the West Coast are Los Angeles and the Columbia River. Gray's Harbor, Washington, Coos Bay, Oregon, and Monterey and Santa Barbara, California, may be mentioned as commercial ports, possessing some resources, which are not fortified.

The Pacific coast harbor defenses are on the average better garrisoned than those on the Atlantic, but none are fully manned. San Francisco is best off in this regard.

The three chief naval centers are connected by rail and road, and considered as a whole afford ample strategical freedom of action to a fleet operating within their zone of support.

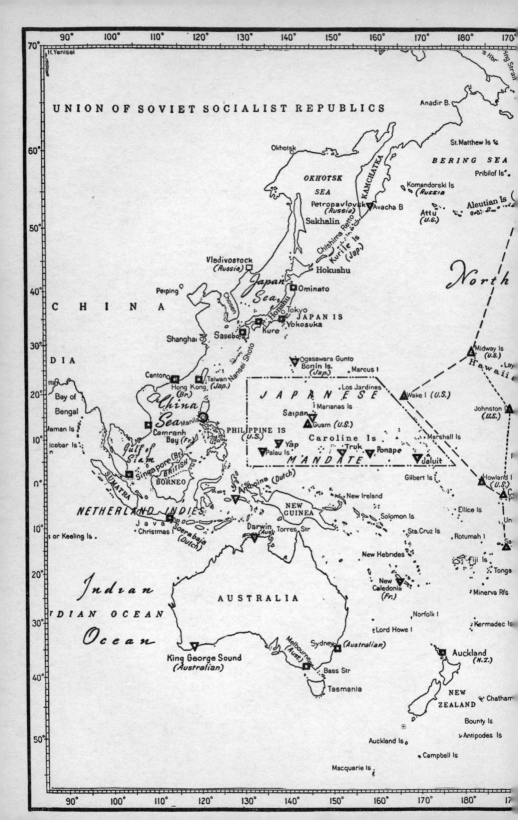

Just as Boston looks to the northeast, so does Puget Sound look to the northwest; and just as Boston is faced by a Canadian base at Halifax, so is Puget Sound faced by Esquimault. The great difference, however, lies beyond. For while the outlying geographical features beyond Halifax are all Canadian or British until one reaches Greenland, the stretch of Canadian coast above Esquimault soon gives way to American territory again, and continues so far out to the north and west until the end of the Aleutian chain is reached at Attu, 2500 miles from Puget Sound direct, 3200 miles by coastal stages.

An ordinary Mercator-projection map of the Pacific, such as that used in this volume, produces a serious distortion in the northern latitudes, because of the vast distances involved. A cylindrical projection of a surface which is actually spherical will present no distortion in the middle (i.e., at the Equator) but a progressively greater distortion as one approaches the ends, or Poles. It is therefore necessary to caution the reader against accepting as precise the relationships shown by this map between positions in the North Pacific; to obtain any really accurate idea of these, a globe must be employed. The reader will notice that the coast of North America, continued by that of Asia, seems to form a great enclosing curve around the upper part of the North Pacific, and might naturally suppose that the shortest route from one side to the other of that ocean would be along the chord of this arc. This is not the case, because of the bulging of the earth at the equator. A considerably less degree of surface curvature, and consequently a shorter steaming distance, is found in proceeding from Puget Sound to Yokohama, for example, by what is called a "great circle" course which, while not following with fidelity the curve of the coast-line, does happen to come very near it in places, especially the outer part of the Aleutian chain. This is the shortest line between American and Japanese ports, and can be controlled from Aleutian harbors more easily than from any other mid-Pacific position. The influence of great circle navigation extends, for so vast an ocean as the Pacific, far beyond such limits as we have mentioned; for example, it is actually about the same distance from Panama to Manila via San Francisco and Yokohama as it is via Hawaii and Guam: though to a landsman looking at a Mercator map, such a suggestion would seem absurd.

Before examining further the strategical conclusions to be drawn from these facts, the question of possible Pacific antagonists must be taken up. Besides ourselves, there is but one first-class naval power whose homeland is washed by the waters of the Pacific—Japan. France—with whom we have no cause for quarrel—has a few positions there, but can hardly extend the influence of her fleet beyond the South China sea, and even that would be a great effort for her. The British Commonwealth of Nations has three great Dominions with Pacific littorals—Canada, Australia, and New Zealand—and moreover possesses many minor Pacific positions. But a Pacific war with Britain is for us beyond the realm of reasonable conjecture, let alone one in which the Dominions would participate. The Netherlands Indies approach closely our present position in the Philippines; but the Dutch navy is inadequate for distant operations, and again there is no foreseeable cause for hostilities.

Soviet Russia has a considerable coastline in the North Pacific, which reaches out almost to touch our Territory of Alaska at Bering Strait. The communications of this region may be said to be nonexistent save by sea—and Russia has at present no high-seas fleet—or, precariously, by air. Russian developments in the Arctic have shown the possibility, however, of maintaining at certain times of the year a route of maritime communications along the north shore of Asia. The time may come when Russian activities in the Far North will constitute a threat of which we must take notice. Just at present Russia has her hands full on her Manchurian frontier; but if Japan goes under in the struggle for continental power and a great Soviet Empire arises in East Asia, it may be that we shall have to remember the demonstration just given us by Russian pilots of the possibility of flying over the roof of the world; or by Howard Hughes of the ease with which properly equipped airplanes can fly from Siberia to Alaska and from Alaska to the United States. Such a threat would be of little account, because of the distances involved, except as a support to a Communist subversive movement in the United States itself, to which Soviet air power might supply leaders, weapons and encouragement. It may seem a long shot: yet longer shots sometimes have come off, in the strange and tortuous history of this troubled planet.

This, however, is hardly an immediate possibility. The one naval power which now confronts us in the Pacific is Japan; and the present conduct of that nation, and the attitude of its civil and military authorities toward other powers, make it quite reasonable to consider it aggressive in immediate act and future intention.

Our Pacific strategy, then, has for the moment a single direction—the defense of our rights and interests in that ocean against Japan.

This established, we return to our great circle navigation and the relations thereto of the Aleutian Islands.

It might at first sight be considered that, as lying on the shortest line between Japanese and American ports, our main outlying naval base in the Pacific should be here located; at any rate while Japan remains our chief possible antagonist.

This however is a theory which does not bear strategical examination. In establishing a military post, just as in building a warship or designing a piece of artillery, the first question to be asked is: "What is this post meant to do?"

The primary object of a great naval base is to give strategical mobility and immediate support to the fleet which is dependent upon it. It must enable that fleet to act offensively against any enemy fleet which may come within its radius of action, of course; but, as we have already demonstrated, this is not enough. The destruction or defeat of the enemy's fleet is but a means to an end: that end being the control of maritime communications and the use of the pressure thereby made possible to compel the enemy to abandon his efforts to injure us and to sue for peace.

Our examination of the Atlantic has shown us how our twin bases — the North Coast and the Caribbean position — enable us to deal with any European enemy's maritime effort against the Western Hemisphere in that ocean, and subsequently to exercise such pressure against his external communications as shall bring him to reason.

Similar considerations apply to our position in the Pacific.

The Aleutian Islands are a purely defensive position as against Japan; they flank the shortest line of approach of a Japanese fleet toward our coast; but offensively, the Aleutians are all but worthless, because our advance along the northern line would not bring our seapower to a position *vis à vis* Japan which would enable it to exercise the pressure of distant blockade. Japan has, in the north, no vital lines of external communications, no very great interests of any kind with the single exception of fisheries. It will hardly be contended that the destruction of Japan's North Pacific fishing fleet, serious though such a blow would be, would bring the Japanese nation to surrender. Nor is an object which may be otherwise accomplished a proper one for the full force of our battle-fleet; and assuredly if Japan is seriously threatened elsewhere, her fisheries may meanwhile be driven from the northern seas by energetically handled light forces, of which our Coast Guard cutters would form an excellent and locally-experienced nucleus.

Even if, in the end, we won a foothold in the Kuriles we

[166]

still could not bring direct pressure to bear upon Japan save by air raids on Japanese cities, a form of warfare against which American public opinion has set its face, and which American airmen would never be willing to carry out unless driven to do so as a measure of reprisal for like enemy conduct.

There can be no comparison between a base which serves a purely defensive purpose, and one which supports both the defensive and offensive forms of war; for the former constrains, while the latter contributes to that strategical freedom of action which to naval warfare is the very breath of life.

A base which admirably fulfills both purposes is found in our present main outlying Pacific position, the Hawaiian Islands.

The center of our power in this archipelago is the island of Oahu, the most formidable maritime fortress and naval outpost in the world. Its two harbors — the commercial port of Honolulu and the naval port of Pearl Harbor — are commanded by powerfully-armed fixed defenses, supplemented by railway artillery which can be shifted to any practicable landing point, and by tractor-drawn mobile guns. The mobile garrison includes a complete infantry division, stationed largely at Schofield Barracks, on a high plateau with a central location. The total strength of the garrison is about 21,000 officers and men, to which may be added a National Guard of 1700. There is a strong army air force, which is being increased as new bases are made available. The naval establishment includes a Navy Yard capable of docking capital ships, a submarine base to which 16 submarines and 4 destroyers are permanently assigned, an ammunition depot, and a naval air base supporting 72 large patrol planes and 11 other naval aircraft.

The hydrographic conditions favor local defense. The one weakness is the nearness of the other islands of the

Hawaiian archipelago; but this is partly offset by the fact that these possess only one all-weather harbor, Hilo Bay, which has both the depth of water and the anchorage room for the large ships of an attacking force. Hilo is 200 miles from Pearl Harbor. Security is being further supported by the establishment of small air bases on the outlying islands, and by training of local detachments of the National Guard. When the measures now in hand are completed, the central position of Oahu with its outlying supports will be as safe as human ingenuity and the great favors of nature can possibly make any isolated fortress.

In position, Hawaii is admirably adapted for our purposes. It is much closer to our home bases than to the home bases of any other power; about 2000 miles, for example, from San Francisco, while 3400 from Yokohoma direct, or 6000 via the chain of advanced posts through the "mandated islands" which a serious Japanese offensive movement would have to follow. On the other hand Unalaska, the best harbor of the Aleutians, is 1700 miles from Puget Sound, while but a little over 2000 from Ominato, the northernmost naval base of the Japanese main islands. Unalaska being one of a continuous chain of positions which extends, almost without a break, from Japan through the Kuriles to Kamchatka and thence via the Aleutians to the tip of the Alaskan Peninsula, it is very much more exposed than Hawaii. Indeed a large naval base at Unalaska might be an almost irresistible temptation to an aggressively minded Japanese high command, at a moment when our fleet was in the Atlantic.

Offensively, Hawaii initiates a line of operations which, prolonged step by step through the Japanese mandates via Jaluit, Ponape and Truk to Guam, would, when we had arrived at the last-named island, establish us in a position but 1300 miles from Yokohoma or 1500 miles from Manila. From this point our cruisers could begin to exercise the pressure of distant blockade upon Japan, operating in the South

China Sea against her trade with Europe, Africa, and Southern Asia, while that with Australasia and South America would already have been cut off as we moved forward from Hawaii. Such a distant blockade could not, in the nature of sea warfare, be completely "air tight;" and it would demand of us a tremendous effort. Nevertheless it could be done, and if long continued would certainly force the Japanese fleet to give battle in the hope of breaking our strangling grip upon the life-line of the Japanese people, increasingly dependent as these are upon foreign markets and foreign sources of raw materials. Notably, in the military sense, the Japanese would have to fight before they were reduced to impotence by the cutting off of their supply of petroleum.

Thus Hawaii affords us the initial means of bringing about a decision favorable to ourselves in the unhappy event of a war with Japan.

It must be emphasized that a war fought across the breadth of so vast an ocean as the Pacific is fraught with very great difficulties. For us to carry out a step-by-step advance through the mandated islands, as suggested, would involve the necessity of fighting for every stepping-stone. We would have to employ considerable forces of troops for this purpose and, as we drew nearer to the source of Japanese power, the resistance would increase in degree and intensity. We would have to keep up a tremendous flow of supplies outward from our West Coast ports to Hawaii, and from Hawaii to our advance bases. This would involve the use of large numbers of merchants ships, which would have to be convoyed by destroyers and escort vessels, imposing a severe burden on the fleet. After each advance, we would be compelled to "mop up" all the adjacent islands; a task whose magnitude may be suggested by the fact that the Eastern Carolines alone number 383 separate islands and atolls. Yet it is a task which would have to be accomplished before the next advance could be made, else the new line of communications would be open to constant attack by Japanese airplanes and flotilla craft.

As each main phase of the advance was completed, we would have to bring forward to the new advance base great quantities of fuel and supplies, and to establish there a temporary repair base by the use of floating equipment. A garrison sufficient to assure the place against raids, and equipped with mobile heavy guns and anti-aircraft artillery, would be required. A regular system of air patrol between the various islands would have to be established.

All this would take time. Presuming — as is indeed certain — that Guam would be taken over by the Japanese in the early days of the war, we might expect that to reinstate ourselves there, to secure the base by clearing the Japanese out of adjacent Saipan, and to begin our distant blockade operations, would take anywhere from a year to two years from the time the first move was made from Pearl Harbor.

Our tenure of Guam would moreover be insecure and difficult, because it would be dependent on a line of communications from Pearl Harbor almost 5000 miles in length, supported by positions having no resources of their own and little natural strength, but entirely dependent upon artificial means for defense and supply. We would be, on the other hand, but 1300 miles from the largest Japanese naval base at Yokosuka (near Yokohama) and about 800 from their fortified advance base in the Bonin Islands.

Therefore our fleet would have to be in readiness to fight at the Japanese "selected moment" with its own average strength; which means that at Guam or perhaps at Truk, as more sheltered from direct attack, would have to be set up and maintained a base adequate to all the needs of the fleet, which could not afford to be constantly sending ships back 5000 miles to Pearl Harbor for repair and overhaul, as too great a percentage would be constantly absent. Great care would have to be taken of the heavy ships (battleships and large carriers) to protect them against torpedo, air and mine attacks. This would require incessant activity on the part of our destroyers, patrol vessels, mine-sweepers and aircraft. Convoy escorts for the line of communications would still be needed, as against long-range Japanese submarines; these could probably be largely furnished by gunboats or Coast Guard cutters, but would need a proportion of cruisers against the chance of enemy cruiser raids. Our cruisers, meanwhile, would not only have to bear the burden of all the distant blockading operations, but also provide some cruisers for such fleet duties as reconnaissance and distant screening. Rapid and extensive new warship construction would therefore be imperative. The writer is unable to estimate the merchant tonnage which would be required to maintain the fleet in this distant position, to supply all the intermediate bases, to transport troops for their garrisons and the necessary reliefs and reinforcements. It would assuredly be enormous.

Yet, when all is said and done; when the magnitude of the effort required of us and the perils to be encountered have been weighed; when the necessarily brief and incomplete picture given above of the difficulty of waging war 5000 miles from our main advance base is considered not only in its primary aspects, but in its implications of the thousand and one troubles and burdens which have not been even mentioned; when there are considered the infinite variety of war, the inevitable set-backs and disappointments, the losses and the failures: it may still be asserted with confidence that such an effort is not beyond the power of this nation if needs must.

And this is the all-important fact of Pacific strategy: that we can, if we have to, direct such an attack against Japan as will be a deadly threat to her security, while Japan cannot do the like by us.

[171]

For the moment the reverse side of the picture is examined, the whole aspect of it changes.

It may immediately be premised that Japan would at the outset occupy Guam and the Philippines (presuming we continue there) and that there is little we could do to prevent it. But beyond that, Japanese difficulties increase with every mile they move eastward. They cannot undertake such a vast combined expedition as would be required to reduce Hawaii until they have disposed of our fleet; the three weeks we would need to bring our fleet from the Atlantic, supposing it to be there, would not suffice for the Japanese to set on foot such an expedition, much less to reach Hawaii with it, and still less to carry that fortress by assault. An assault on our West Coast is out of the question, lacking any base to support it and demanding a far greater effort than an attack on Hawaii. Panama is far out of Japan's reach, being 8000 miles from Yokohama.

What else could Japan do to injure us? She might attempt to seize a harbor in the Aleutians, and from that point conduct raids against our West Coast shipping, or secure a favorable location for basing her fleet for a show-down fight, if her naval staff thought themselves equal to such a contest. But this, again, would require troops, and time, and heavy naval protection. We ought to prepare against it (the initial measures are already being taken) by establishing at Unalaska an air base and a base for the operations of flotilla craft. This will require a garrison and local defenses, which need not be of the formidable character of those at Hawaii, since they have far less to defend. The best reason for believing that Japan will not undertake a major offensive effort here is that Unalaska is distant but 2000 miles from Hawaii, and 1700 miles from Puget Sound, thus coming within the radius of action of our fleet when the latter arrives. Presuming it to be in the Atlantic, the Japanese must make certain of reducing Unalaska within three weeks plus two days for re-fueling and minor preparations plus five days for the fleet to proceed to the vicinity of Unalaska. Even if their expedition sailed in the greatest secrecy, therefore, it would still have to face air opposition and submarine attack on arriving near Unalaska; the troops would have to be landed in the face of our shore defenses, and the base captured, all in four weeks. The greater the expedition the Japanese send, the more certain they will be of accomplishing this object; but the greater the expedition, the more certain we will be to get wind of it before it sails, reducing by from one to three weeks its margin of safety.

The controlling consideration is that for Japan such risks are unjustified by the possible advantages to be anticipated from success; since even if they took Unalaska, our fleet would still stand between it and either Hawaii or our West Coast, and we could quickly establish, at Sitka or Kodiak, advance bases which would bring us much closer. The Japanese fleet being inferior to ours in fighting strength, thus to thrust itself within our radius of action would be foolish in the extreme, because when it got there it could not reap the advantages of its position. The Japanese would have occupied a post which they could not hope to maintain against our tremendously superior resources and from which, meanwhile, they could do us little injury.

Our advance to Guam (above examined), predicated upon battle-fleet superiority, would on the contrary bring the long arm of those resources forward to a position where they could inflict vital hurt upon Japan.

As to other steps which the Japanese might take to injure us, these are largely concerned with attacks upon our shipping. Long-range Japanese submarines and perhaps armed merchant cruisers could operate along the long stretch of sparsely inhabited coast intermediate between Panama and San Diego, perhaps forcing us to adopt a convoy system for this route. It would, however, require seven Japanese submarines to keep one on station in this vicinity, an expensive effort for a result which convoy could quickly render illusory. As the Germans did in the World War, roving Japanese surface raiders could range far afield. They might even penetrate the Atlantic, proceeding no doubt by way of the Cape of Good Hope, and there cause us distressing losses. Daringly employed converted aircraft carriers might make tip-and-run raids on our coastal cities. But these are only pin-pricks to a nation of our size and power. They are troublesome, but not decisive injuries, calculated rather to inspire a determined people to gird their loins for one tremendous effort to extirpate their source, rather than to discourage a continuance of the war.

These are the present conditions. They will continue to be the conditions of Pacific strategy while there is no great change in the relative naval power and supporting resources of the two nations involved. They are as well known to the leaders of Japan as to anyone.

Therefore we may speak of a war with Japan, in a sense, as a war which will not happen, because neither side will start it. The risk of defeat is too great for Japan to contemplate; the advantage of victory too small for us to consider it worth the enormous effort and sacrifice it would demand.

But this happy outlook is entirely conditioned on our readiness to undertake offensive operations if we are compelled to do so. If we allow our fleet to sink below the level of marked superiority to that of Japan; if we fail to keep up the defenses of Hawaii and Panama and to develop our outlying system of covering posts from Unalaska to Samoa; if we do not maintain an adequate system of bases for the support of our fleet: in any of these cases, some day a desperate Japan, or a Japan flushed with victory, or a Japan seeking assuagement for failure in other fields may turn upon us. A military empire with the history and characteristics of

[174]

Japan is at best an uneasy neighbor; it is not a neighbor with whom it is safe to take long chances.

The cost to us of a war across the Pacific would be so great that we must by every means in our power avoid the necessity of actually having to undertake it. It is for this reason that the Philippine question ought to be settled; it is for this reason that we should avoid driving the Japanese to desperation by threatening them with boycotts and embargoes; it is for this reason that we must maintain a level of armament and readiness which will constitute a direct threat to their security if they compel us to employ that armament.

It is not desired to convey the impression that if we have to do this, victory will assuredly be ours. It might not be so. But the chances would be in our favor while our fleet is heavily superior to the Japanese fleet, and it is Japanese knowledge of this fact that makes it unlikely that we shall have to fight such a war.

On the other hand, the chance of our eventual failure is sufficiently great and the certainty of terrible cost sufficiently appalling to make it well worth our while to bend every effort to avoid the struggle. It is this which well-meaning gentlemen ought to consider who urge us to lay an embargo on exports to Japan, or afford more active aid to China. For a proud Oriental nation with its back to the wall may not stop to reckon up costs or count possible losses.

The day may come when we shall have to use our military power to prevent a Japanese aggrandizement across the Pacific which will indeed constitute a threat to us. If it does, that day may be long foreseen and well prepared for. It is not here yet, nor does it seem near. Our present policy should be one of peace and security; and if it must be an armed peace and a watchful security, the fault, in this instance, is not wholly ours.

Before leaving the Pacific area, there are one or two other positions in it which should be mentioned.

One of these is the Galapagos Islands, now belonging to the Republic of Ecuador, and lying about 1000 miles southwest of Panama. While they would not be of much value to us offensively, they might form a base of operations for hostile submarines seeking to intercept our fleet in a passage through the Canal; their lease from Ecuador, previously a subject of discussion, might therefore be a wise precaution.

American Samoa possesses, at Pago Pago, the best and most commodious harbor in the South Pacific. While it does not lie on any route from the United States to Japan, it does flank our communications with Australia and would be a valuable point of support for cruisers and convoys if that trade-route were menaced. It would moreover be useful for stopping Japanese trade with South America if that became necessary. In enemy hands it would be a continual source of danger and trouble. Finally, it is a stopping place for our projected air-route to New Zealand. Samoa has neither garrison nor fortifications at present. It should be noted that Samoa is the southern post of our mid-Pacific air patrol line, Unalaska-Midway-Wake-Canton-Samoa, along which our large patrol-planes can operate to cover the approaches to Hawaii from the Japanese mandated area. This is an important part of our strategical arrangements in the Pacific.

The west coast of Mexico and Central America is of interest to us because of its proximity to our vital sea-line to Panama. On the Gulf of Fonseca, 700 miles north of Panama, we have, by treaty with the Republic of Nicaragua, the right to establish a naval base. If the Nicaragua Canal is built, this right will undoubtedly be exercised. One other position on this line, that of Magdalena Bay in Lower California, has been mentioned as a possible point of support for Japanese submarines and perhaps minelayers. It is a large landlocked gulf, about 600 miles from San Diego, and is frequented by fishing vessels of which many are owned or operated by Japanese. It has no other commercial importance.

The west coast of South America is so much closer to our bases, and especially to Panama, than to the bases of any foreign naval power, that its defense would present few problems; indeed, it is altogether unlikely to be menaced.

With this survey of our strategical position in the oceans which form our military frontiers, we have completed our examination of the incidence of foreign and geographical factors upon the military policy and institutions of the United States. The instruments of that policy, which must give it life and reality, are our next concern. And of these, the chief instrument is man himself — the American man. It is the man behind the gun, behind the range-finder, behind the torpedo-director, or behind the instrument board of the airplane, who is the basic element of military power.

Chapter IX

THE BASIC ELEMENT — AMERICAN MEN IN WAR

Science can never be the master of war, because of the infinite variations of the human factor, which, as long as human minds and human muscles are required to direct machines, must predominate.

MAJOR GENERAL SIR FREDERICK MAURICE, K.C.M.G., C.B.,
British Strategy.

MEN MAKE WAR. The finest weapons, the most perfect technical equipment, are valueless without the human hand, the human eye, and the human mind; more, without the human heart to sustain with fortitude the terrible stress of battle.

In the national sense, weapons and equipment must be adapted not only to the needs of national defense as imposed by strategic exigencies, but to the national characteristics of the men who are to use them. Generations of French leaders strove in vain to imitate the sturdy pikemen of Switzerland, because their human material was not suited to the task; in the British Indian army today, the Ghurka rifleman does not feel himself equipped for war with a weapon which will slay at a mile's range, but must also have his *kukri*, his half-moon-shaped chopping knife.

In the war of tomorrow, America possesses an asset whose

[178]

value will be proportionate to the wisdom with which it is used. War is no longer a matter of pikes or chopping knives; it is a matter of technique — largely of technique in using mechanical and electrical appliances. The young men of America grow to manhood surrounded by the wonders of the machine age; many of them must find their livings from perfecting themselves in various fields of applied mechanics and its kindred sciences. Few indeed among American boys but have their particular and passionate devotion — whether it be to aviation, to automobiles, to ships, to railways, to radio, to electricity, or to photography. All these things are used in war. Perfection in their use may mean the difference between defeat and victory.

And perfection in such things is born, not so much of painful, plodding training in a single operation until letter perfect, as of a burning desire to know what and why and how: arising perhaps from a childish yearning as an airplane hummed high overhead in the blue sky, or a great scarlet truck thundered past a farmyard gate along a dusty road. The toys of childhood become the machines of manhood; the dreams of childhood, the accomplishments of manhood.

The application of mechanical aptitudes to national defense may be dimly glimpsed by a mere repetition of some of the ratings of the navy; gunner's mate, firecontrolman, electrician's mate, machinist's mate, shipfitter, carpenter's mate, coppersmith, metalsmith, aviation ordnanceman, molder, patternmaker, signalman, radioman, pharmacist's mate, storekeeper, aviation pilot. This incomplete list shows how far we have come from the old days when seamanship was everything. Seamanship still has its place, but the day of the old Jack Tar has gone forever. The modern navy is a navy of specialists, a navy of machines and appliances. And as in the navy, so in the army: the infantry is no longer an arm of musket-bearers and bayonet-wielders. Modern infantry has automatic and semi-automatic rifles, light and heavy machine-guns, infantry mortars, rifle grenades, anti-tank guns, all sorts of motor-transportation from light ammunition carriers to three-ton trucks, a bewildering variety of wire and radio communications equipment; it needs mechanics, electricians, radio operators, truck drivers, cooks, clerks, signalmen, cobblers, automobile repairmen, and a dozen other sorts of specialists. The artillery, the tank corps, the air force each has its own particular demands, growing in variety as the variety and complexity of its weapons and tools march on with scientific progress in a hundred fields. Engineers, signal troops, medical troops, quartermaster units, the Chemical Warfare Service and the Ordnance Department call for specialists and more specialists. The cavalry goes to war in a dozen types of armored and unarmored motor-vehicles. The fighting equipment of a coast artillery fort is as complex as the armament of a battleship.

To all this maze of mechanical warfare, American youth brings a natural predilection for machinery, a vast enthusiasm and a boundless curiosity.

An American recruit will be the more easily fitted into his proper niche in the vast organization of the armed forces of his country, for he will seek that niche himself and, once there, he will seek to know all that there is to be known about the job he is called upon to do. He will not be satisfied merely to do his own small share; he will want to know about the job of the man next to him, and especially that of the man above him. He will be part of a team, for all war is team-work; yet it will be a team which will continue to function while one of its members is left, rather than one which will be hopelessly handicapped when a single member is gone.

The American spirit is the free inquiring spirit which is the basis of all advance in science and in the mechanical arts; fostered by a freely competitive system in commerce and industry, by education which looks toward mind-training

[180]

rather than political discipline, and by a wholesome if at times iconoclastic skepticism as to the achievements and worth of past generations.

The American boy lives and finds his standards among his fellows. He must hold his own place; on playground or sports field he is accepted for what he is and can do. He does not march daily in serried ranks, uniformed and regimented to a blind devotion to strange gods; he does not live in an atmosphere of nameless terror, nor are his earliest memories of his elders tinged with the saffron hue of fear: whispers, glances toward door or window, the frantic wails of his womenfolk if an incautious word be spoken. He may, indeed, grow up irreverent of authority, undisciplined, arrogant, and even brutal with the unthinking brutality of the young; but he will not grow up unable to think and plan for himself, regarding "dangerous thoughts" as the root of all evil, his young mind set, ere it has a chance to grow wings, in a pattern of uniform mediocrity.

And this, in war, is his first inestimable advantage over the boy who grows up in a land where the regimentation of childhood is the basis of dictatorial tenure of authority. For war, more than ever before, demands of those whom it calls to its fierce testing-ground self-reliance, initiative, and the ability to think and act without the guiding word of authority. Never before have the responsibilities of the leaders of small groups of infantry been so great as they will be in the battles of tomorrow. Never before has so much depended on the correct appreciation of a complex situation by one young man as may depend in modern war on that of a single airplane pilot.

Those nations which, for the sake of political uniformity, have drilled and bludgeoned these qualities out of the souls of their youth and taught instead a blind and unquestioning obedience to the word from above will pay, in blood and tears and the roaring wrack of defeat and destruction, for the error which has made of their young men a horde of mechanical robots, formidable in mass, helpless when the word from above can no longer reach them amidst the thunderous confusion of the battlefield.

The American youth, then, enters upon the military scene with very great advantages. But there are disadvantages, too. He has a distaste for discipline. He does not like to be forced to do certain things in a certain way because Corporal X. says so. He instinctively resents having to salute Second Lieutenant Y. His respect for his commanders will not be given because of stripes on a sleeve or insignia on a shoulder-strap; it will be earned by those commanders for their personal qualities, when and as and if those qualities become apparent to the commanded. It is, therefore, of the first importance that in an American military force the leaders should be most carefully selected.

As, indeed, they are. But the basis of selection is not conditioned by accidents of birth.

They do not come from the upper layers of the social spectrum, belonging to a class apart from the common run of the nation, finding in the social distinctions of military life merely a continuance of the distinctions of civil existence. They are drawn, in general, from the same sources as those they are to command. It is one of the glories, as it is one of the great strengths of the American military system that it has no military caste; that the service Academies are as attainable by the poor youth as by the scion of wealth. It is true that the bulk of the appointments go to Senators and Congressmen, and that some of these consult political motives in making their choices; yet many conduct competitive examinations for the vacancies, and there are other competitive appointments reserved for enlisted men of the regular and reserve services. The very distribution of the appointments among the members of Congress spreads the sources of procurement over the whole nation, insuring a wide territorial representation and making of the cadet personnel a cross-section of the people of the republic.

Nor are the Academies the only roads to a commission. In the army, under the Thomason law, 1000 young graduates of universities having Reserve Officers' Training Corps are annually selected for a year's active service as reserve second lieutenants, and of these by competitive examination 100 are chosen yearly for permanent commissions. The navy draws a certain number of ensigns for the Supply Corps from universities having naval R.O.T.C. units.

Formerly, enlisted men of the army after two years' service could take the examination for appointment to the rank of second lieutenant, and there were some appointments directly from civil life. The Thomason act seems a better system than the latter; the results have been highly gratifying to all who have had to do with the young officers thus obtained. Commissions for selected enlisted men who are too old for West Point but still young enough to enter on an officer's career ought, however, to be possible.

The broadening of the base of officer procurement which resulted from the World War, following which large numbers of emergency officers were commissioned in the Regular Army, is generally conceded to have been highly beneficial to the service. While West Point should still remain the chief source of appointments to the junior grade, the Thomason system, reinforced by opportunities for the deserving and qualified enlisted man, should have its chance along with the Academy. This is in the best tradition of American military life.

In the navy it is, on the whole, impossible to become an officer of the line except by passing through the Naval Academy. While the requirements of a sea service are somewhat different from those of the army, it is nevertheless to be regretted that some line vacancies cannot be allotted to graduates of the naval R.O.T.C. The old system which permitted the commissioning of a certain number of warrant officers as ensigns is admittedly outdated; for by the time a man has reached warrant rank he is too old to start in competition with men who have been made ensigns at 22 or 23. This has been partially compensated for by provisions which allow a warrant officer to rise after stated periods of service to a final rate of pay equivalent to that of a lieutenant commander.

The growing size of our national defense establishments is indicative of their growing importance as national insurance. They are no longer to be considered the refuge of the unfit, the snug harbor of those unable to face the fierce competition of civil life. They demand the best that the nation has to give, both in the commissioned and enlisted ranks. To obtain the best, and to keep it, the services must offer advantages and prospects equivalent to those of civil life.

This consideration is intimately bound up with the matter of pay and promotion.

The pay of all commissioned officers of the Army, Navy, Marine Corps, Coast Guard, Public Health Service and Coast and Geodetic Survey is now regulated by the Uniform Pay Act of 1923, which establishes equality in pay for the various grades among these several services. This principle is sound and should be continued. The act is however complicated not only by proportioning pay on the basis of length of commissioned service (which is just and reasonable) but by a system of allowances for rental and subsistence which is so adjusted as to work considerable inequalities. The subsistence allowance remains at $18 monthly for all grades of officers without dependents; for those with dependents it rises to $36 and then to $54, thereafter receding, for colonels [1] and general officers, to $36 again (on the theory that such officers' children will be starting out in life for themselves). Rental allowance begins at $40 a month and rises

---

[1] Army titles alone will be used here for the sake of brevity. The pay of corresponding grades in the navy is the same.

slowly to $80 for officers without dependents; for those with dependents it rises more rapidly to $120 for majors of over 23 years' service, and remains at that figure up to the highest grade. These allowances, therefore, are a very large part of an officer's compensation. They are further complicated by a provision for an upper limit; no colonel may receive allowances which will raise his total compensation above $600 per month, a brigadier general is limited to $625, and a major general to $808.33 — which in practice means that (since almost all officers of these grades are entitled to the full rate) a colonel on promotion to the grade of brigadier general receives only $25 more in actual compensation, though the difference in "base pay" is $166.67, which far more accurately represents the increased responsibility and dignity of his new office. At the other end of the line, the second lieutenant's base pay is $1500 per annum, a $200 cut from that under the act of 1908. Rental allowances are not paid when an officer or his family is occupying government quarters, nor to any officer without dependents while on field or sea duty.

The whole question of officer pay requires re-study and adjustment to modern conditions. This will admittedly be a difficult task, since it is all but impossible to set up indices proportionate to the varying conditions of civilian life. However, the basic principle ought to be that of making a service career attractive to the best of our young men.

Into the vexed question of officer promotion, it is impossible to go very deeply in the brief space available. The army adheres to promotion by seniority, all officers (except medical, dental, and veterinary officers and chaplains) being on a single list for promotion purposes, and advancing thus in single file up to the grade of colonel. Promotion to the grade of brigadier general is by selection from the list of colonels, and to major general by selection from the list of brigadier generals. Promotion is now automatic from second lieutenant to first lieutenant after three years' service, and from first lieutenant to captain after ten years' total service as lieutenant. The number of officers in the various grades is fixed by law. The navy promotes ensigns to be lieutenants (junior grade) after three years' service and thereafter all promotions are by selection; this, accompanied with limitations as to "age in grade" and a system by which an officer twice "passed over" is debarred from further opportunity for promotion, causes many officers to be separated from the service in the prime of their usefulness, and in some cases at inadequate rates of retired pay. This has caused many heartburnings, and is now to be adjusted by a new law which will soften some of the more drastic provisions of the old. By way of general comment, it may be said that the army system offers security of tenure, conditioned on proper conduct, but affords no means by which the cream of the service may rise quickly to the top, and brings officers to command rank at too advanced an age; the navy system overloads the retired list with officers who could still render useful service, gives a feeling of insecurity and strain to many officers who might otherwise devote their whole time and thought to their duties, and does not in practice seem to promote officers to high rank at much earlier ages than does the army system, though it undoubtedly produces a higher average of ability in the upper grades. Some service opinion in the navy is turning to the idea of doing away altogether with the idea of promotion as a vested right above the rank of lieutenant; of promoting all officers by seniority that far, and above it selecting carefully for promotion the best qualified men to fill the needs of the upper grades, while permitting others to continue to serve in the lower grades until too old to perform the duties of their rank. This would remove the terrors of being "passed over," since an officer not promoted would still be available for selection at any time that he showed his fitness and, if he felt that his stagnation was his own fault, could turn to and correct his defects, thus qualifying himself for further consideration.

Another plan which seems to have some merit is to make all promotions up to the grade of captain (lieutenant in the navy) by length of service, as is now the case in the army; to fill vacancies in the grade of major (lieutenant commander) on the basis of one promotion by selection to two by seniority; in the grade of lieutenant colonel (commander) one for one; and in the grade of colonel (captain in the in the navy) one by seniority to two by selection. All promotions to general and flag rank to be selection, as at present in both services. This would enable merit to be suitably recognized, while not closing the door of hope to those not selected.

There is one rather unfortunate condition as regards higher rank which ought to be corrected, and that is in the matter of appointments to grades above those of major general in the army. Until the Civil War, the navy was in a position of decided inferiority in the matter of high rank. The highest permanent grade was that of captain, corresponding to an army colonel. Officers assigned to the command of squadrons were given the courtesy title of "commodore," which carried no permanent status. This was because of the prejudice existing against "monarchical" titles, of which that of admiral was felt to be one of the most obnoxious. The vast growth of the Civil War navy compelled the creation of the grade of rear admiral and the permanent rank of commodore. After that war, two higher ranks were created: vice admiral and admiral, one of each, corresponding to a similar provision of one lieutenant general and one general for the army. These two permanent grades were later abolished in both services, but subsequently the device of temporary appointments to the higher rank was brought forward. Under this system, today, the navy has four admirals (the Chief of Naval Operations, the Commander in Chief of the United States Fleet, the Commander in Chief of the Asiatic Fleet, and the Commander of the Battle Force) and three vice admirals (Commander Scouting Force, Commander Battleships, Battle Force, and Commander Aircraft, Battle Force). The army, with a personnel more than half again as large as the navy, has but one such high-ranking appointment — that of the Chief of Staff, who holds the temporary rank of general. These various officers are all permanent rear admirals or major generals, holding the higher grade and drawing its additional pay only during the time they are assigned to the offices to which it appertains. The army ought to have a proportionate allotment of these senior appointments; thus the Commanding Generals of the vitally important Hawaiian and Panama Canal Departments might well be generals, and Commanding Generals of Corps Areas lieutenant generals. The latter rank might be given also to the Commandant of the Marine Corps.

This is the one serious difference between the two services as to rank and compensation of commissioned personnel.

But the pay and promotion of enlisted men is quite as important as that of the officers, while unfortunately the parity between the services which prevails in the commissioned grades does not extend to the lower ranks. This may readily be indicated by comparing the service career of an enlisted man of the seaman branch of the navy, and an infantry soldier. Both start at the basic rate of $21 per month. The navy recruit, however, continues to receive this rate of pay only for about three months, while he is at a training station; when he goes to sea as a seaman, second class, he receives $36, and after a year's service can qualify by examination for promotion to seaman at $54 a month. He can then rise through the various grades of third, second, and first-class petty officer to chief petty officer at $126, plus allowances for length of service. His opportunities for advancement may be indicated by the fact that under the 1939 allotment, 7% of the enlisted men of the navy will be receiving this maximum rate of base pay, and 37.2% altogether will be in the upper three grades, drawing base rates of $72 to $126. The soldier, on the other hand, does not get any increase when he leaves the recruit depot. He continues at $21 per month until there occurs a vacancy in the grade of private, 1st class, in the unit to which he is assigned — which may be a matter of years — and then is raised to $30. He then begins standing in line for promotion to the grade of corporal, at $42, and not until he attains that of sergeant (a highly responsible position), perhaps on his second or third enlistment, does he reach the $54 level which comes automatically (on qualification) to the sailor after 15 months' service. His further opportunities for promotion are much more restricted than in the navy; thus but 0.68% of the enlisted men of the army are in Grade 1 ($126) and but 5.7% in the first three grades. The average pay of a navy enlisted man is $826.81 per annum; of an army enlisted man, $437.29 per annum. Three quarters of the army are in the two lowest pay grades, only one-quarter of the navy.

This situation arose largely from the claims made for the navy years ago that it required a vast number of highly trained technical specialists, and so needed higher rates of pay. But today our mechanized and motorized army, as has been noted, has corresponding and fully equivalent needs, and must not be left in a position of competitive inferiority in the recruit market; quite aside from the demands of justice and equity. The enlisted men of the two services should be placed on the same basis of pay-parity already provided for their officers; not only as to pay in grade, but as to opportunities for advancement.

There is a further advantage which the navy possesses, and that is in the matter of warrant rank. A warrant officer stands between the highest enlisted grade and the lowest commissioned grade. In the navy, he has a well-defined status as an officer; he wears a sword, is addressed as "Sir" and saluted by enlisted men, and lives on board ship in a special warrant officers' mess; if there be none, he lives in the wardroom with the other officers. His base pay begins at $153 per month (more than that of an ensign) and he receives the allowances of an ensign. But this is not all. After six years' service as a warrant officer he is eligible, subject to a qualifying examination, for promotion to the grade of commissioned warrant officer, in which he receives the pay and allowances of a lieutenant (junior grade); after ten years' commissioned service, the pay and allowances of a lieutenant; and after twenty years' commissioned service, the pay and allowances of a lieutenant commander. In this manner he may reach a total annual compensation of $5000; and may, on retirement, receive retired pay as high as $281.25 per month.

The army warrant officer's status is quite different. He has no well-defined position, being regarded rather as a high-ranking enlisted man than an officer of the army. His base pay begins at $148 monthly with the allowances of a second lieutenant, rising to $185 after twenty years' service; at which time his total monthly compensation will be $243, while that of a navy warrant officer of the same length of service will be $356 with further accretions still possible. The highest rate of retired pay possible to an army warrant officer is $138.75, less than half the navy maximum. (This does not include warrant officers of the Army Mine Planter Service, whose compensation is differently arranged.)

Moreover, opportunities for advancement to warrant rank in the army are much less than in the navy. The army is reducing its total number of warrant officers to 600, including 40 band leaders, but excluding the Mine Planter Service, for a total authorized strength of 165,000 enlisted men. The navy has 1526 warrant and commissioned warrant officers for a total authorized enlisted strength of 105,000. Practically, therefore, the mathematical chances of attaining warrant rank in the navy are about four times what they are in the army.

In this matter also the army must be placed in the same status as the navy. A properly constituted corps of warrant officers would not only provide incentive and opportunity to soldiers of ambition and ability, but would be of the greatest service in the performance of many duties which must now be assigned to junior commissioned officers, to the detriment of their training and preparation for higher grades. In the navy, for example, warrant officers not only perform technical duties in charge of stores and equipment on board heavy ships, but act as executive officers, engineer officers, etc., on tugs, minesweepers and other small auxiliaries, and as assistant inspectors of naval material at industrial plants.

The whole question of pay and promotion should be recast along lines which will eliminate the conditions mentioned in a memorandum of the Army Finance Department presented to the 1938 Congress: "The Army is currently required to expend too large a proportion of its limited resources for recruiting, transportation, housing, clothing, feeding and training personnel, who after acquiring a certain degree of skill, take their discharge and sell their Army-acquired skill in more remunerative markets."

In a free country whose military services depend upon voluntary enlistment for comparatively short periods of time, and in numbers are in time of peace limited by law to the absolute minimum consistent with the national security, every effort must be expended to see that the individual quality of the regular services is maintained at the highest possible level. It is not true economy to encourage a rapid turnover of personnel; the army and navy in our country are professional services and must maintain professional standards if they are to be capable of quickly absorbing, without undue loss of efficiency, the large numbers of untrained or partially trained recruits which they would require on mobilization.

If due attention be given to these matters, the United States can create and maintain an army and navy of incomparable quality, for the human material at hand is unequalled by that of any other power. Upheld by the knowledge of the nation's support and confidence, fired by the splendid traditions of both our services, and with the natural American aptitudes for the mechanical processes of modern warfare, such a corps of highly trained professional officers and men will prove in peace the nation's best assurance against the threat of war, in war its sure and unfailing instrument of victory.

Chapter X

THE COMPOSITION OF THE
UNITED STATES FLEET

*Battleships are the backbone of naval power, around which are
arrayed in their proper proportion all the other elements of
naval power to support the battleships and to increase the ability
to employ them under every circumstance.*

ADMIRAL WILLIAM D. LEAHY,
CHIEF OF NAVAL OPERATIONS, UNITED STATES NAVY,
*Testimony before the Committee on Naval Affairs of the
House of Representatives, January 31, 1938.*

MILITARY POWER, to be made effective, must be organized
for united action — i.e., concentration of its striking force —
against any possible enemy. A collection of armed men, without training, discipline and organization, is not an army but
a mob. A comparatively few well-ordered troops can defeat
many times their number of equally well-armed but unco-
ordinated barbarians, as has been proven time and again.

In naval warfare, the unit of power is not the armed man
but the armed ship; the ultimate expression of organization
for war is the fleet, composed of all the necessary classes and
types of armed ships, organized and drilled for cohesive action. A mere collection of ships with guns mounted on their

[193]

decks is not a fleet; as was demonstrated at Lissa, the Yalu and Tsushima.

Naval organization begins with the internal organization of the individual warship. Every officer, every man on board such a ship has his battle station, and is painstakingly drilled in the duties he must perform in action. Not until the captain can depend absolutely on the efficient functioning of every man, of every department — gunnery, engineering, navigation, communications, damage-control, medical, supply — can he feel that he commands an efficient fighting unit, equal to any responsibility which war may bring upon it. The organization differs in size, but not in principle, in the various classes; a destroyer with 150 officers and men, and a battleship with 1500, have the same type of interior organization. The gunnery department of a destroyer may consist of a single lieutenant and fifty or so enlisted men divided into four 5-inch gun crews and a director crew; that of a battleship may have a score of officers and six or seven subordinate units totalling several hundred men, manning turret guns, torpedo-defense and air-defense batteries, and fire control equipment. Both are designed for the same end: that the captain may bring to bear the whole offensive power of his ship, quickly and efficiently, against any objective.

Ships of the same type are grouped in divisions, each having a division commander with a suitable staff. This officer is not in command of any single ship, but devotes his attention to the coordination of the work of several similar ships. Here communication begins to take on a high degree of importance. Within a ship, various electrical communication devices enable the captain, from a central station, to convey his orders to every one of his principal subordinates. The ship is a compact whole, directly under his control. In a group of ships, however, radio and visual signals must take the place of the more direct means of communication, and coordinated action in battle is dependent on the efficiency of these means of conveying the commander's orders.

A division usually consists of three or four ships, except in the submarine force, where six is the usual number.

The next step in organization is the grouping of the divisions of the various types into type-classes, each under a commander assisted by a staff somewhat larger than that of a division commander.

This is the theoretical idea. In practice there are necessary variations. For example, the United States Fleet as at present organized has four divisions of battleships, the senior division commander being in command of the whole; the destroyers, however, being much more numerous than the battleships, require intermediate echelons of command. Two or three destroyer divisions compose a squadron, and four squadrons a flotilla; a squadron has a destroyer of larger type (destroyer leader) as flagship for the commander, while a flotilla commander flies his flag in a light cruiser. The senior flotilla commander commands all the destroyers of the fleet.

Finally, the fleet is divided into organizations arranged on tactical principles, to insure the proper functioning of the several types of ships. These are the Battle Force, the Scouting Force, the Submarine Force and the Base Force; in addition to which there is a Training Detachment and the Fleet Marine Force.

The Battle Force, commanded by an admiral, includes all the battleships, light cruisers and destroyers, the aircraft carriers and their attached air squadons, and the minecraft. The main striking power of the fleet, with those elements necessary to protect it and insure its prompt arrival on the scene of action, are thus concentrated under one commander.

The Scouting Force includes the heavy cruisers and the long-range patrol aircraft with their tenders. Its duties are distant reconnaissance and screening (offensive or defensive). The patrol-planes are assigned to the various shore stations for overhaul and supply, but are provided with tenders which give them a high degree of strategical mobility.

The Submarine Force includes submarine divisions assigned to shore bases for local defense, and other units which operate with the fleet.

The Base Force is composed of the necessary auxiliaries of various types, which make up the fleet's "train" and provide the required supply-link between the fleet and its bases.

The Training Detachment consists of some of the older battleships and a destroyer squadron, and is engaged in the training of naval reservists and midshipmen. It was the only element of the United States Fleet assigned to the Atlantic, with the exception of a few submarines and patrol aircraft, until the recent creation of an Atlantic squadron of light cruisers and destroyers.

The Fleet Marine Force includes two detachments of marines, normally serving on shore at Quantico and San Diego respectively, who would be available for the support of the fleet, if required, in furnishing landing parties for the occupation and defense of advance bases.

Over all this tremendous organization is placed the Commander in Chief who, assisted by his staff, directs its training, controls its operations and insures among the various units that coordination of effort and unity of doctrine which makes the difference between a fleet and a "mob" of armed ships.

The battleship divisions form the backbone of this huge fabric.

The modern battleship represents the most formidable concentration of fighting power yet created by man. Offensively, the range of her great turret guns permits her to hurl her salvos of 1400-pound or 2100-pound shells to a distance of twenty miles. Defensively, her power of survival against all forms of attack permits her to remain afloat and go on fighting under assaults which would destroy less well-protected types.

It is, indeed, in this power of survival that the battleship has her chief title to naval preeminence: for it is apparent that the final issue of any war at sea must be decided by ships with a sustained power of offensive action, able both to give and to endure the heavy blows which modern naval weapons can inflict. To this sustained power, the ability to remain afloat under punishment is fundamental. Without that ability, chance and the getting in of the first salvos would decide every naval action between forces anywhere nearly equal.

The battleship resists attack by gunfire by means of her armor. This is usually heaviest at the waterline (the belt), on the main gun-positions (turrets), at the principal battle-control and navigating stations, and at the funnel bases. The sides above the belt are protected by thinner armor. The vertical armor is supplemented by armored decks, which provide protection against the plunging fire of long-range shells and against airplane bombs. Lateral armored bulk-heads give protection against end-on attack. The weight of all this armor is enormous, being in some ships one-third of the total displacement.

Underwater attack by torpedoes, mines or bombs, striking at the unarmored lower parts of the ship, is provided against by compartmentation. The outer portion of the ship's under-side consists of a sort of outer hull, divided into many water-tight compartments. Next comes the true hull, and within that still a third bulkhead, the spaces between these three "skins" being cut up by many transverse bulkheads into a veritable honeycomb of compartments, each of which, if water be admitted to it from without, may be isolated from its fellows by means of water-tight doors and hatches. A single torpedo or mine, therefore, can rarely inflict enough damage on a battleship to impair seriously her water-tight integrity or to keep her from continuing her place in the battle-line, though it may lower her speed. This system is reinforced by the work of the damage-control crew, which is trained in cutting off damaged portions of the ship, in repairing injuries, shoring up bulkheads, shifting ballast and oil fuel, flooding or pumping out compartments to correct the trim of the ship, and in general minimizing the effect of battle injuries.

The much discussed question of the vulnerability of battleships to air attack depends for answer not so much on whether a sufficient number of bomb-hits could eventually sink a battleship, as the likelihood, under war conditions, of such a number of hits being effected. The chances of this may be thus summarized:

(1) The target must first be located.

(2) The cloud ceiling must be sufficiently high to permit bombing. Actual observation over a long period of years has shown that oceanic ceilings are under 10,000 feet about half the time. Conditions permitting really high-altitude bombing (concerning which so much is heard) are comparatively rare.

(3) Visibility must be adequate.

(4) The target battleship will not be alone; she will be accompanied by other battleships and a large number of lesser craft. All of these will have anti-aircraft guns. The attacking planes must therefore face a very heavy volume of fire, and if they must fly at anything much under 20,000 feet they will suffer severe casualties. At 10,000 feet they will rarely be able to drive their attack home.

(5) Defending aircraft will also have to be considered.

(6) Bombing must be exceedingly accurate to hit a moving target the size of a ship. The greater the altitude, the less accuracy; the lower the altitude, the greater exposure to fire.

(7) Accuracy is impaired by the difficulty of ascertaining exact firing data (velocity and direction of wind, course and

speed of target, altitude of plane, variable air currents between plane and target) .

(8) Horizontal bombing requires a straight course and steady speed for an appreciable period before letting go the bomb, increasing the chances of the anti-aircraft gunner; dive bombing cannot be substituted to any great extent, because a plane large enough to carry large bombs for long distances cannot be made strong enough to stand the strain of pulling out of the dive.

If to all these factors are added the very great powers of resistance possessed by the modern battleship, it may be confidently asserted that the airplane, while able to inflict severe damage under exceptionally favorable circumstances, has no more made the battleship obsolete than has the torpedo vessel or the submarine. It has merely added one more to the remarkably extensive and powerful armory of weapons available to the modern fleet, and will be formidable precisely in proportion to its use in coordination with all the others, as part of the great war-team that the fleet is.

The offensive power of a battleship resides chiefly in her 14-inch or 16-inch turret guns. These are grouped by pairs or threes in armored turrets, which are located on the center line and can be revolved so that the full battery can be brought to bear on either broadside. The fire of these guns is controlled and directed from a central station, by means of a device called a director; which permits a single officer to adjust the fire of the main battery upon any target and to fire the guns either singly, by turrets, or in salvo. Range is determined initially by means of range-finders, and fire is thereafter adjusted by observation of the fall of trial shots; this observation is normally carried on by aircraft, but may in default thereof be conducted from elevated spotting stations. When the target is a hostile battleship, fire for effect (after the range and other firing data has been determined) is normally by salvo: what this means may be faintly imagined by considering that a salvo from the U.S.S. *Maryland* striking such a target means the simultaneous impact thereon of eight armor-piercing shells weighing slightly over one ton each.

A battleship also has two other types of guns: a broadside battery of 5-inch guns for dealing with destroyer attacks, and a "topside" battery of shorter 5-inch anti-aircraft guns, supplemented by anti-aircraft machine-guns.

The resisting power and the offensive power of the battleship must be supplemented by mobility, the means by which these fighting qualities may be transported to the scene of action and there given full scope. Mobility is a factor of speed and fuel capacity. Speed enables the battleship to arrive quickly at the decisive place, and to maneuver in the presence of the enemy after she has encountered him. It has therefore both strategical and tactical value. Strategically, the speed which really matters is sustained sea speed: speed which, without undue strain or excessive fuel consumption, may be maintained steadily, hour after hour and day after day, in good weather and bad, while the great ship hastens to her goal. Tactically, the full speed of which the ship is capable may be called upon.

A ship is always a compromise between various desirable qualities, and this is especially true of warships. Maximum size in the American navy is limited by two considerations: harbor and dock capacities, and the size of the locks of the Panama Canal. Since there is an upper limit on size, it is obvious that ships cannot be built to include the maxima of desirability in all qualities. For every ton allotted to armor, for instance, a ton must be deducted from the allotments to battery, speed and fuel capacity. In the determination of the inevitable compromise between these four principal factors in battleship design, the question to be asked is, as ever: "What is this ship meant to do?"

The answer, as to the battleship, is: "Fight in the line of battle against other battleships."

Therefore guns and armor come first, almost of equal importance. Speed must ever be a secondary consideration. Moreover, speed makes enormous inroads on tonnage. The British navy has two ships which exemplify this very clearly: the battleship *Queen Elizabeth* and the battle-cruiser *Hood*. They carry exactly the same main battery (eight 15-inch guns) and there is little to choose between them in the matter of protection. The designed speed of the *Queen Elizabeth* is 25 knots; her displacement is 31,100 tons. The designed speed of the *Hood* is 31 knots; her displacement is 42,100 tons. It therefore required 11,000 extra tons to gain 6 knots additional speed, with vessels otherwise of similar military qualities. The original cost of the *Hood* was about twice that of the *Queen Elizabeth*, and her annual upkeep cost is about 60% greater.

The tradition of the American navy has ever been to possess battleships of greater gun-power and superior protection to those of contemporary foreign ships. For this, speed has been sacrificed. Our battleships today have on the average top speeds of 21 knots. British battleships range from 22 to 31 knots; Japanese from 22½ to 27. But with the exception of the comparatively new British *Nelson* and *Rodney*, no battleship of either navy has armor protection to equal that of any of the twelve American battleships now with the fleet in the Pacific.

Improvements in engineering, notably in steam boilers, have however enabled our new ships to be given greater speed; this of course looks forward to the day when all foreign battleships will be vessels of 27-30 knots. In the meanwhile, unless employed as a "fast wing", our new ships will in action be tied to the speed of the remainder of the battle-line. That line will not have as high a maneuvering speed as that of other navies; but it will be able to stand a great deal more punishment.

At the enormous ranges at which modern battles are fought, there is not much to be gained by maneuvering the battle-line ten per cent faster or slower, except when one party to the fight wishes to break off the action, as the Germans did at Jutland. But the German withdrawal was successful because of bad visibility and precision of maneuver due to long drill in the exact evolution which was employed, a simultaneous turn by all ships, rather than to superior speed. In future battles at even greater ranges, this matter of visibility will be of very great importance. With aircraft overhead, it is doubtful in the extreme whether one side or the other will reap much advantage from a small margin of speed, which in any case may be lost by injury to a single ship of the line. It will be weight of gunfire, ability to stand heavy blows, and the various factors of visibility (atmospheric conditions, direction of wind, sea, and so on) which will, with the human factors of courage, skill and discipline, determine the outcome. If it comes to running away, a little extra speed may enable a fleet to escape. This is not a major consideration in the design of American battleships.

The tactical doctrine of our navy is based upon maintaining both a numerical and a ship-for-ship superiority in fighting power over any probable enemy. This foresees a preliminary stage in a naval war in which our efforts will be devoted to creating a situation which will compel the enemy to give battle or yield to us the control of his maritime communications. If he eventually chooses the former, we are desirous of leaving as little as possible to chance, for chance is the hope of the weaker party to a contest; we desire to reap the full benefit of our superior striking power. We are therefore concerned with having battleships which can inflict the maximum of punishment on the enemy, while receiving the minimum of punishment themselves. We are not concerned with having battleships in which too much fighting power has been sacrificed to the ability to break off the action, because we do not expect to desire the action to be broken off. If the enemy, on the other hand, desires to quit, pursuit by destroyers and especially by aircraft can be much swifter than by any imaginable battleship force, and should be able to inflict sufficient injury on a retiring foe either to enable our battleships to come up, or force him to the demoralizing expedient of abandoning his lame ducks. If night intervenes, as at Jutland, the ability of our fleet to continue the action in the morning will be based far more on accurate information of the enemy's course from our light forces, and on accurate appreciation of his intentions by our Commander in Chief, than on an extra two or three knots speed for our battle line.

There is, however, another point to be considered in this matter of speed for armored ships. The German navy now possesses three 10,000 ton "pocket battleships" capable of 26 knots, with main batteries of six 11-inch guns and cruising radii of 10,000 miles. There have been persistent reports that Japan is building armored ships which are an improvement on this type (15,000 tons, six 12-inch guns and 30 knots speed). Such vessels, operating as commerce destroyers, would be extremely difficult to deal with, as they could not be overtaken by our battleships, even if we were in a position to detach battleships in search of them, while they could easily destroy our heavy cruisers. If such ships are constructed in any number by foreign powers, we will have to provide against them as the French have provided against the German "pocket battleships", by building fast, powerful, armored ships especially designed to deal with them.

Such vessels should be of sufficient size, speed, armament and protection to deal with any foreign ship of their class. They should be able to dominate any situation in which enemy battleships are not involved; just as the British battle-cruisers did in the World War, notably on the occasion of the Heligoland Bight action and the battle of the Falkland Islands.

As to the number of battleships we require, that is entirely dependent on the numbers others may build. Safety requires a decisive numerical superiority as against any conceivable enemy in either ocean, having regard to the great distances over which we should have to operate.

The present Japanese navy includes ten battleships; ours has fifteen. Japan's new construction program is as yet unknown, but is reported to include four battleships (two of 40,000 and two of 43,000 tons). We have two battleships under construction (*North Carolina, Washington*) and four more (*Indiana, Massachusetts, Alabama, South Dakota*) shortly to be taken in hand: all of 35,000 tons.

This will give us a margin of 21 ships to 14 over Japan.[1] Considering that three of our ships (*New York, Texas, Arkansas*) are now by reason of their low gun-elevation and advancing age hardly fit for active service without extensive refits (which would not justify the expense save in emergency) the immediately available ratio will be 18 ships to 14. This is by no means excessive, as the reader will realize if he will remember the circumstances, earlier described, under which a Pacific war would have to be fought.

In the Atlantic, we might possibly have to face a coalition of Germany and Italy. When ships now building are completed, Germany will have five battleships, plus three "pocket battleships", and Italy eight. This is almost exactly the same fighting power as the Japanese will possess. Only two German battleships are now ready, and two Italian.

If by some now inconceivable combination of circumstances we were compelled to fight Great Britain, we should not be quite so well off. The British have fifteen capital ships at present, and are building ten. But at least five of these are

---

[1] For details of the world's battleships, see table on Pages 207-208.

to be permanently stationed in the Far East, which leaves twenty to face our eighteen; no overwhelming odds, considering our superiority in armor and individual gun-power as against the older British ships, and the fact that the British could not effect a junction with their Far Eastern detachment without meanwhile leaving their vital Atlantic trade routes open to us.

We may therefore conclude that for our immediate purposes, and having regard to even remotely possible antagonists, our present and contemplated battleship strength is adequate, though not overwhelming.

The upper limit of the new Navy Bill (630,000 tons of underage battleships) will permit us to have exactly 18 battleships of 35,000 tons each; some of them may be larger, as our fleet will for some years to come include certain of our present battleships of 32,000 tons or thereabouts, and the Navy Bill provides for an additional 30,000 tons if the larger ships are found necessary. The question of whether to build larger ships or not depends on what others may do. The enigma here is Japan; no other nation possesses or is known to be planning a battleship larger than 35,000 tons. If reports as to the proportions of the new Japanese ships turn out to be true, it will be necessary for us (and Britain) to increase the size of future ships, as both offensive and defensive qualities may be greatly increased as tonnage increases. We cannot afford to give away such advantages. Seaworthy battleships as large as 50,000 tons can be built which will pass through the Panama Canal, by decreasing the proportion of beam to length.

The strengths of the other elements of our fleet (except aircraft carriers) do not depend so much upon numerical ratios with foreign navies as upon our own requirements, based on our battleship strength and on geographical conditions.

Next in importance to the battleship ranks the cruiser. It has been said that no naval commander-in-chief in war ever had enough cruisers; Nelson's continual cry was for frigates and more frigates (the frigate being the cruiser of his day).

The American navy has two types of cruiser, heavy and light. The heavy cruiser is a vessel of 9000-10,000 tons, 32-35 knots speed, armed with 8-inch guns in her main battery, and with 5-inch anti-aircraft guns. The light cruiser is 7000-10,000 tons, about the same speed as the heavy cruiser, but with a main battery of 6-inch guns. We have 18 heavy cruisers and 19 light cruisers, built and building, with four more of the latter class authorized. This is probably ample for all fleet duties: that is, for distant reconnaissance and screening, protection of aircraft carriers from enemy cruisers and destroyers, support of destroyer attacks on enemy battleships, and battle reconnaissance. But cruisers will also be required for a variety of other duties, such as raids on enemy bases, the protection of our commerce by patrol or convoy, and attacks on enemy commerce. It is true that some of these, notably attacks on enemy commerce, would not begin to be really exigent until the enemy's fleet was disposed of, when the greater part of the cruisers required for fleet duties could be released; but the examples already given of the Brazilian manganese convoys and the protection of our shipping on the Panama route indicate that many cruisers will be needed for such tasks from the very outset of a naval war. There is not much chance of any peace-time provision being sufficient for all war needs: if we maintain a ratio of about one heavy and one light cruiser to each battleship, for fleet duties, plus 50% for other tasks, we shall have a figure which will reconcile economy with military necessity about as closely as possible in a calculation based on so many inponderables.

BATTLESHIPS OF THE WORLD

No. of Ships	Main Battery of Each Ship						Tonnage (standard)	Designed Speed (knots)	Armor		Year of Completion
	11"	12"	13"	14"	15"	16"			Turrets	Belt	
United States											
1		12					26,000	20.5	12"	11"	1912
2				10			27,000	21	14"	12"	1914
2				10			29,000	20.5	18"	13½"	1916
2				12			32,600	21	18"	14"	1916
3				12			33,000	21.5	18"	14"	1917-19
2				12			32,000	21	18"	14"	1920-21
3						8	32,000	21	18"	16"	1921-23
2*						9	35,000	28	18" (?)	16"	1941
4*						9	35,000	?	?	?	1942
21		12		124		78					
Japan											
4				8			29,330	26	10"	8"	1913-15
2				12			29,500	22.5	12"	12"	1915-17
2				12			29,990	23	12"	12"	1917-18
2						8	32,720	23	14"	13"	1920-21
2*						10 (?)	40,000 (?)	?	?	?	1940- (?)
2*						12 (?)	43,000 (?)	?	?	?	1941- (?)
14				80		60					
Germany											
2	9						26,000	30	12"	10"	1938
3*					8		35,000	30 (?)	?	?	1939-41
3**	6						10,000	26	7"	4"	1933-36
8	36				24						

BATTLESHIPS OF THE WORLD (Continued)

No. of Ships	Main Battery of Each Ship						Tonnage (standard)	Designed Speed (knots)	Armor		Year of Completion
	11"	12"	13"	14"	15"	16"			Turrets	Belt	
Italy											
4	..	..	10†	...	..	...	23,622	27	11"	9¾"	‡1913-16
2*	..	..	...	...	9	...	35,000	30	?	9"	1939
2**	..	..	...	...	9	...	35,000	30	?	?	1941
8	..	..	40†	...	36	...	......	..	..	..	......
Great Britain											
2	..	..	...	...	6	...	32,000	28	11"	9"	1916
1	..	..	...	...	8	...	42,100	31	15"	12"	1920
5	..	..	...	...	8	...	31,100	25	11"	13"	1915-16
5	..	..	...	...	8	...	29,150	22	13"	13"	1916-17
2	..	..	...	...	..	9	33,500	23	16"	14"	1927
5*	..	..	...	12	...	...	35,000	30	?	?	1940-41
2**	..	..	...	...	...	9 (?)	40,000 (?)	?	?	?	1941
3*	..	..	...	...	...	?	?	?	?	?	1942
25	..	..	..	60	100	36	......	..	..	..	......
France											
3	..	12	...	...	...	...	22,189	20	12½"	10¾"	1913-14
1	..	..	8§	...	...	...	22,189	20	17"	10¾"	1916
2	..	..	10§	...	...	...	22,189	20.5	17"	10¾"	1915
2	..	..	8	...	...	...	26,500	29.5	14"	11"	1937-38
3*	..	..	...	...	8	...	35,000	30	?	16"	1940-41
11	..	36	44	...	24	...	......	..	..	..	......

* Building.   ** "Pocket Battleships."   † 12.6".   ‡ Completely rebuilt, 1933-39.   § 13.5".

Composition of the U. S. Fleet

The new limit on cruiser tonnage will be 412,500 tons. Allotting 180,000 tons to the existing 18 heavy cruisers and 90,000 to the nine 10,000 ton light cruisers now in service or building, this would permit us to have, in addition, about 18 new cruisers of an average of 8000 tons (when the 10 older ships of the *Omaha* class are all replaced): a total of 45 cruisers. This is a rather low limit and will probably require the retention of the *Omaha* class in service for some time to come.

The remaining classes of fighting ships which form part of the fleet come under the heading of flotilla craft. The general definition of these is that their main weapon is the torpedo, bomb or mine and not the gun.

Torpedo-vessels are divided into surface and sub-surface: that is, destroyers and submarines. The modern American destroyer is a ship of 1500 tons, 36½ knots designed speed, armed with four 5-inch guns and sixteen 21-inch torpedo tubes. For squadron leaders a slightly larger type is built (1850 tons). The sea-keeping qualities of these new ships are much superior to those of the old destroyers of the World War, which nevertheless contrived to batter their way through the storm-swept Atlantic with convoy after convoy. The fleet requires large numbers of destroyers: while no exact ratio can be laid down, eight per battleship are none too many. Offensively, the duties of destroyers include torpedo attacks on the enemy's heavy ships, offensive screening in conjunction with cruisers and aircraft, and the firing of star shells to illuminate night targets for their battleships. Their defensive duties include submarine screening of their heavy ships (all-important in waters where any number of enemy submarines may be operating, as for example in the area studded by the Japanese mandated islands), repelling enemy destroyer attacks, and providing an outer barrage of anti-aircraft fire. The laying of smoke screens may have an offensive or defensive purpose.

[209]

It is rarely economical to employ these fast, heavily-armed, expensive ships for other than fleet duties. Their speed is not needed for convoying coastwise shipping, which is better performed by gunboats or specially designed convoy vessels; nor for anti-submarine duties in the vicinity of our coasts and outlying possessions, for which again special ships of less expensive type are equally well suited. For raiding enemy convoys, destroyers lack fuel-endurance.

We have at present, built and building, 81 destroyers of modern type (including 13 destroyer leaders), and 8 more appropriated for. We also have 161 older destroyers of World War design, of which 58 are in commission and the others in reserve at San Diego and Philadelphia. As long as any of these older vessels are serviceable they can be employed for convoy and miscellaneous duties. They are however rapidly wearing out.

Our new destroyer tonnage limit is 228,000, providing for about 150 destroyers of 1500 tons (including one leader of 1850 tons to eight of the regular size). Considering the high proportion of time that these comparatively delicate, machinery-filled ships must spend undergoing overhaul in Navy Yards or alongside destroyer tenders, this number will be none too many for an active fleet of 18 battleships.

Our modern destroyers have cruising ranges of 6000 miles at economical speeds. It is this which so strictly limits the radius of action of a fleet; since obviously it cannot go more than 3000 miles out from its base, and in practice the necessity for the use of high speed and of maneuvering would cut this to the figure heretofore given of 2000-2500 miles. Battleships have cruising ranges of 10,000-15,000 miles, and cruisers almost as much; but a fleet in war must be complete in all classes of ships, and destroyers are an absolute necessity to it.

Another type of surface torpedo vessel is the coastal motorboat, used for inshore operations in the defense of harbors and coasts. They are "skimming" boats — i.e., they are driven by powerful motors at such high speed that they rise and skim the surface of the water. They cannot be very large, as there is a natural limit to the weight which can be made to skim; they depend on their very high speed for safety against enemy gunfire. They are not long-range or heavy-weather vessels. Their work may be supplemented by larger types of torpedo-armed patrol boats, similar in design (though not in armament) to the admirable 165-foot patrol boats now used by the Coast Guard. These may also be used for coastal convoys, or anti-submarine duties.

Funds have been appropriated for experimental work with ships of these types. Construction in large numbers in time of peace would not be economical, as there are many small shipbuilding firms which can turn them out rapidly, if needed, from type-designs.

Submarines are vessels of peculiar qualities, which, like those of the airplane, are likely to be overrated if not clearly understood.

The principal advantage of the submarine is her ability to approach a target, or effect a reconnaissance, unseen.

Against this, the limitations of the type may be summarized as follows:

(a) Lack of speed, especially submerged. No submarine in the world can do better than 11 knots under water; since the normal cruising speed of battleships is 15-16 knots, the submarine has to intercept such a target; she cannot overtake it except on the surface, exposed to attack.

(b) Low cruising endurance when submerged. A submarine is driven on the surface by Diesel or other motors which require air and cannot be used when air supply is cut off. Therefore their submerged power comes from electric motors, drawing current from storage batteries. It is the capacity of these batteries which limits the submarine's underwater radius of action. In modern ocean-going submarines the batteries will last 35 to 40 hours at very low speeds (two or three knots). If higher speed is required, the batteries are much more quickly exhausted.

(c) Vulnerability to gunfire. A single hit may prevent the submarine from diving, converting her into a slow and unhandy surface vessel, inadequately armed.

(d) Vulnerability to underwater attack. The chief enemy of the submarine is the depth charge, aided by the detector. The former is an explosive charge set to explode at a fixed depth under water. The latter is a listening device which detects and locates the submarine by the beat of her propellers. It must be remembered that unless she can lie on the bottom, a submarine cannot remain submerged with her engines stopped. The laws of buoyancy then take charge, and she either comes up or goes down. At depths greater than 300 feet, the pressure becomes too great even for the sturdiest hull; prolonged submersion to a greater depth than 200 feet is not considered safe. In deep water, therefore, such as the Pacific and much of the Caribbean, the submarine must keep going. These two factors of vulnerability explain why even a small patrol boat with a single gun, a few depth charges, and a detector, is so deadly an enemy for a submarine of twenty times her displacement.

(e) Poor vision. On the surface, the submarine presents no elevated position from which any radius of vision may be attained. Submerged to periscope depth she is dependent entirely on the limited vision provided by her periscopes. Submerged below that depth she is entirely blind and has to depend on hydrophones to detect the presence near her of other vessels.

The submarine is not a particularly valuable weapon in a fleet action, as she is a danger to friendly ships when the latter are maneuvering at high speed; she is in such an action strictly a weapon of opportunity — for example, a commander encountering a weaker fleet and desiring to prevent the enemy from breaking off the action might be able to slip a squadron of submarines around on the enemy's disengaged flank and by subsequent maneuvers compel the enemy to withdraw in the general direction where the submarines were lurking. Even then the submarines might be unable to drive home their attack because of their low speed; they would however be very dangerous to any damaged ship.

In the close defense of bases and coast lines submarines have great value. As was proven at the Dardanelles, vessels engaged in supporting a landing force by gunfire, or in close blockade or bombardment of shore positions, are excellent submarine targets. In defense of coastal shipping, submarines can cruise in an area likely to be the operating ground of raiders, seeking opportunities. They can also operate successfully where shipping is compelled to converge into narrow waterways, as in the passages leading into the Caribbean, which they could make perilous for enemy vessels. This is especially the case when the adjacent shore-lines are not in possession of the enemy, who is thereby inhibited from organizing a local patrol-service to deal with the submarine menace.

The great value of the submarine to the United States will be for local defense, and as affording the means of imposing caution and delay on enemy operations if we are involved in war in an ocean where our fleet is not present. *Fear* of the submarine impeded the operations of the British Grand Fleet in the North Sea far more than its actual accomplishments. Fear of our submarines would make hostile battleships very chary of entering the Caribbean Sea or of operating too close to any of our Pacific bases; far more would such fear put reins of caution upon the approach to those areas of the slow unwieldy mass of transports necessary to convey a large body of troops. The submarines could not, of course, *prevent* such operations; their limitations are too numerous and too great. But they would assuredly gain us much time, which, in the two-ocean, one-fleet strategy imposed upon us, is all-important.

Long range (offensive) operation of submarines is a more debatable subject. If they can keep station off an enemy port containing any portion of his fleet they may be able to inflict serious injuries; this may however be countered by patrol and minefields. British submarines so operating in the Heligoland Bight had some successes; German submarines on the contrary were never able to torpedo a capital ship of the Grand Fleet, though, as has been said, fear of them restricted its movements and made heavy demands on destroyers for screening purposes.

The submarine as a commerce-destroyer will still be dangerous but can hardly be so employed effectively save with the ruthlessness displayed by the Germans in the World War. This would not be initiated by the United States, but might very well be forced upon us as a measure of reprisal.

We have at present 35 of the newer type submarines, built and building, with several more authorized. We also have 68 older submarines, of which 32 are in commission and 36 are laid up at the Navy Yard, Philadelphia. Estimates of the number required must be based on the needs of local defense, plus fleet requirements, plus a certain number of long-range submarines for offensive operations.

The number on hand should approximate war requirements and allow some margin, as it will be all but impossible to build submarines rapidly in case of emergency. Only two Navy Yards (Portsmouth and Mare Island) and one private firm are now equipped for and experienced in the building of this class; they are difficult ships to design and construct. They are, moreover, quite expensive, two to two-and-one-half times per ton more costly than battleships, while they have but half as long a life.

Our authorized tonnage of submarines is 81,957, enough

for a total of 56 ships of the new 1450-ton type (*Sargo*); since small submarines of limited cruising radius will be of little value to the American navy, the individual tonnage will hardly be less in future ships. In view of the importance of the submarine in our strategy, this seems decidedly too small an allowance, though adequate for a war which begins and ends in the ocean where the fleet is present. Since this happy circumstance cannot be assured, our limited facilities for building submarines should be expanded and the authorized tonnage gradually stepped up to allow at least 80 underage submarines to be available.

At present our submarines in commission are divided among the fleet, the Asiatic Station, and the submarine bases at New London, Panama and Hawaii. (The latter two operate under the Commander-in-Chief of the Fleet.) The submarines out of commission at Philadelphia are kept in serviceable condition as far as possible, the difficulty in preparing them for active service would be to get experienced crews. No very great expense would be involved in putting these vessels on a reserve status, with skeleton crews, including for each ship 5 or 6 "key" petty officers. The time required to complete them for sea would be very appreciably reduced by this measure: but it would be only a stop-gap, as many of these ships will be worthless in a few more years.

The mine is an important naval weapon. It may be used offensively (in enemy waters, as in the channels leading from his bases) or defensively, to deny him certain waters in which we do not need to operate. The naval mine is of the contact type, exploding when touched by a passing ship. So-called "controlled" mines, operated from the shore, are used in defense of our own harbors and are the responsibility of the army. The provision of mine-layers for our navy has been somewhat neglected; at present the mine squadron with the Battle Force consists of one old converted merchant vessel, four light mine-layers converted from wartime destroyers, and four mine-sweepers. There are four more light mine-layers in reserve. At least one large mine-layer with a considerable cruising radius and capacity for ample equipment and mine supplies is urgently needed, not only for operations but for training—"that the art of mining be kept alive," as the Chief of Naval Operations put it to the Naval Committee of the House.

The naval mine is anchored to the bottom, and floats at the end of a cable, the length of which may be adjusted to the depth of water. Mined channels are cleared by "sweeping," for which specially designed ships are used. The ones we have are little more than ocean-going tugs; newer and faster ships are needed. Like many other small types, however, large numbers of mine-sweepers are not required, as they can be turned out rapidly if needed once experiment has shown the proper design.

The remaining "flotilla" classification is the aircraft. Those used by the navy are of two types, shore-based and ship-based. The most important shore-based aircraft are the large patrol-planes, which are given strategical mobility by the use of tenders which form temporary floating bases for them. At the present time we have five patrol wings in service, including a total of eighteen squadrons (usually of 12 planes each). These wings are stationed at Panama, Hawaii, Norfolk, Seattle and San Diego. There are also 15 patrol-planes at the Naval Air Station at Pensacola.

Ship-based aircraft are of two types—carrier-borne and catapulted.

The aircraft carrier is a huge floating hangar and repair shop, as well as a sea-going landing field, since she has a flight deck from which her aircraft can take off and to which they can return. She must have high speed, since she has to turn into the wind to fly her planes off or on and must then be able to regain station rapidly—regain, that is, the protection of the battle-fleet. For a carrier, by reason of her great bulk and her comparative lack of armor, is the most vulnerable of all big ships; she must be protected by other ships against attacks by gunfire or bomb or torpedo. The loss of one carrier would be so great proportionately that every precaution must be taken to guard against it.

The airplane carrier is a type in which our required numbers are directly affected by the construction programs of other powers as well as by the circumstances under which our fleet may have to operate. Probably, in a naval war of the future, the earliest contacts between hostile fleets will be made by planes, and there will develop a struggle for air superiority upon which may hang the whole issue of the coming battle. If either fleet is operating beyond the radius of its shore-based aircraft, it will be entirely dependent in the air upon its ship-borne planes; if these are destroyed or so reduced in number as to be able to operate only under difficulties, the fleet will be sadly handicapped as to reconnaissance, artillery observation, and defense against hostile air attack. Initial superiority in the air will be a tremendous advantage, because such superiority will tend to grow proportionately in action.

In a Pacific war, offensive operations by our fleet would very likely be within range of many small Japanese islands where seaplane tenders or small carriers might lurk. It would be the task of our patrol-planes, based on our small outpost islands, to "get the jump" on these opponents, but it would also be necessary for our fleet to have a force of carrier-borne aircraft superior to that of the Japanese fleet.

The controlling figure is therefore not so much the number of carriers as their total plane capacity.

The United States at present possesses two very large carriers (*Lexington, Saratoga*) of 33,000 tons and 33 knots speed. They were our first large carriers, and were originally designed as battle-cruisers; both are now badly in need of modernization to increase their efficiency. Three other carriers (*Ranger* of 14,700 tons and *Enterprise* and *Yorktown* of 19,900 tons) have subsequently been added to the fleet; all three were designed for their purpose, and are more efficient, ton for ton, than the big ships. All five carriers have the same plane complement at present — 80 planes each: of which 8 planes are assigned to special duties, the rest forming four squadrons of 18 planes each. One fighter squadron, one of torpedo-bombers, and two of scout-bombers is a typical distribution, though there are variations. If appropriations are made for their modernization, *Lexington* and *Saratoga* can probably handle five squadrons without overcrowding — say 100 planes per ship. This is also the full capacity of *Yorktown* and *Enterprise*. *Ranger* and the one carrier now under construction (*Wasp*) can handle 80 each. Our total capacity for carrier-borne planes will therefore be 560.

The Japanese navy has two large carriers of 27,000 tons, one designed as a battleship and the other as a battle-cruiser, with capacities of 60 and 50 planes respectively. Subsequent Japanese carrier construction was much smaller in individual size than ours, both because they did not want to put too many eggs in one basket, and because they wanted ships able to conduct operations in shallow waters (Chinese coastal waters and rivers). They have, built or building, five small carriers of 7000-10,000 tons; one carries 24 planes, one 30, the others 40 each. Finally, though there is no official news obtainable, they are reported to be building four more carriers; and if, as seems reasonable from the reported size of their battleships, they are now building ships for oceanic warfare, with at least as great plane capacity as any existing Japanese carrier, we may credit these new carriers with 60 planes apiece, very likely more. This figure gives a tentative Japanese strength of 524 carrier-borne aircraft. Our margin of superiority is hardly great enough for comfort. The 40,000 tons of additional carriers provided for in the Vinson bill should therefore be laid down as soon as possible; assuming two ships about the size of *Yorktown*, this will give us 200 additional planes: a total of 760 against Japan's 524. Our superiority should be at least as great in carrier-borne aircraft as in battleships; greater, if possible, considering how many more islands Japan possesses in the probable theater of operations than we do, and how near we should probably be to the Japanese main bases before they would be compelled to fight a decisive fleet action.

In an Atlantic war we should be much better off, if our opponent were Germany: this nation has two 19,250-ton carriers under construction, which will probably carry 50 or more aircraft apiece. Italy has no carriers, and none are planned. Great Britain, however, has five carriers in commission, with a total capacity (estimated) of about 190 planes; five more are under construction, reported as able to carry 70 planes each, but probably equal to caring for 100. Total, 690 planes. The French navy has one carrier with a capacity of 40 planes, and is building two with capacities (estimated) of 60 each. Total, 160.

In addition to our carriers' planes, a great deal of reconnaissance and other work will be done by catapulted planes carried in cruisers. All our heavy cruisers, and the new light cruisers, carry four aircraft each. The older light cruisers carry two. When ships now building or appropriated for are completed, the total number of scouting planes so borne will be 144. The 18 battleships will carry three spotting planes each. Total, 216 catapulted aircraft.

The Japanese fleet will have about 128 such planes; the German, 38; the Italian, 70; the British, about 130; the French, 82.

Since the total number of aircraft for the navy allowed by the Vinson bill is 3000, and since the eventual needs of the fleet, as above stated, are something under 1000, the reader may wonder what is to be done with the remainder. There are no complete published data as yet, but since the figure of 3000 planes represents about a 50% increase over the old maximum of 2050, we may conjecture that 50% more pilots, and therefore 50% more training planes, will be needed, or a total of say 525. The Marine Corps squadrons will doubtless receive some increase from their present strength of 110 planes—say 200 in all. In training reserve units, 187 planes are now employed—if this is increased a little over 50%, it may come to 300. About 100 planes will probably be employed on miscellaneous duties. The proposed Tactical School will require about 80 planes. This gives a total of 2205.

There remain the patrol-planes. The number now considered necessary for the Pacific is 428. The Atlantic has very few—18 at present besides those used for training duties at Pensacola. If four patrol wings of four squadrons each were to be organized for the Atlantic—one at a new northeastern air base, one at Norfolk, and two for the Caribbean—this would total 192 planes plus 48 spares, or 240. Add one patrol wing for a possible new base in the Aleutians, and the total number of planes required of all classes is 2933.

These figures are of course based purely on the writer's conjecture, and are set down here, not in any attempt to anticipate official announcements, but to show that the figure of 3000 planes asked by the navy is by no means disproportionate to the requirements of proper defense. Certainly if war comes to us in the Atlantic when our fleet is in the Pacific, an adequate number of long-range naval planes will be immediately required for defending our coastal waters, locating the activities of the enemy, and covering the arrival of the fleet through the Panama Canal.

No description of the fleet would be complete without

reference to the auxiliaries. Briefly, these consist of the following types:—

(1) Repair ships, able to carry out major repairs and even, by the use of coffer-dams, to execute underwater repairs in some cases. In war, their major function would be to provide the fleet with immediate repair facilities for damaged battleships, cruisers and carriers, sufficient to enable these either to return to duty in an emergency, or to make their way to a base for further repair. The importance of such ships to a navy which may have to operate at great distances from its bases is apparent. Four repair ships are required for the fleet.

(2) Destroyer tenders. Destroyers have few facilities for making their own small repairs, limited stores and little accommodation for sick and injured men. They also have limited fuel supplies. Destroyer tenders are therefore required in a proportion of about one for 18 destroyers (two squadrons) to care for these needs and shortcomings. Without tenders, destroyers would have to spend a large part of their time in Navy Yards and in coming and going.

(3) Submarine tenders. Submarines, because of their cramped interiors, are even more dependent on "mother ships" than destroyers. One tender is needed for each 12 submarines.

(4) Seaplane tenders. These are floating bases for the big patrol-planes (flying boats); they do not transport the planes, but can hoist damaged planes on deck for repairs. The use of tenders permits the patrol-planes to operate with the fleet instead of being tied to shore bases. In addition to the duties outlined for other tenders, quarters are provided for the crews of the planes. Both large and small seaplane tenders are required; the latter can operate with detached squadrons, and can use harbors and anchorages too shallow for the large tenders. A large tender can serve two squadrons of 12 planes each; a small tender can serve one squadron,

but can carry only a limited amount of stores and repair facilities.

(5) Oilers. The constant replenishment of fuel and lubricants is a prime necessity for the efficient operation of the fleet, and of great strategical importance. The need is for fast oilers which can keep up with the fleet. None of sufficient speed are now available, nor can the merchant marine fill the need in war since commercial tankers do not allot space which can be filled with profitable cargo to provide extra speed which they do not require. The Standard Oil Company is, however, now building 12 tankers of 16½ knots speed under agreement with the Maritime Commission. Six navy oilers are required for the peace-time needs of the fleet.

(6) Store ships, cargo ships, hospital ships, ammunition ships, transports and fleet tugs are other types of auxiliaries whose names are self-explanatory. Specially fitted submarine rescue vessels are needed in the proportion of one to each squadron of submarines.

The principal defects in the auxiliaries now available for the fleet are lack of speed and advanced age. At least 16½ knots speed is necessary to enable the train to keep station with the fleet. Seaplane tenders require 18-20 knots. Of our present large fleet of auxiliaries, only two destroyer tenders, one submarine tender, one repair ship and one hospital ship can be considered satisfactory. It is more difficult to dramatize a prosaic, workaday vessel like a repair ship than it is a mighty battleship or a dashing destroyer; Congress and the public must be brought to understand the needs of the fleet in this respect, for the deficiencies are becoming serious and must be made up if the fighting ships are to operate efficiently in war.

Let us now recapitulate the composition of the fleet, as provided for by the Naval Expansion Act of May 17, 1938.

Under that act (translating tonnage figures into ships) we shall eventually have an under-age fleet of:

Composition of the U. S. Fleet

        18 battleships,
        45 cruisers (or thereabouts),
       150 destroyers,
        56 submarines,
         8 aircraft carriers,
      3000 airplanes.

This is the first time that a comprehensive naval building policy for the United States, based on our own actual requirements, has ever been enacted into law.

The provisions of the old law were confined within the closed field of treaty limitations, which were a matter of negotiation and did not always represent the American point of view. Now we have an American naval program — and it will be noted with what precision the limits set by the act meet our needs as described in this chapter.

Tremendous economies are made possible by such a considered program. When future building needs can be foreseen, both Navy Yards and private shipbuilders can arrange their facilities and labor problems accordingly. The old method of letting naval strength drop in time of peace, building hastily and wastefully in time of war, and then wasting more money in keeping large numbers of aging ships in service until once more rush replacement is necessary, will now gradually be abandoned in favor of small annual increments necessary to keep up to an established level.

Take the matter of destroyers. The life of a destroyer is considered to be 16 years. A total strength of 150 can therefore be maintained by the annual replacement of about 9 ships — that is, a squadron of 1 destroyer leader and 8 destroyers. This is the system which has been consistently followed since the World War by the British navy, and it results not only in very great economies, but in each successive squadron representing numerous little technical advances on its predecessor, the ironing out of little kinks which have been discovered in service. The destroyers actually in service will not require excessive expenditures to keep them fit, as do many of the ancient craft of this type now on our Navy List, nor will they have to spend excessive periods of time undergoing overhaul.

We shall have a larger fleet, a better fleet, and it will cost us, both for new construction and for upkeep, a great deal less in the long run than by following our old hit-and-miss method.

Moreover, released from treaty requirements as to scrapping of over-age vessels, we shall be able to retain the best of these in a reserve status, or out-of-commission (using some of them for the training of the Naval Reserve), keeping them by careful and inexpensive maintenance methods in fit shape for immediate use, and thus building up a reserve naval strength which may be of incalculable value in an emergency. In the World War the British and French navies both found use for every one of their pre-dreadnought battleships and old-style armored cruisers, though these had been scornfully written off as "obsolete and useless" by naval commentators of the pre-war period. At the outbreak of the war comparatively few of these ships were in full commission.

But it is not enough to formulate and enact a law based on sound principle; that law must be supported by suitable annual appropriations to maintain the level of naval strength it prescribes. It is here that the support of public opinion is required. The National Defense Act of 1920 marked a tremendous advance in the formulation of sound military (army) policy for this country — was, indeed, something quite unprecedented in our history — yet it was subsequently emasculated, as to many of its wisest provisions, by lack of appropriations. The necessity for flexibility is recognized; future conditions may be such that reductions will be possible, or that economies will seem forced upon us even at the compromise of safety. In these matters, however, Congress on the whole reflects the will of the nation; this is another reason why an established policy, of the wisdom and necessity of which the people at large are convinced, is so greatly superior in the long run to the old way of doing things in which naval appropriations so largely depended upon the naval-mindedness of the President and his ability to induce compliance with his views by Congress. Once the annual naval replacement increments come to be regarded as fixed charges, essential to the national safety, as much an absolute need as the Post-Office or the Federal Courts, a much healthier condition will have been attained; the defense services will no longer be the first to feel the pruning knife of economy, as they so often have been in the past. Before this happy state of affairs can be assured, however, it is necessary that our people should have a sound understanding of our naval requirements, and that it should become as politically dangerous to strike out the annual replacement of — let us say — nine destroyers as to reduce the pension rates or abolish the Social Security Act.

This would in no way preclude the reduction of our fleet if at some future time the international naval situation became such that reduction was a safe and sound policy. Nor would it preclude future increases proportionate to increases which may be made by other powers. The basic necessity is not so many battleships or so many destroyers to be laid down in this year or in that, but a firm policy, flowing out of correct principle and commanding the support of public opinion, for maintaining our fleet at a level relative to other navies, and to our strategical problems, which shall enable it to perform its necessary missions in war.

Only when this becomes fact — and we are making long strides toward that goal — may we be assured of possessing a complete and well-balanced fleet, proportioned to our needs and to the enemies it may have to encounter.

It is well, however, to bear in mind that the fleet is not everything. Behind it there are other elements of naval power, necessary to its functioning in peace and war; and to these we must now turn our attention.

Chapter XI

OUR MANY-SIDED NAVY

The Navy's field of action and its whole work are peculiar, and therefore its organization must be peculiar also. It combines in itself so many branches of knowledge and of labor, that it is quite impossible for one man, however great and wise, to be proficient in them all.

CHARLES B. BOYNTON,
The History of the Navy during the Rebellion.

IN CONSIDERING our naval policy, no subject is more important than that of administration and planning: the work of the "high command."

Under the Constitution, the President is Commander-in-Chief of the Army and Navy. The Navy Department is one of the executive departments of the Government, and at its head is a Secretary, a political officer appointed by the President, and changed with each change of administration, as is likewise the Assistant Secretary. It is of course impossible that, in so highly specialized a field, the various Secretaries who come and go should have any comprehensive knowledge of the technical details or military requirements of the navy. It is their task, rather, to exercise that control which, in a republic, must ever exist, of the civil over the military power. The Secretary, as the direct representative of the President, assigns general missions to the navy: he states what the Government wants done, not the details of how it is to be done.

He makes the broad decisions, defines the general policies. In so doing, he of course requires both military and technical advice. His military advisor and chief naval assistant is the Chief of Naval Operations, who in practice has a relation to the Secretary and to the Navy similar to that of the Chief of Staff toward the Secretary of War and the Army.

The difference is one of theory rather than of fact. The Chief of Staff has a definite legal position, deriving from the old office of Commanding General of the Army. He is the superior officer of every head of department and supervises every activity of the War Department other than those concerned with non-military matters (such as the rivers and harbors work of the Chief of Engineers). All access by department heads and other officers to the Secretary must be through the office of the Chief of Staff.

The Chief of Naval Operations is not by law established in a similar position. The several Bureaus of the Navy Department are legally independent; their chiefs may have direct access to the Secretary. The defined duties of the Chief of Naval Operations include the operations of the fleet and of other vessels of the navy, the preparation of war plans, the supervision of the Office of Naval Intelligence, the preparation of Navy Regulations and general orders, advice as to the military features of new ships, and as to the military features of dry docks and other supporting elements of the shore establishment directly concerned with the operations of the fleet.

In practice, however, these duties are so extensive that the Office of the Chief of Naval Operations becomes in effect a Naval General Staff. Its divisions include War Plans, Intelligence, Communication, Inspection, Fleet Training, Fleet Maintenance, Naval Districts, Ships' Movement, and

Technical. Approximately 140 officers of the navy and Marine Corps are assigned to this Office. The Chief of Naval Operations himself is selected from the rear admirals and has the rank of admiral while so assigned. He usually serves a four-year term.

There also exists, as an advisory body to the Secretary of the Navy, an organization known as the General Board, which consists of five or six officers, usually of flag rank; and as ex-officio members the Chief of Naval Operations, the President of the Naval War College, the Director of Naval Intelligence and the Major General Commandant of the Marine Corps. The General Board existed long before the Office of Naval Operations was created. It has now become in a sense an anachronism, and there remains no reason why its functions cannot be absorbed by the latter office.

The technical and administrative work of the Navy Department is performed by eight Bureaus.[1]

The comparative independence of these Bureaus, and the interlocking nature of their work when it is extended into the ships and shore stations of the navy, has given rise to much criticism. In particular, there has been some lack of coordination among the three material bureaus (Ordnance, Engineering, and Construction and Repair) in the matter of new ship construction. It has been proposed that these three be combined into a single great organization, eliminating friction and increasing efficiency and cooperation. This would, however, present serious problems. It is questionable whether such a Material Bureau would not be too big and cumbersome. At present an effort is being made to coordinate the work of these three Bureaus under the Assistant Secretary of the Navy; the difficulty here being of course the short tenure of office of a civilian officer who has little original knowledge of the navy's problems.

[1] For details see Appendix "A."

The Marine Corps is administered by the Major General Commandant. It is the land-fighting arm of the navy, and its duties include the provision of detachments of marines for the battleships, carriers and large cruisers to perform guard duty on board and form the nucleus of the landing-force; the guarding of Navy Yards, naval stations, ammunition depots, and the like; the protection of American lives and interests in foreign "disturbed areas" where shore operations are involved (as in China at this moment); and finally, the maintenance as an arm of the United States Fleet of the Fleet Marine Force, previously mentioned. The first two duties are definite and fixed in their demands on the total strength of the Marine Corps, and in consequence the Fleet Marine Force has suffered, having now but 22% of the strength required on mobilization.

The strategical problems of the United States, already discussed, will have made clear to the reader the very great importance of naval bases, and in particular the various situations in which the extension of our sea-power into distant waters may require the use of advance bases, which, if in enemy hands, must be seized to begin with, and in any case must be quickly put in a state of defense. Initial operations of this type, until the army can reinforce, are the main function of the Fleet Marine Force. It is therefore obvious that this force must be ready to act promptly; it will take some little time anyway to embark it and transport it to its field of action; there should not be added a long period of delay due to the embodiment of numerous raw recruits. The Fleet Marine Force should be kept in the same state of readiness as the other units of the Fleet.

The organization considered necessary for this force is that of two reinforced brigades, one at Quantico, Virginia, and one at San Diego. Normally each brigade should include two regiments of infantry, artillery units comprising base-defense and anti-aircraft batteries, an engineer company, a signal company, a tank company, a chemical company, and an air component.

When the almost completely defenseless state of Guantanamo, Culebra and Saint Thomas in the Atlantic is considered, and of Samoa and the Aleutians in the Pacific, to say nothing of the need for a force in the Pacific area able to seize and hold island advance bases, it is obvious that a reinforced brigade of about 9000 men on each coast is barely adequate for initiating the necessary war measures. The present strength of the Fleet Marine Force is about 4100, and the Fleet Marine Reserve can add about 4200 more. For the Fleet Marine Force to be able to discharge its responsibilities, its strength should be raised to approximately 12,000, and that of the Fleet Marine Reserve to 6000.

The authorized enlisted strength of the Marine Corps is fixed by law at 27,400; the appropriations this year however provide for only 18,000, an increase of 1000 over last year. Of these, about 3100 will be required for service afloat, 7000 for guard duty ashore in the United States, 2900 for foreign service, leaving 5000 for the Fleet Marine Force. A further increase of 7000 men is therefore necessary for the Marine Corps if the Fleet Marine Force is to be brought to its minimum required strength. As the continual addition of new ships to the fleet will also require additional marine detachments, not wholly compensated for by the decommissioning of older ships; and as the enlargement of naval shore facilities to care for the increased fleet also demands more marine guards, the Marine Corps should be advanced within a five-year period to its full legal quota of 27,400 enlisted men, with a proper proportionate increase of its officer personnel. The requirements of foreign service (both emergency, as in China, and normal, as in our outlying possessions) will fluctuate from time to time, and, especially as to emergency service, cannot be foreseen with any accuracy. The least that can be done is to bring the Marine Corps up to a level at which it can discharge its forseeable war missions.

The naval forces which do not form part of the United States Fleet are the Asiatic Fleet, the Special Service Squadron, the squadron temporarily serving in European waters, the Naval Transportation Service, vessels on special duty, and vessels and aircraft assigned to the Naval Districts.

The Asiatic Fleet is charged with protection of American lives, property and interests in the Far East. It is based on the naval station at Cavite, on Manila Bay. It consists at present of 2 cruisers, 4 gunboats, 6 river gunboats, a destroyer squadron of 13 ships, and a submarine division of 6 ships, with a few auxiliaries. Its strength is of course wholly insufficient for a contest with the Japanese navy.

The Special Service Squadron takes care of American interests in the Caribbean and on the west coast of Central America. Its station is the Canal Zone; it consists of two new gunboats and one destroyer.

The Spanish Civil War has required the temporary assignment of a squadron to European waters; it includes one cruiser and two destroyers.

The Naval Transportation Service performs duties appropriate to its title. It includes 2 transports, 1 ammunition ship, 2 cargo ships, and 3 oilers.

Vessels on special duty include surveying ships, station ships, tugs, and ships assigned to experimental duties.

The Naval Districts form the framework of the shore activities of the navy. The Continental United States is divided into eleven such districts (of which three in the South Atlantic and Gulf are grouped under a single command); Panama, Hawaii and the Philippines form a district each. Each district is commanded by a rear admiral, who administrates naval and Naval Reserve activities and coordinates defense plans with the army commanders within his district. The district commandants at Panama and

Hawaii perform dual functions; as district commandants they report directly to the Navy Department, as commanders of units which belong to the Fleet (submarine and air bases, etc.) they are subordinates of the Commander-in-Chief.

It is obvious that the efficiency of the fleet will be dependent upon the support which it receives from the several shore stations. The location and facilities of our naval bases have already been commented upon. These will require proportionate enlargement as the fleet grows. There are, for example, not enough drydocks in the Pacific area to care for the fleet's possible needs if a considerable number of ships were to be damaged in action. Moreover there exists no large floating drydock which could be towed to an advance base if that became necessary. Such a dock should be provided, and an additional graving dock at Pearl Harbor is essential also.

The building capacity of our Navy Yards is largely concentrated on the east coast. Detailed discussion of the vexed question of government building vs. private building is outside the scope of this book; both will probably be needed, and the proper encouragement of the private shipbuilding industry is a real contribution to national defense, since unless such an industry flourishes in time of peace it cannot be rapidly expanded in war. Nor can the government maintain sufficient building facilities in peace to meet war requirements; to attempt to do so would mean so vast and unproductive an expenditure as to be prohibitive. It is all very well, however, to say what ought to be done; the actual methods by which undue private profits on the one hand and wasteful public expenditure on the other may be eliminated require a great deal of study and attention. The writer does not pretend to be able to present a solution of this problem; but he does assert that the maintenance and indeed the expansion of our private ship-building industry is an absolute essential of our national defense, and that it does not seem beyond the bounds of possibility to adjust that industry's relations with the Government on a basis which shall be fair both to investor and taxpayer.

The provision of additional submarine, destroyer, mine and naval air bases is, under the provisions of the 1938 Navy Bill, now being studied by a board of naval officers headed by Rear Admiral Hepburn, and a report on this subject will be transmitted to the new Congress. Such bases will greatly contribute to the mobility and freedom of action of the fleet.

One of the most important functions performed by the Naval Districts is the training of the Naval Reserve.

The navy will of course require many more officers and men in war than in peace. Active ships, which have complements of about 85% of their war requirements, must be filled to war strength; ships in reserve or out-of-commission status must have crews; ships under construction will be rushed to completion, and new ships such as patrol vessels, motor torpedo boats, escort ships, and others of which only type "samples" are maintained in peace-time will be hurriedly put in hand; finally, numbers of auxiliary vessels must be purchased or otherwise acquired for naval service. These needs will expand very rapidly in a war of any duration; at the beginning of the World War, for example, the Naval Reserve had 1662 officers and 12,206 enlisted men, and at the end of the war had attained a total of 21,985 officers and 273,094 enlisted men.

The present plan for placing the navy on a war footing proposes, when emergency arises, to immediately begin the intensive training of officers and men on a basis of a training course of 120 days. The existing Naval Reserve will be called up at once to fill the immediate needs of mobilization; it should therefore be maintained at a strength adequate for all requirements over a 120-day period.

The Naval Reserve is divided into three classes — the

Organized Naval Reserve, formerly called the Fleet Naval Reserve; the Merchant Marine Naval Reserve; and the Volunteer Naval Reserve.

The Organized Naval Reserve is maintained on much the same basis as the National Guard. It is organized in "divisions" of about 5 officers and 70 men each; these are grouped where possible in battalions, or assigned to Naval Reserve aviation squadrons. From 48 to 60 paid drills per year, and a 15-day annual active-duty training period, are provided. Armories are maintained for battalions and separate divisions; some units have old naval vessels assigned for training purposes. At present each division is supposed to provide a nucleus complement for one of the laid-up destroyers; but this arrangement is subject to alterations: certain divisions might be assigned to battleships or cruisers. As the old destroyers become unserviceable, the need for the Naval Reserve to fill the complements of the fleet to war strength will be increasing, as the fleet will be growing the while. In a few years there will be a question as to whether it will not be highly advisable to construct more patrol-vessels of the 165-foot or larger type for training the Organized Naval Reserve. This would make immediately available a strong force of these vessels, and on mobilization their crews could be largely supplied by new men, with a small nucleus of trained reservists, leaving the balance available for the fleet. The present approximate strength of the Organized Naval Reserve is 750 officers and 13,000 men; this is insufficient to meet the needs of mobilization and should gradually be built up to 35,000. Officers for the Organized Naval Reserve are principally obtained from the graduates of Naval R.O.T.C. at our colleges, and from the ranks.

The Merchant Marine Naval Reserve is made up of officers and men who are actually serving in the nation's merchant ships. It has a present strength of about 3500 officers; there are very few men. The question of building up the enlisted force of this component is involved with a decision, as yet unreached, of whether in war the merchant vessels needed by the navy as auxiliaries will be purchased and operated with navy personnel, or obtained by charter. The shipowners favor the latter course, as assuring them better profits. But it has certain objections, of which the main one is the necessity for naval control and discipline in all ships forming part of, or operating with the fleet. Another is the matter of obtaining suitable personnel. Why, a merchant seaman well may ask, should I go to sea in a chartered ship, taking the same risks which a navy seaman assumes, but without the protection for myself and my family which is provided by navy retirement and pension laws? There seems no way of solving the problem save by using navy crews; and these crews can best be obtained by building up in time of peace a Merchant Marine Naval Reserve which in war will serve on the same ships either as naval auxiliaries, or as cargo ships operated in commercial service by the Government.

It is necessary to say quite plainly that a very bad state of discipline now exists in our merchant marine. This is not altogether due to union activities; the American shipowner has his share of the blame, for the miserable working and living conditions which have been permitted to obtain on certain ships, as well as for failure to back up ship's officers in the enforcement of discipline. If war came, it would be necessary to dispense with many of the men now serving in our merchant ships, either for disciplinary reasons or for lack of physical fitness. A Merchant Marine Reserve of 20,000 men would be adequate to fill the key positions on such ships as the navy might require, including ships necessary for all military purposes such as carrying cargoes of strategic materials. The balance could be made up from young recruits. But this is not enough; commercial service must continue. Much of our foreign trade now carried on by foreign-flag ships will have to be taken over by the American merchant marine. Some of these ships if not all of them may have to be operated in the same manner — that is, by nucleus navy crews. Our coastwise shipping must also be kept going. There must be no interruption of essential services.

Consider for example the matter of fuel. Today the city of New York and the other great centers of our northeastern section are almost wholly dependent, not only for power, but for heat, motor-transportation, and other needs, on oil brought in tankers from Texan ports and on coal brought from Norfolk and Newport News by sea. These ships must be kept running; the railroads cannot possibly take up the slack. Under war conditions, with many of the ships, officers and men drafted away to the navy, this fuel must keep moving; it is the very foundation of our industrial, commercial and even residential life. Laid-up ships will have to be put into service, and crews must be found for them. There can be no half-measures, no trifling with disaster, no lengthy negotiations with disloyal elements. An additional 15,000 Merchant Marine Naval Reservists would provide assurance that our necessary maritime commercial services would continue to operate.

To obtain these men, it will be necessary to provide inducements for them to enlist, such as active duty training, retainer pay, and assurance against their use as strikebreakers in time of peace. The training of 3300 officers and men of the merchant marine by the Coast Guard, in cooperation with the Maritime Commission, is a step in the direction of improving the character of our merchant crews; it is to be hoped that further progress may be made.

The Volunteer Naval Reserve constitutes a reservoir of personnel, fitted either for general naval service by reason of experience, or for some special service. It has a present strength of about 2500 "general service" officers, 4700 "special service" officers, and 12,000 enlisted men. The greatest need is for more funds for training; if 25% of these officers and men could have an annual 15-day training period, this component of the reserve would be much more valuable. No pay is provided for the Volunteer Naval Reserve in time of peace except for active duty.

The "transferred" elements of the Naval Reserve—men with 16 or 20 years' naval service—number about 14,000. They are not available for general service, for the most part; the 16-year men average 49 years of age, and are 87% chief petty officers or first class petty officers; the 20-year men average 53 years of age and are 96% chief petty officers. Their great value would be as instructors for the young men who would be rushed through the 120-day training courses on the outbreak of war.

The United States Coast Guard is administered in peace by the Treasury Department, but comes under the Navy Department in war. It is our oldest marine service, and its ships, officers and men have distinguished themselves in all our wars. It provides a large number of ships of the gunboat, escort and patrol types, adequately manned by personnel of the highest quality (about 10,000 officers and men). The large cruising cutters, of 1700-2000 tons, are especially well adapted for convoy duties. The latest of these ships have speeds of 20 knots and a war armament of four 5-inch guns and two 3-inch anti-aircraft guns. They form our reserve of the gunboat, or sloop, class—vessels adapted for high-seas convoy work, fast enough to keep up with merchant shipping, with armaments equal to dealing with enemy destroyers or submarines. The gunboat class was formerly much favored in our navy, as being able to give protection to our interests in foreign parts, notably in Latin America, without being expensive to maintain. At the time of the Spanish War the navy included no less than 17 gunboats of 800-1700 tons. As Latin American conditions have become more stabilized, and as the needs of the fleet for cruisers and destroyers grew, there has been a falling off in gunboat construction. Today there are but two in the Caribbean, and four (of which one is really an armed yacht) in China: exclusive of very small river-gunboats for service on the Yangtze. The World War, however, proving that convoy is the answer to submarine attacks on merchant shipping, showed the necessity for adequate provision for this sort of service. The cruising cutters of the Coast Guard will take up the slack between the opening of war and the time when new gunboats (which can be quite rapidly turned out by yards which could not possibly build cruisers or battleships) will begin to be delivered. The patrol boats of the Coast Guard will be available for convoying coastwise shipping, for anti-submarine duties in the vicinity of our ports, and general patrol service. There are now seventeen 165-foot patrol boats, 27 of 125 feet, 74 of from 65 to 100 feet. The Coast Guard has its own air service, with about 50 aircraft.

The personnel of the navy is being gradually increased to take care of the expansion of the fleet. The total number of officers of all branches (except the Marine Corps) was 9840 as of September 30, 1937; this includes warrant officers. For the fiscal year 1938 the enlisted personnel will number 105,000.

The system of training and instruction in the navy is very highly developed. Line officers are obtained through the Naval Academy, where after a four-year course they go to sea with the rank of ensign. After three years' service they are promoted to lieutenant, junior grade, and return to Annapolis for a year at the Post-Graduate School. This takes the place of the basic course at the "school of the arm" (Infantry School, Cavalry School, etc.) in the army. The fleet itself takes the place of the army's Command and General Staff School; it is here that the officer receives instruction in the best way that such instruction can be imparted: in the actual performance of his duties under the very severe conditions of tactical exercises. Finally, for the theoretical study of strategical problems, there is the Naval War College at Newport, Rhode Island, with senior and junior courses. Officers are also attached for instruction to the Office of the Chief of Naval Operations and to the various Bureaus. Selected officers are given courses at various civilian technical institutions, such as the Massachusetts Institute of Technology. Other courses are given at the Naval Gun Factory, the Naval Medical School, the Naval Research Laboratory, the Marine Corps School, and the Finance and Supply School. Naval and Marine officers are detailed to many of the army's schools, and some are sent abroad for special instruction.

Officers of the Construction and Civil Engineer Corps usually are obtained by transfers from the line, though the latter has a few direct entries from civil life. The Supply Corps draws its junior officers partly from the Naval Academy and partly from graduates of Naval Reserve Officers' Training Corps. Medical officers are obtained from officers of the Medical Reserve Corps who have undergone a special training course. Chaplains are directly appointed.

Officers of the Marine Corps come partly from the Naval Academy, partly from civil life, and partly from the ranks. Whether Academy graduates or not, all must undergo a special training course of one year at the Marine Corps School at Philadelphia before being assigned to active duty.

Warrant officers of both the navy and Marine Corps are with very few exceptions chosen by competitive examination from specially recommended enlisted men of senior grade and high qualifications.

Enlisted men of the navy enter through the training stations at Newport, Norfolk, Chicago and San Diego, where they receive three months' preliminary instruction. There are many schools for the various specialist ratings, and on board ship men are carefully prepared by courses of instruction for advancement to higher grades. No man may be promoted until he has demonstrated his fitness by examination, as well as by his efficiency in his immediate grade.

The Marine Corps training stations are at Parris Island, South Carolina, and San Diego. Subsequent instruction is quite as carefully arranged for as in the navy.

Aviation instruction is, in its preliminary stages, largely centralized at the Naval Air Station, Pensacola, Florida. Subsequent instruction both for officers and enlisted men is with the fleet and at the various naval air bases, though there are many special courses. A large number of student pilots are now sent through the course at Pensacola and thence to the fleet as aviation cadets; after temporary service in this grade, they revert to civil life with commissions as ensigns in the Naval Reserve. The navy regularly trains a proportion of enlisted men as pilots. The growth of the naval air service makes necessary a new Air Tactical School, which, it is to be hoped, will be provided in the near future.

Perhaps the greatest unifying force in the navy is tradition. The entering midshipman at Annapolis is surrounded by reminders of the navy's great past from the moment he sets foot on the grounds of the Academy. Tradition guides his every waking hour, marches beside him in the ranks, sits at his elbow in class, speaks to him in the very shriek of the wind and splatter of salt spray on his training cruises. He himself gradually becomes a living part of the tradition and spirit of the navy, accepting them as his priceless heritage, to receive, to guard, to cherish, and to pass on unsullied to those who shall come after him.

Likewise does the enlisted recruit feel the force of tradition. He learns first of all to do certain things in certain ways — to lash his hammock with a certain number of turns, to tie his neckerchief in a certain fashion, to keep his seabag and its contents neat and clean, to answer "aye, aye, sir" instead of "yes, sir" to commands—in a word, to do things navy fashion. He learns something of the history of the navy, of its opportunities, of its high standards; and before he has left the training station he is beginning to acquire that vague but essential quality which is called the navy spirit. Not, however, until he joins his first ship does he really begin to understand this spirit. Then it is that he first realizes the meaning of that good old navy word "shipmate," and of the love of the sailor for his ship. The average navy enlisted man will tell you at once that he is serving on the finest ship of her class that ever floated the seven seas. He will relate to you marvelous tales of her incredible accomplishments in the way of speed, seaworthiness, and the like. It makes no difference how old she is, or how decrepit, or how soon her name will figure in that last sad entry in Naval Orders: "Stricken from the Navy List."

To the young sailor, then, the navy spirit is first of all a ship spirit. Later on, as he rises in rank, as perhaps the "fore-and-aft rig" of a chief petty officer is acquired, he acquires also a broadening of vision; his navy spirit becomes in essence indistinguishable from that of the officer. And to officer and enlisted man, the very well-spring of that spirit is loyalty: loyalty to superiors and to inferiors, loyalty to messmates, shipmates and service-mates, loyalty to ship, division, squadron and fleet, loyalty above all to the navy and to the nation which the navy serves.

It is worth while, in indulging in these comforting reflections on the character and tradition of our navy, to consider another aspect of that tradition — its fighting aspect. A military service which draws so great an amount of its spiritual strength from a great past will inevitably seek to apply to present problems the time-honored methods which have given it victory in years gone by. This may not be so much a matter of plan and intention, as it will be of the almost instinctive reaction in the making of emergent decisions, by those in whose very blood that tradition flows.

The fighting tradition of our navy is above all else an offensive tradition: and it is this which in war has ever been the navy's most formidable quality. It is as ancient as the existence of the republic. John Paul Jones, flaunting the flag of the infant nation within pistol-shot of British shores, began it. Truxtun carried it on, and Preble in the Barbary wars. When war came with Great Britain again, in 1812, the idea of the Cabinet was "On to Canada, but lay up the ships — no use fighting the tremendous sea-power that won the Nile and Trafalgar." The navy thought differently, and the eloquence of Bainbridge and Stewart convinced President Madison that our handful of frigates and sloops must go out to seek the enemy, be he never so superior. What that handful did, went further to the building up of a fighting tradition. So it was in the Civil War: Farragut at New Orleans and Mobile Bay, Dahlgren at Charleston, Foote on the western rivers, Porter at Fort Fisher — ever the same reaction to the problem — "Damn the torpedoes! Go ahead! Four bells!" And mark how the torch passed from hand to hand. When Truxtun's *Constellation* — that frigate of which one of her youthful lieutenants wrote, "We would put a man to death merely for looking pale aboard *this* ship!" — was battering the French *L'Insurgente* into surrender off Nevis in 1799, her foretopmast was struck by a French ball, and Midshipman David Porter scrambled aloft to cut away the wreck amidst a hail of small arms fire. When *Essex*, Captain David Porter, swept the South Seas clear of British trade in the War of 1812, and later fought, till her decks ran red with the blood of more than half her crew, two British ships which totalled twice her force, there was serving in her Midshipman David Farragut. When Flag-Officer Farragut led his thundering column past the forts at New Orleans in '62, Lieutenant George Dewey was "watch and division" officer in the frigate *Mississippi*. When Commodore Dewey, in the black of night, led a squadron of his own up to the entrance of Manila Bay, thinking the while of Spanish batteries and Spanish mine-fields, he asked himself "What would Farragut do?" — and the blazing wrecks of the Spanish squadron proclaimed next morning the answer that he found.

True heir to this tradition, Commander Taussig, with the first American destroyer division to serve overseas, stood into Queenstown Harbor after a stormy Atlantic passage in May, 1917. "How soon will you be ready to go on patrol?" asked the British Admiral Bayley, expecting to be told "in a week or ten days." "We will be ready when fueled, sir," said Taussig. And he was.

It is this sort of answer which the United States Navy has ever returned to the question: "There is the enemy; what shall we do?" It will return the same answer if war comes tomorrow: another reason why America, if compelled to make war, must make offensive war. Her navy does not know how to make any other kind.

And what of the navies which it may meet in that war, if it comes? Of the Japanese navy, we may say at once that it too is a fighting navy, an offensive navy. Its traditions in one sense are older than ours, in another not so old; they center, today, around the memory of Heihachiro Togo, the victor of Tsushima, who has become almost a god to the officers and men of his service. It would be a very great mistake — a mistake which none of our naval officers who have served in the Far East will make — to underrate the Japanese navy. Its officers must not be judged by the performances of certain of the officers of the Japanese army in China — reserve officers, for the most part. The naval officer is a very different breed. He is intensely serious, wrapped up in his profession to the exclusion of all else. But he knows that profession, and he remembers with a glowing pride the victories over China and Russia. Above all, he knows how to wait, how to bide his time: as Togo waited, week after week, in storm and freezing blast, outside the harbor of Port Arthur; waited again, in the Strait of Korea, when every passing day seemed new assurance that Rodhjestvensky had after all taken the outside route to Vladivostok. In all-round technical efficiency the Japanese enlisted man does not equal ours, because of the lower standard of education among the population; but the discipline is magnificent, the spirit high. The submarine service, for which the personnel is most carefully selected, may be expected to display particular efficiency. The air service, on its record in China, will be full of enterprise but not up to our standards of performance. The Japanese navy has had a great deal of experience, in all its wars, in joint operations with the army.

The German navy's traditions are those of the World War. In the professional qualities of its officers, and in technique, it stands very high. Insofar as it may be said to have any outstanding quality, that quality is one of almost unbelievable precision. As a whole it will probably not be inclined to the taking of long risks; not from any lack of courage, but from too meticulous weighing of chances. It is a navy which regards Jutland as a tremendous victory because its High Seas Fleet escaped without too much injury.

The Italian navy is almost without tradition, save for the well-remembered dare-devil exploits of Commander Rizzo and his motor-boats in the Adriatic. Of Lissa it prefers not to think. It produces an impression of smartness and efficiency on the observer; but the test of war has yet to weigh its fighting qualities. The verdict must be: "Not proven."

Of the magnificent traditions of the British navy, little need be said save that today most British officers wish they had Jutland to fight over again, and are burning with anxiety to show that what some call the timorous attitude of the government in the face of Mussolini's Ethiopian defi-

ance does not represent the navy's spirit. The result may
well be that in another war the British fleet will be inclined
to the undue taking of chances. Certainly it will operate on
Nelson's principle "that no captain can do very wrong if
he lay his ship alongside one of the enemy" — not literally,
of course, for modern naval battles are not fought yard-arm
to yard-arm, but the Royal Navy is assuredly grimly resolved
to show the British people and the world that it has not
lost the "Nelson touch." Its principal weakness is probably
its spirit of intense conservatism, especially in the higher
ranks. The figures of catapulted aircraft, given in the pre-
ceding chapter, are but one indication of how this works
in practice. Its Fleet Air Arm is, in the judgment of many
observers, not to be compared with the aviation services of
certain other navies — the disparity being not in quality of
machines or personnel, but in tactical doctrine and cooperation with surface forces.

Of the French navy—rich in heroic tradition—it is possible to say little more than that there has been a tremendous all-round improvement since the World War, and
that it is today, ship for ship and plane for plane, one of
the most formidable sea-services in the world. Its doctrine,
however, is inherently defensive because its chief problem
is to protect the shipping lanes between France and North
Africa. French naval practice has always inclined to the
accomplishment of ulterior objects rather than the destruction of the enemy's sea-power; that is, it has sought to
achieve ends without first making sure of the means.

Among these various navies, it is not too much to say
that our own ranks with, if not above, the best, in spirit,
in tradition, in technique, and in quality of commissioned
and enlisted personnel. The intellectual and educational
standards of our naval officers may be judged by comparing
with similar foreign publications, month after month, the
remarkable articles on naval and foreign affairs contributed

to the navy's principal professional magazine, the *Proceedings of the United States Naval Institute*. Our system of naval education, both for officers and men, is far ahead of anything possessed by any other navy. Our ships, year for year, compare favorably in paper qualities and in actual technical achievement with foreign ships. Our naval aviation is without a peer in the world.

That the navy is not perfect, no one knows better than those who serve in it; some of its shortcomings have hereinbefore been mentioned, but they are, in general, national shortcomings rather than those inherent to the naval service. Certainly there is no better navy in the world; probably not one as good.

Chapter XII

THE MISSIONS OF OUR ARMY

Our object ought to be to have a good army rather than a large one.

GENERAL GEORGE WASHINGTON,
To the President of Congress, September 15, 1780.

IN ORDER TO understand the place which the army occupies in the national strategy of an insular state, we must for a moment revert to our previous examination of British policy during the nineteenth century.

The British army was required to maintain garrisons for the outlying possessions of the Empire, sufficient to secure them against attack until they could be reinforced, and to maintain internal order among the native populations; in the British Isles it provided a force for home defense, including the defense of the fortified ports, and depots for the supply of recruits to the overseas garrisons. The home army was supposed to be sufficient for such comparatively small expeditionary forces as might be required for intervention in particular phases of a Continental struggle, as was done in the Peninsular and Crimean Wars. A citizen force of militia and volunteers reinforced it for home defense purposes, and the growth of this force was always notable at times of danger and strained relations.

Very similar are the present missions of our own army. Strategically speaking, these missions may be stated as follows:

(1) The defense of our outlying possessions.

(2) The defense of the home bases of our navy.

(3) The defense of the mainland of the United States against direct attack, either by raiding forces (air, land or sea) or a serious attempt at invasion.

The primary purpose underlying these missions is to give the navy that complete freedom of action which is essential to it, and enables it so to act as to maintain control of the sea-communications by which, and only by which, any serious danger may approach our shores. But if the navy be defeated in battle, the army must be able to assume the full burden of the defense of our coasts. Similarly it may be called upon to defend one coast for a greater or less period of time, if the navy be engaged in the other ocean, or detained by any injury to the Panama Canal. The army will always have to be ready to deal with swiftly delivered raids.

The defense of our outlying possessions centers around two major points: Panama and Hawaii.

Panama is the more important, as commanding the vital link between our two maritime frontiers. Its situation is remote from the bases of any possible enemy. From the easternmost Japanese outpost in the Marshall Islands to Panama is 6600 miles; from the nearest point on the Continent of Europe, 4300. There are, it is true, European possessions in the Caribbean Sea, but it is impossible to conceive the collection there of so formidable an armament as would be required for an attack in force on Panama, under our very noses and within air range of our own bases in that area.

A base for an attack on Panama must therefore be obtained in the territory of some Latin American power within a reasonable distance; and here again one cannot imagine such a thing being done without our obtaining ample notice of what was going on. None of the adjacent countries has any great military strength of its own; none would be capable, without outside aid, of launching such an attack even should any become so minded. The outside aid must come by sea, must come from the bases of a great naval and military power capable of undertaking such an effort. Therefore we are back where we started — Panama, by virtue of its geographical position, of its much greater proximity to our own bases than to those of any possible antagonist, is secure from attack in force: that is, by a great joint expedition, navy plus troops.

In any case, it may be remarked, such an attack could have but one object — denial of the use of the Canal by our navy and shipping. No power could hope thus to obtain the Canal for its own use, since our garrison, if defeat stared it in the face, would hardly be so kind as to leave the Canal intact to fall into the hands of the enemy.

Since therefore denial of the Canal to our use must be the only object of an attack upon it, it remains to be seen whether this object can be attained by any other means than an attack in force.

Air attack naturally comes first in mind. Such an attack would be intended to destroy or injure some essential part of the Canal by bombing from the air.

An air attack would have to be launched either from aircraft carriers or from a shore base previously established within bombing range of the objective. It might have one of two general characters: it might be delivered on a small scale, using only a few bombers and seeking to attain its object by surprise; or it might be a large-scale attack, which would equally make use of surprise if it could, but would employ sufficient force to smash its way through to its objective against the opposition of our air force and anti-aircraft guns.

The character of the possible objectives determines the scale of attack required to give a chance of success. The most vulnerable points of the Canal are the locks, six in number — three at Gatun, on the Atlantic side, and two at Miraflores and one at Pedro Miguel on the Pacific side. They are massive concrete structures, with elaborate systems of culverts and valves for admitting water or letting it out again, and great steel gates weighing hundreds of tons which are really big boxes divided into many interior compartments. To disable a lock from the air, one of two things is required: either a sufficiently powerful concentration of heavy bombs to produce a general demolition effect, or direct hits on the gates. The first method would demand a large number of bombs, since concrete structures are not easily damaged by exterior, untamped explosions; the second would equally require a large number, since the chance of scoring a direct hit on the upper surface of a gate (only 67 by 7 feet) is not high.

Another vulnerable point which may be mentioned is the spillway dam which holds back the waters of Gatun Lake. This has 14 small gates, about 19 feet wide, upheld by a series of 13 concrete pillars about 10 feet square. If a sufficient number of these gates were destroyed, the water level of the lake would be lowered and the Canal might run dry. This possibility is however somewhat discounted since the completion in 1935 of the Alajuela dam, containing in Madden Lake a vast reserve of water to maintain the level of Gatun Lake. The problem of air attack on the spillway dam is quite similar to attack on a lock: success demands either a heavy concentration, or a number of direct hits on very small targets.

This disposes of the attack on a small scale, which would have little chance of success, would more likely serve merely to put us on our guard against the enemy's greater purposes.

A large air base could hardly be established secretly within striking distance of the Canal. It may therefore be concluded that an attack on the Canal must come from carriers, approaching stealthily within range.

Modern carriers have cruising ranges about equal to those of heavy cruisers; perhaps 15,000 miles at economical speeds. This would enable Japanese carriers which had refueled in the Marshalls to reach the Canal Zone and return, with a small allowance for incidents. Since however returning would hardly be calculated upon, that factor need not be considered. European carriers would have no difficulty as far as mere distance to the Canal was concerned. Approach undetected from either side would however be very difficult, as the Canal is a great focal point of maritime traffic. The daily average of transits by ocean-going vessels (exclusive of Government vessels) has been 14 over the period 1933-1937 inclusive; of the ships making up this total, about one-third were American, and one-quarter British, Scandinavian or Dutch. Almost all such ships carry radio, and the queer ungainly outline of an aircraft carrier is quite unmistakable. Any American merchant skipper who saw a foreign carrier near the Canal would report her immediately; so, in all probability, would a "neutral" skipper, who would be primarily interested in maintaining the free traffic of the great interoceanic waterway. Approach by night will not help much, as the hours of darkness in the latitude 10° north are only seven or eight; say a run of 200 miles for a fast carrier, which would not be enough so that she could commence it at a point outside the focal influence of the Canal.

As a matter of fact, a single carrier would probably not be enough. The planes of at least two carriers of average size would be needed, perhaps more, since the bombers would have to have a pursuit escort. Surprise therefore becomes very difficult, if not impossible, and without surprise the attack is foredoomed to failure. But assuming the bare possibility, still enough bombers must be launched to win through anti-aircraft barrage-zones and deliver a sufficient volume of fire to effect their purpose, despite the further opposition of our pursuit aviation.

If the attack be delivered against the locks — the best chance — both sides of one lock (which are all double) or two gates (one in each channel) must be destroyed to stop the traffic. This must be achieved by the first effort; there will be no repetition, for the army bombers and navy patrol-planes will certainly locate the carriers before a second attack can be launched, and either destroy them or so cripple them that they will be easy prey for submarines or surface torpedo vessels.

It comes back, therefore, to the weighing of risks. On the one hand, the absolutely certain loss of the carriers, a hundred-odd planes and three to four thousand highly trained officers and men. On the other hand, the bare possibility (by no stretch of the imagination a certainty or anything like it) of stopping our use of the Canal. Possible military gain — four to five weeks' additional time before our fleet can arrive in the ocean to which the enemy desires to impede its access. Whether the gain will be worth the risk depends entirely, of course, on what use the enemy can hope to make of this extra time.

Our proper defense policy at Panama against air attack, perhaps the most serious danger to be apprehended, is to increase both the element of risk and the size of the force required for any chance of success, to the point where the proposition will appear even less attractive than at present.

Before attempting to determine how this may be done, one other possibility may be considered. That is the collection in the territory of the Republic of Panama or one of its neighbors of a small "dare-to-die" expeditionary force, intended to make its way through the jungles and mountains which flank the Canal Zone to north or south and by a sudden, surprise attack, obtain possession of one set of locks or of the spillway dam and hold it long enough to effect its complete destruction by regular demolition methods; or alternately, a similar attempt by a small landing force.

The Canal Zone, unfortunately, is but five miles wide on either side of the Canal, which does not give much freedom of action to our mobile ground forces. On the other hand the terrain of approach, while affording a good deal of cover, is so tremendously difficult that no very large force could hope to reach the Zone at all; certainly not undetected. A thousand men in single file on a jungle trail will string out for a mile or more. Assuming that the men would carry with them all their weapons, ammunition, explosives and rations, thus eliminating pack animals, they would still have to be sufficient in number not only to seize a lock, but to hold it for several hours while furnishing working parties to place the explosives. If the party is reported while on the march by native villagers, or spotted by our air patrols, it is done for. If when it enters the Zone it runs into even slight opposition, it will have little chance of reaching its goal, since alarm plus even a slight delay will enable our troops to reach the spot, or at least produce the intervention of an attack squadron. If it does reach a lock, or the spillway dam, it must be prepared to meet immediate attack by whichever of the two regiments of infantry in the Zone garrison is the nearer (say 2000 men), also air attack, and the arrival within a very short time of the other regiment. The chances are decidely not in favor of success, even granting the almost impossible — a strength of 1000 attackers.

The use of a small landing-force would be restricted by the necessity of landing outside the Zone — that is, beyond the reach of our sea-coast artillery — and its subsequent operations would be controlled by the same considerations as those of a force coming overland. It might however be somewhat larger in size, since it would not have to go so far through the bad terrain carrying all its equipment.

Combination of some of the above methods — perhaps the landing-force or the overland column, or both, supported by air attack from carriers directed, not against the locks, but to the impeding of the movements of our troops — sounds formidable, but would be very difficult to coordinate and almost certain to lose the advantage of surprise. Nevertheless it must be considered.

There is of course the problem of bombardment by enemy warships. The locks at Gatun are 6½ miles from the Atlantic outlet of the Canal, those at Miraflores 8 miles from the Pacific outlet. The maximum range of the modern 16-inch naval gun as mounted in battleships is about 35,000 yards, or something under 20 miles. The same gun mounted on shore has a somewhat longer range. At either end of the Canal are well-sited fortifications armed with 14-inch and 16-inch guns, supplemented by guns of lighter caliber. These will keep any attacking warships at a distance, and will certainly be able to prevent any bombardment of the locks, since an attacking ship within extreme range of Gatun Locks would be but 24,000 yards from the shore batteries, and as a practical matter would have to come much closer in to register any percentage of hits. On the Pacific side, where some of the batteries are on islands in the Gulf of Panama, there would be no chance for bombardment of the locks.

The possibility of the Canal being damaged by spies or some other secret means must not be forgotten; but the vulnerable points are few and well guarded, a duty in which the garrison has the help of the excellent Zone Police. The population of the Zone itself is small; that of the adjacent cities of Panama and Colon is rather mixed and contains elements which will bear watching. Ships passing through the Canal are carefully inspected, especially in any period of international tension. The measures taken for the defense of the Canal against secret attack may be considered as covering all foreseeable possibilities.

The present garrison of the Panama Canal Zone includes:

(a) Two regiments of coast artillery, one at each end of the Canal; each regiment has an anti-aircraft battalion of four batteries, and a harbor-defense battalion of three batteries.

(b) A mobile force, consisting of two regiments of infantry, a battalion of pack artillery with three batteries of 75-mm. howitzers, and a regiment of engineers.

(c) An air force, including 2 reconnaissance squadrons, 2 pursuit squadrons, 1 bombardment squadron and 1 attack squadron.

Total strength, about 13,000 officers and men.

The anti-aircraft artillery force is insufficient, since to stop a surprise air attack what is needed is a tremendous volume of fire produced very quickly; there may be no time to bring reinforcements from the other end of the Canal. There should be a full regiment of anti-aircraft artillery stationed at each end. The harbor-defense troops are also insufficient to provide full manning parties for the heavy guns and mines which deny the nearby waters to enemy warships, and which would, if our fleet were coming through the Canal in the face of opposition, insure its unmolested deployment into battle-formation. Assuming for this the possible transfer of personnel between the two coasts, since it is not likely that the harbor-defenses on both sides will be simultaneously engaged, still a harbor-defense regiment for each end (say 6 gun batteries and 1 mine battery) is not too much.

The mobile ground force, in view of the necessity of instantly smothering a surprise attack, should have a third infantry regiment. The anti-aircraft units are of course mobile, and in case of a circuitous air attack which seeks to approach from the land side, they will take up positions already selected; to some of which the engineers have to keep open the jungle trails. The field artillery component is probably sufficient.

The air force now in the Canal Zone requires reinforcement, and plans for this are in hand, but must await the gradual increase of the total number of planes available under the existing procurement program. Assuming an air increase of 1000 men, the total increase required to assure the defense of this all-important position is only about 5000 men, or 18,000 in all.

To recapitulate — Panama must be made absolutely secure against surprise attack. Its position gives it security against a grand attack in force, as it is remote from possible hostile bases and close to our own. Against surprise, only the force actually present can be counted on. No local citizen forces are available.

The problem of the defense of Hawaii, our island outpost two thousand miles out in the Pacific, is a very different one. Here the time element is clearly involved: Hawaii, on which an attack in force is conceivable in the absence of our fleet, must be able to resist the heaviest possible assault until such time as the fleet can reach it from the Atlantic — say five weeks altogether, with some allowance for the chapter of accidents.

The defense is based on holding the central island, Oahu, which contains the great Pearl Harbor naval arsenal. The garrison includes the following elements:

(a) Coast artillery. Two harbor defense regiments of 3 batteries each (one for Honolulu and one for Pearl Harbor); one railway regiment of two batteries; one regiment of tractor-drawn 155-mm. guns of 6 batteries; one anti-aircraft regiment of 9 batteries.

(b) Mobile force. One complete infantry division of 4

infantry and 3 field artillery regiments, a regiment of engineers, a tank company and other necessary units.

(c) Air force. Two pursuit, three bombardment, two reconnaissance and one attack squadrons.

Total strength, about 21,000 officers and men.

This organization and strength seems adequate, save for the air force, which will receive some increase as the new planes are provided, and as the new bombardment base at Hickam Field is completed.

Hawaii has certain defense problems which are absent in Panama. One is the defense of the outlying islands, which afford possible bases for a hostile attack. As already noted, these have but one harbor — Hilo Bay — which is adequate for the use of large ships, and this is 200 miles from Oahu. The outlying islands are the particular responsibility of the army and navy air forces at Oahu, and this is one reason why these should be augmented.

There are a certain number of local troops available: about 1700 men of the National Guard (4 battalions of infantry) to begin with, which could quickly be recruited up to 3500. There are 562 reserve officers in the islands, who could be used as a framework for additional citizen forces if these were needed.

The population of the islands (estimate of June 30, 1937) is 396,715, including about 60,000 Hawaiians and part-Hawaiians, 151,000 Japanese, 27,000 Chinese, 30,000 Portuguese, 53,000 Filipinos, 7500 Puerto Ricans, 6600 Koreans, 57,900 Americans, British, Germans and Russians, and a scattering of other nationalities.

This mixed population constitutes, in itself, a military problem, especially the very large Japanese element. There is no reason to suppose, however, that this matter has not received careful study.

To recapitulate: The defense of the Hawaiian Islands

is based on the fortress-island of Oahu, which is the strongest maritime place of arms in the world; Singapore is nothing beside it. The outlying islands must be defended by air and by mobile naval forces. The time element is essential; the place must be able to hold out against a full-dress attack until the fleet can arrive to relieve it — that is, about five weeks. It could probably hold out until the fleet had made the circuit of Cape Horn if it had to. There is a serious internal problem. Certain local troops will be available. Reinforcement by air from the United States, even in the absence of the fleet, is possible.

Other responsibilities of the army for the defense of outlying possessions may be briefly dealt with.

Alaska has at present a small force of about 400 men, mostly infantry. If an army air base is to be created there, additional troops will be needed. If there is to be a naval base in the Aleutians, a garrison of coast artillery troops will be required to defend it against raids. It need not be made into a great fortress like Oahu, for reasons already discussed. Probably 1200 men would form an adequate artillery garrison — 3 harbor-defense batteries and 3 anti-aircraft batteries, plus a mine battery and headquarters.

Puerto Rico has at present an infantry regiment of about 900 men. If the Puerto Rico-Saint Thomas-Culebra area is to be made a naval outpost, coast artillery will be needed. The number cannot be properly estimated until the nature of the naval establishment has been determined, but if at least two points are to be defended, 1500 men will probably be the minimum; rather more than less. An advantage here not possessed by the Aleutians is the possibility of augmenting the garrison by the use of Puerto Rico National Guard troops.

The provision of a defense force for the Philippine Islands is not considered here, since the continuance of our garrison there is a subject bound up with the determination of the political future of the islands. Existing plans call for the withdrawal of the garrison in 1946, or before. If those plans are altered at some future time, the strength of the defense force to be maintained will have to be considered in the light of conditions then obtaining.

The old system of periodically relieving the regiments in the outlying possessions by other regiments has long been discontinued in favor of keeping certain regiments permanently stationed there, and effecting relief of personnel by drafts. This has the great advantage of maintaining always a percentage of personnel of all grades who are familiar with local conditions and defense plans.

The needs of the Regular Army for outlying possessions may be summed up as follows (allowing an estimated figure of 1500 additional Air Corps personnel for Hawaii):

Panama 18,000
Hawaii 22,500
Others, say 4,000
———
Total 44,500

For the Continental United States, the strategical requirements divide themselves into three groups:

(a) Harbor defenses and anti-aircraft defense,
(b) Air force,
(c) Mobile ground units of infantry, cavalry, artillery, etc.

To these must be added the necessary "overhead" of the whole military establishment; the personnel needed for the instruction of the so-called "civilian components" — National Guard, Organized Reserve, Reserve Officers' Training Corps, and Citizens' Military Training Camps; the "overhead" of the nine Corps Areas, which are the territorial administrative units by which the work of the War Department is decentralized; general and special service schools, general hospitals, depots, arsenals, procurement agencies, disciplinary barracks, the Military Academy at West Point, officers and men on Civilian Conservation Corps duty, finance offices, and bands.

There are three ways in which a maritime frontier may be defended.

First, by the use of naval force. But the navy must act offensively, and to do so must remain concentrated; it cannot scatter itself up and down the coast, to have its fractions destroyed in detail by concentrated enemy force. It is an error to speak of the navy as "our first line of defense" unless the application of the term "defense" be very broad and general.

Second, by the use of mobile land and air forces. But any sort of mobile force is subject to the same considerations as the navy; it must remain strategically concentrated, ready to meet a concentrated enemy effort. If to the mission of providing a concentrated force of this sort is added responsibility for the defense of the bases of the navy and our great commercial harbors, we shall need a far larger army than would otherwise be necessary.

The third and proper method is by a "team-work" defense system which includes the navy, the air forces, and a mobile ground force, and which is supported by a system of fixed defenses covering the navy's bases and the great seaport cities. This is by far the most economical and efficient plan, making use of every weapon within the limits of its powers and supplementing each by the coordinated efforts of the others.

The harbor defenses of the Continental United States differ from those in the outlying possessions in two general respects. First, they form strong points in a general system of coast defense of wide extent. Second, their garrisons need not be entirely composed of the Regular Army, as troops of the National Guard are available.

The purpose of harbor defense fortifications is widely

misunderstood. Their missions may be stated as follows:

(1) Defensive: To protect against invasion by denying the enemy the use of suitable harbor facilities; to defend cities and harbor works against bombardment by warships; to afford secure ports of refuge for our commerce.

(2) Offensive: To free the navy from all responsibility for the immediate defense of its bases or other seacoast cities, thus contributing to its freedom of action; and to afford it secure bases from which it can operate, or in which crippled, defeated or outnumbered ships can take refuge.

(3) Political: To give the populations of the great seacoast cities a sense of security which could otherwise only be provided by mobile forces (naval, military or air), hampering these forces in the discharge of their proper functions and methods of operation. This consideration cannot be ignored in a democracy, if full offensive use is to be made of the mobile forces.

The location and armament of harbor defenses must be considered, not as a separate subject, but as part of the scheme of defense of the whole coast-line on which they are situated. The sea affords easy access to any part of a maritime frontier, and reconnaissance agencies available to the army are not of very long range. An enemy approaching by sea will have an initial advantage, since it cannot be known where his blow is going to fall, and even when his forces are located his mobility enables him to make use of feints to deceive the land forces.

However, by no means all of the coast-line is a likely object for attack, as may be seen from the following classification of harbors and coastal areas for the purposes of a defense plan:

(1) Fortified harbors,
      (a) Those containing naval bases,
      (b) Other fortified harbors (usually places of commercial importance);

(2) Unfortified harbors,
- (a) Those located within striking distance of military objectives which might attract a strong enemy effort,
- (b) Those which are cut off from such military objectives by mountains, arms of the sea, distance or otherwise;

(3) Open beaches suitable for landing, subclassified as for unfortified harbors;

(4) Positions so remote, by reason of sparse population or lack of communications, or both, as to be more or less out of touch with the rest of the country, but which are suitable for an enemy air base, and are within bombing range of an important objective;

(5) The remainder of the coast-line.

It will be found that the portions of our coast-line which are of critical strategic importance are of limited extent. Comparatively few areas are suitable for landing, and of these only a few are conveniently placed with regard to possible enemy objectives. The harbor defenses, therefore, in denying an enemy the use of convenient methods of landing, force him to the precarious expedient of landing over an open beach and subsequently supplying his forces by the same difficult and uncertain means; while even in this he is confined to particular and limited areas by topographical, hydrographical and strategical factors.

Defense of cities and harbor works against bombardment is usually achieved by siting the fortifications at a point where warship guns cannot reach these targets unless the ships themselves come within comparatively short range of the forts. Most of our seaports lend themselves to this arrangement; two which do not are Miami and Los Angeles (including San Pedro and Long Beach).

The weapons of harbor defenses are of two kinds: artillery and mines. Harbor defense artillery of large calibers can usually be given a slightly better range than ship-mounted guns. Formerly the practice was to mount them on "disappearing carriages," which permitted the gun to be loaded behind the parapet and to rise over it at the moment of firing, when the recoil threw it back to the loading position. This type of mount however is not capable of giving the gun the high elevation needed for long-range firing and is not used in modern ordnance construction, though many of the old disappearing guns are still mounted in our various harbor forts and can give an excellent account of themselves against any enemy they can reach.

The development of air power has tended to induce a dependence on concealment rather than on the protection of thick parapets and deep emplacements for coast artillery. Some large guns are now sited in the open, without parapets; they would in war be skilfully concealed from air observation by camouflage, though this will not serve once the gun has opened fire. Danger from a ship's guns is limited to a direct hit on the gun-emplacement, very unlikely at the extreme ranges imposed on the ship by the fire of modern coast artillery; the danger from the air is greater and can be better provided against by concealment than by fortifications with a regular trace which can be easily spotted either by the the eye of a trained observer or by aerial photography. There are some students of the subject who would go even farther, eliminating fixed guns altogether and replacing them by mobile guns on railway carriages or tractor-drawn mounts. To this procedure, however, there are serious objections.

First, in defense of a harbor there is not an infinity of satisfactory gun positions. Those to be occupied must be carefully selected to give a good field of fire, sufficient "command" (i.e., height of site), and to insure interlocking arcs of fire which shall sweep the entire sea-approaches to the harbor without leaving any dead space. Once the gun positions have been chosen, fire-control installations must be made, including observation stations and base lines which have reference to fire from the chosen positions. This affords one of the great advantages of seacoast artillery over fire from ships. Much greater precision in training, operation and supply is obtained by the use of fixed installations; a greater volume and greater accuracy of fire. Mobile artillery is moreover subject to errors induced by enemy feints; if an enemy develop such a feint, let us say toward Point A, the temptation to rush to the defense of that point the mobile artillery assigned to the defense of Point B may become irresistible. If both points have a certain amount of fixed defense, neither can be left wholly open to attack. The contrary tendency, to tie up too many guns and men in fixed installations, must of course likewise be avoided. The ideal situation is one in which every harbor which requires defense shall have the minimum fixed defense necessary to deal with a surprise attack, while a reserve of mobile artillery exists which can be rushed to reinforce any harbor threatened by a serious enemy effort, which will take time to develop.

This general principle is however subject to certain limitations. Not all desirable gun positions are accessible to railway artillery, nor can they all be made so, since the heavier types of railway weapons impose severe strain on culverts and bridges, and it is difficult to conceal from air observation the tracks leading to the gun positions. Tractor-drawn artillery requires roads, likewise difficult to conceal. Some types of railway artillery have very limited arcs of traverse, a serious defect in firing at a moving target such as a ship. Curved track emplacements may be used to increase the arc of fire, but shifting the gun takes time and the emplacements cannot be concealed. Very heavy guns (10" and upward) are not suitable for tractor-drawn operation. Ammunition supply for mobile artillery is a serious problem, in the absence of protected magazines immediately at hand.

[265]

The strength and disposition of our harbor defenses, therefore, should be initially based on the selection of the harbors to be defended, then on the tactical problems presented by the local requirements of each harbor; assigning to each a proportion of fixed defenses considered adequate for its needs, and with due reference to the military, economic and political importance of the positions which it is sought to protect. The reserves of mobile artillery should be proportionate to the tactical use which may be made of them with reference to particular localities.

The artillery assigned to fixed harbor defenses is of three general types, classified by objectives:

(1) Long-range heavy guns of 12″, 14″ or 16″ caliber, intended to keep hostile armored ships at a respectful distance and inhibit them from bombarding the port or from covering a landing-attempt by their fire. The object here is to provide guns of such great range that such hostile operations will be rendered impossible, and of such great striking power that hostile battleships will not be risked within their reach.

(2) Guns and mortars of less range and caliber (6″, 8″ and 10″ guns, 12″ mortars) intended to prevent a raid by hostile cruisers, to deal with an attempt to "run by" the forts, and to support the heavier guns in attacking armored ships if the latter come within range. Guns of these calibers are also useful for "interior" fortifications, intended to deal, within a defended harbor, with enemy ships which may have passed the outer fortifications. The guns act against the side or deck armor of battleships and cruisers; the mortars, which are curved-fire weapons, against the decks only.

(3) Rapid-fire guns intended to defend mine-fields, to deal with enemy torpedo-craft and other light vessels, and to support mobile troops in repelling attempts at landings. These guns are of 3″ to 6″ caliber.

The controlled mine is an important harbor-defense

weapon. Mine-fields usually include outer and inner fields, the outer performing the usual duty of a military obstacle in holding the enemy under the fire of the defense, the inner closing the channels of approach and affording opportunities to attack enemy ships which may enter them. Mines have a great moral effect, imposing caution and restraint on all naval operations where their presence is known or suspected.

Non-controlled mines (normally laid by the navy) are used to close passages and navigable areas not used by friendly shipping, and to close off large areas far offshore or in deep water. Where such areas are required as deployment space for our naval vessels, controlled mines must be employed. Mines are useful for checking the operation of hostile submarines, or giving warning of their presence.

A mine-field must be well defended by batteries of rapid-fire guns, otherwise the mines may be swept up and removed. Searchlights must be provided for night control of mine-fields.

Controlled mine projects are laid by vessels called mine-planters, manned by highly trained Coast Artillery personnel and operating under the orders of harbor defense command-ders. The mine defense of harbors is planned in time of peace, and the mine project is laid when ordered by superior authority.

Anti-aircraft defense of harbor forts is normally provided by mobile batteries of guns and machine-guns, and mobile searchlights. A certain number of fixed guns of larger caliber than are suitable for mobile employment may be used. All fixed defenses should have anti-aircraft machine-guns for emergency use against low-flying air attack.

In addition to the normal activities of the Air Corps in defense of a coastal position, spotting aircraft will be required for the adjustment of artillery fire, especially that of the long-range guns. While it will not be making the best use of the great flexibility of the air arm to assign planes permanently to each harbor-defense, bases for their use should be provided in the vicinity thereof, and frequent training provided for, in which naval, air and coast artillery units may participate.

The fire-control installations of fixed defenses are elaborate and extremely accurate when manned by training personnel. They include position-finding systems, observing, plotting-room and pointing instruments, spotting devices, and the intricate communications net which connects the gun emplacements, observation stations, spotting stations, and command posts. Two-way radio is used for communication with observing airplanes; when captive balloons are observing fire, direct telephone communication is possible.

The present condition of the seacoast defenses in the Continental United States is not satisfactory. This is due chiefly to lack of personnel. Prior to the World War we had one of the finest and most complete systems of harbor defense in the world, manned by 170 companies of the Coast Artillery Corps totalling, with headquarters units, 19,321 officers and men, or 27.8% of the authorized strength of the Regular Army. At this time the Coast Artillery Corps had no other duty than harbor defense. During the war, however, this corps was assigned heavy mobile guns for use in the field, railway guns, anti-aircraft artillery, heavy trench mortars, and sound-ranging. All these (except trench mortars) are still responsibilities of the coast artillery, while its present personnel is but 18,908 officers and men, or 10.7% of the strength of the Regular Army. Of this total, only some 5300 are assigned to harbor defenses in the Continental United States, or about one-third the pre-war figure; and this 5300 includes four batteries of railway and two of tractor-drawn artillery.

The correct method of determining the strength of harbor-defense personnel is not, however, on the basis of a fixed percentage of the Regular Army, but rather on the minimum number required to care for the equipment and armament provided, to maintain proper training standards, to train the National Guard and Organized Reserves, and to provide at least a skeleton garrison sufficient to man the armament, lay the mine project, and beat off any initial attack which might be made upon the harbor. Behind this should be a sufficient increment of National Guard troops, stationed in or near the city to be defended, to provide a full manning party for the whole armament. The proper basis is a 100% garrison of the Regular Army for the fixed defenses of the outlying possessions; at home 100% for the mine commands and 50% for the gun commands, the other 50% being made up by the National Guard.

The numbers now assigned fall far short of this, in fact have been reduced to a point where the situation may be described as one of the most serious defects in our present defense establishment. Many harbor forts are manned by mere maintenance parties, or have infantry garrisons, or are not garrisoned at all.

The total of the National Guard harbor defense artillery is just over 5000 men, divided among 11 states. But harbor fortifications cannot be dependent on National Guard troops for their *initial defense;* like the navy, they must be sufficiently manned by regular forces to meet the first shock of war. Otherwise there will be inevitable delay, inefficiency, and perhaps disaster to some of our great cities. The intricate organization of a harbor defense is much like the armament of a battleship; it requires so many men to handle it; personnel is a function of materiel. So considered, the harbor defenses of the Continental United States require for their regular garrisons about 20,000 Coast Artillery troops of the Regular Army, which should be reinforced by about 18,000 of the National Guard, distributed among the cities to be defended, spending their active-duty periods in the forts in which they will be used in war, and with the closest sort of liaison between the Regular Army and National Guard units at all times.

The harbor defense commander should be fully responsible for the training of the National Guard units assigned to his command; he should furnish the commissioned and non-commissioned instructors, and officers and men of the National Guard should be encouraged to visit the forts at all times and to take part in drills and special instruction courses.

The armament and equipment of many of our harbor defenses are still pre-war, though some new guns have been mounted. A great deal of this equipment has not been used for years, and is merely kept painted, greased or otherwise looked after as far as possible by the caretaking detachments. It is of course slowly deteriorating, though in general still serviceable. Deficiencies of personnel thus produce deficiencies of materiel also. More long-range guns are needed, also modern fire-control and communications equipment, searchlights and mine equipment.

An estimate of the cost of a proper harbor defense system for the Pacific coast was made in 1936, and totalled $15,-610,000; part of this has been appropriated. A similar estimate for the Atlantic and Gulf coasts amounts to $34,000,000. These programs should be proceeded with, of course spread over a period of three or four years. Like the building of battleships, harbor defenses cannot be deferred till war begins; it takes three years to construct a battery of 16-inch guns.

Modern harbor defenses, fully armed and equipped and with trained garrisons sufficient to operate the armament, are highly unlikely to be attacked from the sea. But harbor defenses with their armament on a maintenance basis, unready, without personnel, do little to lessen the temptation which may beset an enemy to strike a savage and terrible blow at the vast accumulation of riches, resources and population which lies behind, exposed, save for the forts, to a dashing raid. Though they may never fire a shot, the harbor defenses of our great cities and naval bases must be ready. "If these defenses are strong enough," remarks Admiral Schofield, "they will never be attacked. But harbor defense earns fully, in the battles it may never fight, the cost of its construction and maintenance." [1]

Another very great deficiency of our defense system is in the lack of anti-aircraft artillery and equipment. There are at present in the Continental United States five regiments of anti-aircraft artillery. Each of these regiments at full strength is supposed to include:

3 gun batteries with 4 75-mm. guns each,
4 machine-gun batteries with 12 machine-guns each,
1 searchlight battery with 15 searchlights.

Three of our regiments have at present, each, 1 gun battery, 1 machine-gun battery and 1 searchlight battery; another has 2 gun batteries, 2 machine-gun batteries and 1 searchlight battery; the remaining one is a new regiment now in course of formation at San Francisco.

There are 10 National Guard regiments of anti-aircraft artillery, none of which has anywhere near its war equipment.

The seacoast defenses also require a considerable number of both fixed and mobile anti-aircraft guns; very few are available.

The guns and searchlights are not the only requisite; fire-control equipment for anti-aircraft is complicated and extensive, including directors, height finders, listening apparatus and communications materiel. The critical anti-aircraft shortage is in materiel, which cannot be hastily improvised but requires months or years to fabricate. The Chief of Staff, Gen-

---

[1] Rear Admiral F. H. Schofield, U.S.N., *Naval Strategy and Tactics with Special Reference to Sea-Coast Fortifications.*

eral Malin Craig, told the House Appropriations Committee in January, 1938, that this was a matter of "the utmost concern." The last Congress appropriated $23,000,000 for this purpose; $52,000,000 is required to complete the anti-aircraft armament (including ammunition) to the minimum strength consistent with safety. If this sum seems large, let us reflect upon the British Army Estimates for 1938, which included $215,000,000 for new weapons, equipment and ammunition for that one year alone; a very large part of this was for anti-aircraft. Let us reflect, and be thankful that we have but to protect our women and children, our great cities, our naval arsenals, our industrial centers, our railways and our power-plants against raids by ship-borne aircraft, and not against full-power air attacks from the great bases of a neighboring enemy — and let us not grudge the cost of making that protection as complete as we can.

The anti-aircraft regiment is a highly mobile unit, able to move quickly to any threatened point. The peace-time distribution, however, should be sufficiently dispersed to provide a certain amount of anti-aircraft protection near every one of our major seacoast cities, and those near the coast. The war requirements for the Continental United States are estimated at 34 regiments; of which 5 now exist in the Regular Army and 10 in the National Guard. There are 19 "inactive" Regular regiments, without equipment or enlisted men but with a certain number of reserve officers assigned to them, all of whom have had some anti-aircraft training. The number of Regular regiments of this arm should be raised to 9, and the National Guard regiments to 18; this will give one Regular and two Guard regiments to each Corps Area. These should be maintained at full war strength (about 1800 men per regiment) because anti-aircraft artillery may be "first to fight" and must be instantly ready. There may be no time for it to absorb and train recruits. The equipment for one additional regiment for each

Corps Area should be provided and placed in store; this regiment can be formed on an "inactive" basis, with Reserve officers assigned and perhaps key noncommissioned officers and specialists from the Enlisted Reserve Corps. The nine Regular regiments will require 16,200 men. It should be possible to complete this project in from three to four years.

The very great value of anti-aircraft artillery as an immediate and effective defense against air attacks has been repeatedly emphasized in the course of the war now raging in Spain. This nation cannot afford to neglect the defense against air raids which it can so cheaply provide—in comparison with what others must do.

The next component of the army to be considered is the air force.

The principal combat unit of our Air Corps is known as the General Headquarters Air Force. At the present time it consists of three "wings," with headquarters respectively at March Field, California; Langley Field, Va.; and Barksdale Field, La. It includes bombardment squadrons, the main striking arm of the force, to whose operations the other components generally conform; attack squadrons, intended for the low-flying attack of ground troops; pursuit squadrons, the arm of aerial combat; and reconnaissance squadrons. Its total strength in combat airplanes when the present Air Corps project is complete in June, 1940, will be 947.

The headquarters of the G.H.Q. Air Force has recently been moved to Scott Field, Ill., so as to have a more central location. This force is intended to provide a powerful air unit capable of exercising to the full that power of strategic concentration which is inherent in the air weapon, based on its high mobility; it is therefore an offensive weapon admirably adapted to the use of surprise, and its flexibility enables it to act over a wide front. It is quite possible, for example, that enemy ships operating off, let us say, the capes of the Chesapeake, might be attacked by planes of the G.H.Q. Air

Force on one day, and the next day those very same planes
might deliver an attack on another enemy squadron in the
Gulf of Mexico. Such qualities require unified command and
thoroughly efficient and coordinated staff work, if their full
value is to be realized. An air force dispersed among a
dozen small commands will merely fritter away its efforts
without accomplishing any great purpose.

The G.H.Q. Air Force is what is called an "M-day" unit:
that is, it must be ready, at full strength, the day war arrives.
Like the navy, it must stand or fall on what it is then.

The present Air Corps project, which is considered sufficient for present needs, calls for a total of 2320 serviceable
planes, exclusive of those awaiting salvage, undergoing experimental tests or overhaul, and those determined under
existing regulations to be obsolete. Of these, 1226 were on
hand December 31, 1937, and 1022 on order; also on hand
were 547 obsolete planes which were still usable for some
purposes. Deducting estimated losses from crashes and obso-
lescence, the full projected number of 2320 planes will be
on hand by June 30, 1940; possibly before.

Of these, 171 will be assigned to the National Guard — 19
observation sqadrons of 9 planes each. The remainder will
be Regular Army planes, except a few used for the Organized Reserve. In addition to the 947 required by the G.H.Q.
Air Force, about 300 will be assigned to Hawaii and 200 to
Panama; the rest will be cargo and training planes, and observation planes assigned to units of ground troops. Approximately 600 of the total will be bombing planes, 500 pursuit,
300 attack, 85 "basic combat," 250 observation, 200 cargo,
100 primary training, and 300 basic training.

The personnel needed for the Air Corps at this strength
will be 2368 officers and 25,728[1] men, in addition to 1304
reserve officers on active duty. The present strength is 1430

---

[1] Including about 5000 officers and men in outlying possessions.

officers and 17,576 enlisted men. It is of course foolish to provide the planes without trained personnel for their operation, maintenance and repair.

Is this force of 2320 planes really sufficient for our needs? For dealing with raids, the answer must be yes. It will provide a striking force of about 1000 planes, under a single command and capable of rapid concentration on either coast (for which additional bases must be made available) ; this can do all that can be done against raiding aircraft from ships, if supported in local defense by sufficient anti-aircraft artillery. It can direct a powerful attack against any enemy air base which may be established in the territory of our neighbors, or our own, before the enemy base can begin to function. Success in establishing such a base would depend on careful preparation, the effecting of surprise, and very swift exploitation of such initial success as might be gained. Whether such an operation will succeed will depend very largely on other factors than the size of our air force, which will be adequate to deal with the beginnings of any attempt of the sort however great the number of planes which may be lying knocked down in the holds of the ships. The force is markedly superior to the greatest number of carrier-borne and catapulted aircraft possessed by any naval power, or conceivable combination of powers. Its losses can be made up much more rapidly by our very extensive airplane industry than can the losses of any attacking force. As to dealing with a serious attempt at invasion, the latter factor will be of great importance, and will give us a superiority which will increase proportionately with the passage of time.

The question of whether we shall within the foreseeable future be liable to air attack by direct flight across the oceans may be answered by a decided negative, as far as anything more than tip-and-run raids are concerned. The record for distance flying (airline) is 6295 miles, set by the Russian aviators Gromov, Youmachev and Daniline in their flight from Moscow to California. But for war operations, the military radius of action is roughly about one-fourth of the maximum range; that is, the plane must go out from its base and return, which cuts the range in half, and it must be prepared to face enemy opposition, to fight if need be, to maneuver, to encounter bad weather (which is no respecter of air-staff plans), to waste time searching for its objective, to be impeded by low ceilings, to be driven off its course, and to sustain damage. These exigencies will average a loss of another 25% of the maximum range. But maximum range is also a function of fuel-load; and if damage is to be inflicted on the enemy, part of the fuel-load must give way to military load — bombs and ammunition. Therefore the maximum radius of action of 1500 miles, which might be thought possible on the basis of the existing world's record, must be still further reduced in war. When it comes to the operation of large formations of planes, these are kept to the performance of their least efficient ships. While it is theoretically possible for single planes to fly across the Atlantic with a very small military load, drop a bomb or two, and return, as a practical operation of war even this is out of the question, and will remain so as far as can now be foreseen; a serious attack by a large air unit is still less to be envisaged. Planes which did not expect to return might raid our coasts, but no nation has enough long-range bombers and highly trained crews to waste them in enterprises of this nature, for which the military return is likely to be incommensurate with the results achieved, still less so with the loss of the whole attacking force.

The respective zones of activity of our army and navy aviation must be carefully defined. In general, naval aviation works with the fleet, as an integral and necessary part thereof; while coast defense, even though it involves flying over the sea, is a function of the army. However this is subject to some modification in practice, where the use of patrol-planes is considered. The patrol-plane is a flying boat. It can alight only on a water surface. As size increases, the advantages of the flying boat, by reason of its stream-lined hull without shore landing-gear, also increase (as to fuel consumption and therefore range) over the land bomber. The flying boat can alight in any sizable bay, lagoon or inlet, or on the surface of the open sea under suitable weather conditions. Its base may be in any sheltered waters where its tender can proceed. It does not need (as do the very large army bombers) a large, specially prepared field; and it can have considerable advantage in wing-load and power-load, since it does not have to take off from a restricted area and perhaps clear obstacles bordering that area. The flying boat is a long-range naval weapon, admirably suited for operations over water, and is properly, therefore, operated by the navy even when based at shore stations. In war its range could always be extended by the use of tenders.

The work of the navy patrol-planes and the land-based planes of the army in coast-defense operations will of course be closely coordinated; as indeed must the work of all the various elements, army and navy, which take part in such duties.

We have now considered certain basic elements of the army's part in our national defense: the garrisons of our overseas possessions, the harbor defenses, the anti-aircraft defense and the Air Corps.

The strength of these elements as determined by this survey should be as follows:

REGULAR ARMY

Overseas garrisons	44,500
Harbor defenses (home)	20,000
Anti-aircraft (home)	16,200
Air Corps (home)	23,000
Total	103,700

National Guard

Overseas garrisons	4,000
Harbor defenses (home)	18,000
Anti-aircraft (home)	32,400
Air Corps (home)	2,400
Total	56,800

Let us see how these tie in together in that coordinated military framework which it should be our object to achieve.

The overseas garrisons are primarily to give mobility to the navy and to protect our communications by sea. The harbor defenses also contribute to the mobility of the navy, and protect our seacoast cities from bombardment. The anti-aircraft artillery helps to protect our vital centers and internal communications from air raids. The air force assists in the defense of all these points, and provides a powerful, concentrated striking force which can be hurled at any enemy approaching our coasts, before he comes close enough to do much damage, since great land-based bombers will always have a longer range than carrier-based planes.

What remains to be done? Is there a chink in this armor?

There is. For just as the navy cannot be everywhere, neither can the air force. Moreover it is handicapped by its inherent limitations of range, carrying power and continuity of action and its susceptibility to weather conditions. The harbor defenses can do little beyond the range of their guns. They can deny; they cannot strike. If our navy is defeated or absent, it will still be possible for a hard-fighting, determined enemy to gain a foothold, either on our shores or in some adjacent territory where he can set up an air base and harass our cities, and from which he can launch more ambitious projects.

There is, therefore, a need for a body of mobile ground

troops, sufficient in number to care for any one or more of the following responsibilities:

(1) Defense of such areas of our coast as may be exposed to attack and are not covered by the fire of harbor defenses.

(2) Ejection of an enemy from any nearby island base he may have seized, which would first require the restoration of naval command of the intervening sea by our navy.

(3) Ejection of an enemy from any base or position he may have seized on our coast, or that of Canada or Mexico; and such further assistance against attack as either of those countries might need.

(4) Reinforcement of the garrisons of our outlying possesions.

(5) Reinforcement, by means of mobile artillery, of one or more of our harbor defenses.

(6) Occupation and tenure of advance bases for the use of the fleet in cases where the strength of the Fleet Marine Force is inadequate to the task.

Probably any initial attempt at landing on our coast would be made either for the purpose of establishing an air base, or to attack harbor defenses in rear and thus obtain possession of a suitable port for landing a larger force. It is conceivable that in a case where our fleet had been totally defeated and was no longer capable either immediately or eventually of restoring control of the sea, such an attempt might be made; or that an attempt to land a larger force than would be necessary for such a limited purpose might be contemplated even on open beaches, such as are afforded by parts of the Long Island, New Jersey and Delaware coasts.

A force adequate to deal with such an attack would assuredly be adequate also to deal with any of the other above-mentioned missions. The required size of our mobile force is therefore that which will be able to repel any such attack upon our shores.

This is not fixed by the size of the various foreign armies,

[279]

but by the number of troops that, considering all the various factors of the situation, can possibly be transported across either ocean to attack us. Two cases must here be considered: first, direct attack by troops landed from trans-oceanic ships; second, an attack delivered from a nearby base (say in the West Indies) previously seized, at which the expeditionary force has been assembled.

The first case is conditioned by the fact that Great Britain need not be taken into account since she has not a regular army large enough to attempt such a thing, and we can create larger citizen forces than she can. No other power, or combination in one ocean of two powers, can assemble for such a purpose (having regard to their commercial needs) more than 2,500,000 gross tons of merchant shipping suitable for carrying troops and supplies across the ocean. The usual allowance for the sea-transport of troops is one man for every 4 gross tons, plus an equal allowance for guns, motor transport, animals, and the normal supplies carried in corps and division trains. To this total, for a great overseas expedition, must be added a 50% allowance for aircraft, base equipment, special landing devices such as armored barges, movable piers, cranes, etc., and reserve stores and ammunition. The full force that might possibly be brought against us is therefore in the neighborhood of 200,000 combat troops.

The attacker is constrained by the forces available to us which have been heretofore mentioned. Even though our fleet has been defeated, it is not likely to have been wholly destroyed. Some remaining elements of it will be lurking in a defended port ready to pounce upon what opportunity may offer. Submarines and long-range aircraft will harry the convoy when it comes within their reach. The harbor-defenses deny the enemy the use of any convenient harbor. As he approaches the shore, the enterprising use of aircraft and light surface craft will increase his troubles. Anti-aircraft artillery will take toll of his air operations. Only limited sections of the coast are available to him. Mines may lurk beneath the surface of the most innocent-looking waterways.

Yet all these obstacles, or at least obstacles similar in proportionate importance, have in the past been overcome by disciplined and determined men, and may be so again. The enemy landing forces may be able to come to grips with the troops defending the shore-line.

The advantages of our defending troops in such a case would be very great. They would have at their back the whole resources of a great country, instead of merely supplies carried in ships; the rail and road net would make these supplies available wherever needed along the coast instead of only where boats could land them on a beach; the landing force must arrive by driblets, its rate of landing being controlled by the capacity of its boats and barges, while the defending force has entire freedom of maneuver and can concentrate its whole effort against part of the attackers; the anchored transports are admirable targets for submarines and bombardment aviation, as are the crowded boats for attack aviation; the attacking force in the opening phases of the fight has only the support of naval artillery, repeatedly proven unsuitable by reason of its flat trajectory for fire against field fortifications (as at Gallipoli), whereas the defenders have the support of all sorts of light, medium and heavy guns, machine-guns and infantry mortars. Even though, as a prerequisite to making the attempt, the enemy has gained a local and temporary air superiority by previously establishing an air base, he cannot be sure that the situation will not be suddenly reversed, perhaps at a most embarrassing moment, by the arrival of air reinforcements from the other coast, or even from some of our outlying possessions.

We may therefore say with assurance that as against anything like equal forces, such an attempt is foredoomed to failure; and to provide such equality, we require mobile ground troops numbering 150,000 to 200,000.

The second case above noted is exactly similar in tactical possibilities, since, island base or no island base, the landing must be attempted from ships in the end. We have, however, to consider the chances of the enemy having built up a larger force than 200,000 men at such a base, and thus having reinforcements immediately available to throw in behind his initial attack. But this implies a considerable period of preparation, during which we will have time to raise more troops, to build more planes, to train more pilots, and otherwise to prepare ourselves to meet the added threat. Therefore it makes no change in the size of our required peace-establishment.

The whole of our mobile ground force need not be provided by the Regular Army; part of the responsibility may be assumed by the National Guard, since if it is needed for the purpose just discussed, there will be at least time enough for the National Guard to be called up.

Further examination of this subject cannot be made without first considering the organization of the National Guard and its relationship to the Regular Army in peace and war. This is therefore the appropriate place to consider the proportion of responsibility which, in our whole scheme of defense, may be assigned the citizen soldier.

Chapter XIII

THE ARMY AND THE CITIZEN SOLDIER

There can be little doubt that Congress will recommend a proper peace establishment for the United States, in which a due attention will be paid to the importance of placing the militia of the Union upon a regular and reasonable footing. . . . It is essential . . . that the same system should pervade the whole.

GENERAL GEORGE WASHINGTON,
To the Governors of the several States (1783).

THE WISE RECOMMENDATIONS of General Washington, above quoted, were not followed. "The moment independence was established," notes General Upton, "all the States hastened to resume nearly every attribute of sovereignty."[1] The result, from the military viewpoint, was the militia system which was to prove a veritable curse in every subsequent war up to and including 1898. In the World War, however, a new plan was adopted: the National Guard was fused with the Regular Army and with the troops raised directly from civil life into one great Army, in which the original component parts became almost indistinguishable. Although certain divisions were called Regular, certain National

---

[1]*The Military Policy of the United States.*

[283]

Guard, and certain National Army, officers and men were freely shifted about and replacements assigned as required.

It was with the success of this, our first well-fought war, in mind, that the National Defense Act was passed in 1920. This Act created the Army of the United States, to consist of the Regular Army, the National Guard and the Organized Reserves. The National Guard, under this Act, continues to be a force apportioned among the several States, subject to State laws, and with officers appointed by the respective Governors. The Federal Government however provides arms, ammunition, equipment, uniforms, etc., and pays the officers and men one day's pay of their rank for each armory drill, and at the regular rate for the annual 15 days' training period. In order to obtain this Federal support, each unit of the Guard must maintain certain standards of efficiency; each officer must be Federally recognized, and under later amendments of the act must receive a commission in the National Guard of the United States (as well as his State commission) for which he must qualify by examination; all personnel must meet the physical standards of the Regular Army. The Regular Army provides officer and noncommissioned officer instructors for duty with the National Guard. The War Department allots to the States the number and character of the units they may maintain, in order to provide the components of 18 divisions, 4 cavalry divisions and certain corps, army and G. H. Q. reserve troops.

The National Guard of the United States, under these wise and far-sighted provisions, has become a totally different military organization from the old militia. Its efficiency has improved year by year since the World War. It is today truly a national force, with an excellent spirit and pride, and its divisions take the field in maneuvers alongside the troops of the Regular Army with creditable results.

Yet within each State, the National Guard is still subject to the call of the Governor for use in maintaining order;

and some Governors have used the Guard and its Federal arms and equipment for purposes hardly in accordance with the reputation for impartiality and dissociation from politics which is the Army's pride. The more the Guard becomes a part of the Army, the less does the Army desire to see it involved in local troubles and partisan disputes. Inevitably arises the simple question with which the military mind ever confronts its instruments: "What is this force meant to do?"

If the National Guard is primarily an instrument of national defense, then it should be divorced from all other duties, save in case of serious disorder or insurrection. To do this, it will be necessary to provide that arms, ammunition, uniforms and equipment furnished by the Federal Government to the National Guard of the several States cannot be used when the Guard is called out by order of the Governor, except in such cases as may be authorized by the President. This, in effect, would end the calling out of the National Guard except in cases of disorder of so grave a nature that the President's permission might be obtained — conditions such as may always arise justifying the reinforcement of the civil by the military power.

It would leave many States, it may be objected, without the means to deal with minor disorders of various sorts beyond the capacity of the local authorities to handle. The answer is State police: such uniformed, disciplined, permanently embodied forces as now exist in New York, Pennsylvania, New Jersey, Massachusetts, Connecticut, Michigan, Maryland and several other States. Some States may have insufficient revenue to maintain such forces; but the divorcement of the National Guard from such work is so greatly to the advantage of the Federal Government that on this count alone, to say nothing of better law-enforcement, the Federal Government might well adopt the system now used in Great Britain. There the central government allows what is called a "grant in aid" annually to the various counties and municipalities, for the partial support of their police forces. In return, the counties and boroughs are required to keep their police forces up to certain standards of discipline, efficiency and numbers; three inspecting officers make periodical inspections to see that this is done. A similar Federal grant to the various States would enable them to maintain State police forces and require proper standards; a Governor or Legislature which permitted inefficiency or corruption in the State police and so lost the Federal grant would have difficulty explaining such conduct to indignant taxpayers. The law controlling this matter should of course be very carefully drawn, so as to eliminate all possibility of Federal *administrative control* over the State police forces. A great national police force run from Washington would present many points of danger to the liberties of the citizen. The States should have entire control of their police, with Federal aid granted purely on the basis of maintaining certain fixed standards. Numbers (in proportion to population and other conditions) ; discipline; physical, moral and mental qualifications of officers and men, including qualifications for higher grades; equipment and methods; freedom from graft and politics; tenure of office independent of changes in administration — are some of the points to be considered. An independent bi-partisan long-term Police Commission should be appointed to administer the act, something on the order of the Interstate Commerce Commission or the Federal Trade Commission. The Commission could appoint its inspecting officers, and could make surveys to determine the minimum strength required by the police needs of each State. This strength should always be sufficient to provide a mobile reserve force to deal with serious disorders. Thus local police would always have a reliable reinforcement in case of trouble, and the National Guard would be called on as infrequently as it has been in New York since the New York State Police was organized in 1917.

Such a system would certainly induce States not now having State police forces to organize them. They could not, of course, be coerced; but the withdrawal of the right to use the National Guard's arms and equipment would be a great incentive to the seeing of the light.

The National Guard would benefit in another way: in the opening of its ranks to union labor, which in some communities now shies away from it for fear of being called out to "break strikes." Under the suggested plan a man might join the Guard to do his patriotic bit in defense of his country, without fear that he would be called upon for a policeman's work, which would be and should be performed by those enlisted for that purpose, trained for it and able capably to discharge it. The skilled tradesman is of vital importance to the modern mechanized army.

The time has come to face this issue squarely, to insist that the army in all its components, professional and citizen, be devoted to the purposes of national defense, and that no portion of it be made the tool of local politics, or used for duties which should be better performed by police.

This is not to say that the writer wishes to break up the State ties of the National Guard and make it merely a reserve of the Regular Army. Local pride and sentiment, the fine *esprit de corps* of many of the Guard regiments, are assets which we would be foolish to throw away. But also the ties between the Guard and the Regular Army must be strengthened; they must become in peace, as they will in war, flesh of one flesh — one army, serving one nation.

This high purpose can be furthered in other ways than by relieving the Guard from police work. To examine these possibilities in detail, let us for the moment revert to our figure of 150,000 to 200,000 men as required for our mobile ground forces in the Continental United States.

In order to express this desired total in military terms, we must translate it from terms of men into terms of fighting organizations — battle-teams. The battle-teams of our army, those in which the several arms are grouped for coordination and control, are called infantry divisions and cavalry divisions. The infantry division is a heavy fighting unit of which the chief components are infantry and field artillery, with proper proportions of other elements; it is the mainstay of our fighting army. The cavalry division is a light, swift-moving force devoted to the duties of reconnaissance and of striking swift hard blows. Its chief components are cavalry (either horse or armored-vehicle units, or both) and field artillery. The relations between these two types of divisions are much the same as between the Battle Force and the Scouting Force of the fleet.

These divisions are grouped into corps (normally three infantry divisions or two cavalry divisions). The corps has certain troops of its own, mostly artillery of the medium calibers (155-mm. guns and howitzers), anti-aircraft artillery, engineers, and observation aviation. Army and G. H. Q. reserve troops include various types of artillery, engineer units of specialist types, observation aviation, and heavy tanks.

The infantry division as at present authorized has been changed only in detail since the World War, when a new organization was adopted suited to European conditions and analagous to that of our associates in the war. This division has been criticized as being too large and unwieldy, as having too long a marching column to enable the rear elements to come into action on the same day in which the advance elements might, at any time before noon, encounter an enemy. Experiments have been taking place with a much smaller and more mobile division, the so-called "P.I.D." (Proposed Infantry Division); but this, too, has not been satisfactory to all officers who have studied its "trial run" in Texas. The infantry units are too small, it is said, and the division would be too quickly "burnt out" in action; the results of General Franco's present shortage of infantry, which has paralyzed all his operations, are pointed to as indicating the dangers of this. The artillery component, also, is considered in some quarters as insufficient to support the infantry. The tendency at present seems toward a somewhat larger division.

There is general agreement that the reduction of the number of infantry regiments from four to three is sound, but not the reduction of the component elements of those regiments. There is also general agreement that a reconnaissance unit of some sort is needed in the division. The grouping of all the heavy machine-guns and mortars of an infantry regiment in a separate battalion is not so widely approved; it is probable that these weapons will, at least in part, be restored to the rifle battalions. The elimination of all animal drawn transportation, and an increase in the number of motor-vehicles available for carrying troops and ammunition, seems likely to be continued. The infantry regiment will need an anti tank organization. The infantry rifle company will probably continue at around its present strength of 200 men, with possibly a different interior organization. The divisional artillery will include only the lighter types of guns (75-mm. guns and howitzers, 105-mm. howitzers); the 155-mm. howitzer will become a corps weapon. Probably the division will continue to have certain divisional trains of its own; the grouping of all trains under corps control does very well at maneuvers but might result differently in war.

A division organized on these general principles — and while they are not certainties, they may be accepted as fairly accurate forecasts — will be something like the present division, less one infantry regiment, one regiment of 155-mm. howitzers, one infantry brigade headquarters and headquarters company, and with proportionate reductions in the other components. Such a division, entirely motorized as to transport, and with a reconnaissance unit added, would number approximately 16,000 officers and men, at war strength; perhaps a little more. This figure we may use for purposes of calculation without being too far astray.

The war strength of the cavalry division may be put at about 5000.

The United States is divided, for purposes of military administration, into nine corps areas. These are well-established and functioning organizations, based on the principle of having approximately equal military populations. They ought not to be disturbed if it can be avoided. If in each of these corps areas we had one infantry division, plus four cavalry divisions for the whole country, we should have a war force of mobile troops totalling, as to these divisions, 164,000 men. When corps and army troops were added this would be ample for all the contingencies hereinbefore considered.

At present we have three infantry divisions and one cavalry division of the Regular Army more or less organized, and eighteen infantry and four cavalry divisions of the National Guard. These are by no means at war strength. Presuming that the infantry company will continue to have a war establishment of about 200 men, the average Regular company has about one-half that, the average Guard company about one-third. The strength of other units is comparable, though not exactly in the same proportion. What this means is that every unit, both Regular and Guard, would on mobilization have to absorb at least its own present strength of more or less raw recruits. Not until these recruits had been whipped into shape could the unit take the field. Our present army, therefore, is a nucleus army, a skeleton which lacks the flesh which will give it life and strength.

So far we have been lucky. In 1812 we went to war with an enemy (as far as land forces were concerned) too weak to attack us seriously; only our frontier suffered at first, though later our capital was burned. In 1846 we had plenty of time to create an army for aggressive war; we had nothing to fear ourselves. In 1861 the Civil War took place between parties almost equally unprepared. In 1898, 1846 repeated itself: we had merely to create the instrument wherewith to attack a weaker foe. In 1917 we had Allies who held the ring while we got ready.

Next time our luck may desert us. Next time we may be faced with a foe who is as strong as we are in the elements of military preparedness, who will not give us time to fill up our skeleton ranks. Next time we may have no Allies. There is no reason why we should put up with a makeshift, unready organization when we can have something better.

What we need, as Washington wisely said, is not a large army but a good one. Today that means a highly trained, thoroughly armed, well-officered army, equipped with all the thousand-and-one weapons and devices of complex modern war and ready to take the field on a few hours' notice. It does not mean an army which has to train thousands of recruits after war begins. Such an army may be ready too late. War today comes with lightning swiftness, moves thereafter with the speed not of the sailing ship, the horse and the foot soldier, but of the airplane, the swift cruiser, the armored car. It is well to keep this in mind, for to forget it may be dangerous.

European nations, living in direct and uneasy contact with powerful neighbors, have to absorb all their young men into their military structure. They solve the problem by maintaining strong professional cadres of officers, noncommissioned officers and specialists, who train the young men who are called up every year as they reach military age. Thus a European army (the British excepted) consists at any given time of the professional framework plus one or two of the annual conscript classes, according to the term of military service (average, two years). When the conscripts have finished their army service, they pass to the reserve, graduated in classes according to age. Each regiment is recruited from a certain territorial area, and maintains in that area a permanent depot, wherever the regiment itself may be stationed. On mobilization, the reservists belonging to the regiment have merely to repair to the depot, draw their arms and equipment, and are then sent to join their units. Those not required to raise the regiment from peace to war establishment may remain at the depot as a reservoir to replace casualties, or may be formed into reserve regiments. In time of peace the reservists are frequently called up for training.

It is not necessary for us to thus regiment our entire male population, and for that we should be duly thankful. But the system of mobilization just described does have one feature which we well might copy: the provision of a trained and organized reserve to fill our fighting units to war strength. Given such a reserve, we do not need to keep our Regular Army at war establishment. Nor, to obtain it, do we need to recast our whole military system along European lines; for we already have such a reserve force in our National Guard. All that is needed is to tie the units of Regular Army and the National Guard closer together, in permanent association one with the other; the professional and the citizen soldier, side by side, equal partners in the grave and honorable responsibility of defending their country.

At present each corps area furnishes two divisions of the National Guard; that is, eight regiments of infantry, six regiments of field artillery, two regiments of engineers, and certain other units.

The cavalry regiments are scattered throughout the Union; and there are some additional infantry and field artillery regiments, which may for the moment be disregarded.

If the standard infantry division is to be reorganized, it will be necessary to reorganize the National Guard to fit the new system. Assuming that the number of divisions is not to be increased, the number of regiments will have to be reduced. This is a problem which has to be faced anyway, and a solution found for it. Let us for the moment assume that the number of regiments will be reduced, and that therefore there will be in each corps area only six regiments of National Guard infantry, and four of field artillery. (This assumes that the regimental organization of field artillery will be continued on a six-battery basis, and that the whole of the field artillery of a division will not be grouped in one regiment of nine or twelve batteries, as has been suggested.)

Let us further assume that there are to be nine divisions of the Regular Army, and that one is to be stationed in, and locally recruited from each corps area. This means that there will be in each such area three Regular infantry regiments and two field artillery regiments.

These Regular units need not be at war strength. If, as is now proposed, an infantry rifle company is to have four platoons and a company headquarters in war, with a total of about 200 men, it might have two platoons and a somewhat reduced company headquarters in peace, with a total of, say 110 men. If it is to have three platoons of the old strength, with a war establishment of 193, in peace it might have two platoons, with 120 men. This would be sufficient for training. A battery of field artillery with a war strength of 136 men might in peace, by eliminating spare cannoneers and the extra ammunition section, function quite comfortably with about 100. Field artillery combat trains could be reduced to a mere cadre. Carrying out such ideas through the whole organization, the peace strength of the Regular division might be 8500 men. It would need 7500 more in order to take the field.

There will be two National Guard regiments for each

Regular regiment in the corps area. Suppose that these regiments were, so to speak, affiliated. The commanding officer of each Regular regiment might be made responsible for the training of two National Guard regiments. He would furnish their instructors from his own unit. While the senior instructors should not be frequently changed, additional instructors might be assigned for special purposes, to give courses in weapon-training, signaling, physical training, etc., and thus many of the other Regular officers would from time to time have an opportunity to serve with the Guard units. The Guard officers should be encouraged, when their civil occupations permitted, to perform extended tours of active duty with the Regular regiment, thus replacing the Regular officers on duty with the Guard. Noncommissioned officers might be similarly "exchanged." The Regular colonel should not be considered as commanding the National Guard regiments at all; he would simply be responsible for their instruction as far as the Regular Army could impart that instruction.

Assuming that the National Guard units are maintained at half the war strength of the Regular units, a certain number of the enlisted men of each National Guard regiment should be selected to form a reservoir of reinforcements for the Regular unit. In a company of 100 men, 30 or 35 might be told off for this purpose, for example. On mobilization, the Regular regiment would immediately be brought to war strength by being joined by these additional men, already trained and ready to take their places in the ranks, in duties with which they would be sufficiently familiar to enable them to be immediately useful. By confining this procedure within the geographical limits of a corps area, and by each regimental staff carefully working out a mobilization plan down to the last detail, it should be possible to bring the Regular Army to war strength within twenty-four hours.

But where will this leave the National Guard? It will

leave it about where it is now. At present National Guard units are much below the strength of Regular units. If the number of regiments is to be decreased, the unit strength can be increased without much difficulty. Assume the war strength of an infantry regiment of the Regular Army to be 3000, the peace strength 1700. The Regular regiment will require 1300 men on mobilization. It will draw 650 from each of two National Guard regiments, maintained at half the Regular war strength, or 1500, leaving each with 850 men — nearly the average strength of National Guard infantry regiments at this moment. The ranks of these units can then be filled up by recruits in the time-honored manner, and they will be available as reinforcements if they are needed. If there is immediate need for a certain number of National Guard troops, transfers from one regiment to the other of each pair can be effected to hasten the process.

Everything possible should be done to cultivate the closest and most fraternal relations between the Regular and National Guard units. They should be imbued with a single spirit. The thought that both are part of the same army, linked together in common purpose, should in every way be emphasized. The National Guard should never be allowed to feel that it is merely a reservoir of recruits for the Regulars; its identity, spirit and traditions should be the constant care of every Regular officer associated with it. Only by such a spirit may friction be avoided in a system which calls for the transfer of personnel between units on mobilization. The underlying feeling ought to be: The Guard cannot, under any conceivable arrangement, be ready to fight on M-day. But it can help the Regular Army to be ready, while the Guard, in its traditional manner, is recruiting to war strength. It thus has a dual mission as part of the Army of the United States: to help the Regulars bear the first brunt of the attack, and to prepare itself to meet later eventualities.

[295]

The men to be transferred should of course be those volunteering for such service as far as possible. Local recruiting of both Regulars and National Guard will do away with much of the feeling of going to serve among strangers which might otherwise prevail. There will be difficulties to be overcome, of course; but when one contrasts the National Guard of today with the State Militia of the Spanish War, the progress made toward unity of spirit, toward the one-army ideal, is so amazing that one hesitates to believe further progress impossible.

It might seem better from the standpoint of strict efficiency to transfer only privates from the National Guard to the Regular Army on mobilization, leaving the National Guard with its full quota of officers and noncommissioned officers to train recruits; but as this would make appointment as a noncommissioned officer in the Guard automatically act as a withdrawal from the first line of defense, the moral effect would be bad. As the Guard regiments will be maintained at 50% greater strength (approximately) than at present, the noncommissioned officer allowance can be proportionately increased, and the drafts sent to the Regulars on mobilization can include these additional noncommissioned officers, while leaving the Guard with the same proportionate number that it has at present. As for officers, if each company unit of the Guard be allowed an additional lieutenant, these will be available to fill up the officer personnel of the Regular regiment without unduly handicapping the Guard. If the existing number of Guard regiments is reduced, there will be plenty of surplus officers who can be assigned to the remaining units.

To fill the National Guard units to their war complement of officers, there are two immediate sources of supply: the "inactive" National Guard, which has at present 942 officers, and enlisted men who have qualified for commissions, totaling 1324. The Officers' Reserve Corps should be able to take care of all vacancies which cannot be filled from these sources.

This scheme will give us nine divisions of the Regular Army ready within 24 hours, and behind them 18 divisions of the National Guard which can be brought up to war strength in anywhere from 30 to 60 days.

The nine divisions of the Regular Army will form three corps. If one regiment of medium artillery, one battalion of engineers, and one regiment of special-type artillery (portée, pack, railway, heavy tractor-drawn, etc.) be allotted to each corps area, this will in total provide 3 groups of corps troops, each of 3 regiments of medium artillery and 1 battalion of engineers, and one group of army troops of 9 regiments of special-type artillery and 6 battalions of engineers (camouflage, water-supply, pontoon, topographical, etc.). This will be sufficient for immediate purposes. Twice this number of National Guard regiments and battalions will be needed in these categories to be linked with the Regular regiments as suggested for divisional units. The anti-aircraft artillery and observation aviation will come from sources already considered. Other units (medical, train, general service engineers, military police, etc.) for corps and army allotments can be quickly built up on mobilization and need not be maintained in peace except in the inactive status, with proper assignment of reserve officers. Signal troops should be provided on the basis of one battalion for each corps and two for the army.

The peace strength of a Regular Army group of corps troops on the above basis would be about 3500; the war strength 6000 (exclusive of units on an inactive status in time of peace). A National Guard group of corps troops would require 3000 men in peace.

The army group would number for the Regular Army about 11,000 men in peace, and 19,000 in war; the National Guard peace strength would be 10,000.

The cavalry divisions cannot be handled on this basis. First, the cavalry of the Regular Army cannot be allotted proportionately over the several corps areas; the bulk of it must be kept in the vicinity of the Mexican border. Next, as to mechanized cavalry, this is a new arm requiring a great deal of highly complicated material and highly trained personnel; it is still in the experimental stage in the Regular Army, and it is not practicable at present to organize National Guard units with their limited training opportunities. There can be very little difference between peace and war establishments, since like a coast artillery installation, personnel is a function of material. Mechanized cavalry is a swift-moving striking force with a high concentration of offensive power, and should be maintained at war strength to conserve these qualities. As to horse cavalry, the question of the feeding, training and care of animals is paramount. National Guard cavalry at present has about 65 enlisted men per troop, and an average of perhaps 15 or 20 animals. A certain number of private or State-owned mounts are available. Since such a troop must take the field with about 135 fully trained men and horses, it is obvious that National Guard cavalry presents a difficult problem. It is not an arm which may come into service slowly; it will be needed, if an army is needed at all, in the very earliest stages of the operations. If it is furnished with its full quota of horses, paid caretakers must be provided to feed, water, exercise and groom these animals daily, and they must have ample stable accommodations — this for mounts which are to be used once a week for a couple of hours' drill. Obviously this is not an economical proceeding. On the present basis, it is highly questionable whether the National Guard cavalry could take the field inside of three months. The question therefore arises whether National Guard cavalry should be maintained at all.

Four cavalry divisions of the Regular Army — two horse and two mechanized — would provide a considerable amount of mobile fire power which could be concentrated swiftly against any enemy on our shores or those of our neighbors. Since these four divisions would require but 20,000 officers and men, it seems that they would represent a much more economical expenditure of money than the maintenance of reduced strength cavalry divisions and regiments of the Regular Army and National Guard, which would require a long time to prepare or else would have to take the field with insufficient numbers of men, horses and equipment.

Similar considerations apply to infantry tank units. There is one company of light tanks which forms an integral part of each infantry division of the Regular Army and National Guard. In both, these companies should be maintained at war strength, both in men and equipment. The National Guard tank companies would be available to reinforce the Regular divisions at once if they were needed, without waiting for their divisions to recruit. But there are also needed certain independent tank units, and these ought to be supplied by the Regular Army and kept at full establishment. They are required for the support of the infantry in battle; the long-distance armored striking force is supplied by the mechanized cavalry. Probably three infantry tank regiments (two of medium tanks and one of light tanks) would be enough for a force of nine divisions, though the proportion of tanks to infantry is still a subject of study and experiment. The strength of these units may tentatively be put at 1600 each.

What, in total, will be the strength of the combined army, citizen and regular, which this plan envisions?

The allotment of the Regular Army to overseas garrisons, harbor defenses, anti-aircraft and air force has already been considered, and totals 103,700. To this must be added:

```
 9 infantry divisions at 8,500 ...   76,500
 4 cavalry divisions at 5,000 ....   20,000
 3 groups of corps troops at 3,500   10,500
 1 group of army troops ......       11,000
 3 tank regiments at 1,600 .....      4,800
 Overhead ...................        12,200
                                    _____
      Sub-total ...............     135,000
 Already considered (see above) .   103,700
                                    _____
      Total ...................     238,700
```

The National Guard allotment already considered comes to 56,800. To this must be added:

```
18 infantry divisions at 8,000 ....  144,000
 3 groups of corps troops at 3,000     9,000
 1 group of army troops at 10,000     10,000
                                     _____
      Sub-total ................     163,000
 Already considered (see above) ..    56,800
                                     _____
      Total ...................      219,800
```

The mobile force which could, in 24 hours or thereabouts, be produced from the above set-up would total:

```
 9 infantry divisions at 16,000 ..   144,000
 4 cavalry divisions at 5,000 ...     20,000
 3 groups of corps troops at 6,000    18,000
 1 group of army troops at 19,000     19,000
 3 tank regiments ............         4,800
                                     _____
      Total ...................      205,800
```

Behind this would still be 18 divisions of the National Guard of 4250 each which would be the framework for such additional citizen forces as might be needed.

Their actual strength would really be somewhat greater, since on mobilization about 1000 men per division can be made up from an enlisted reserve force, to be paid a retainer pay of $24 per annum (as now authorized for the Regular Army Reserve) and consisting of men for such positions as mechanics, truck drivers, hospital attendants, cooks, clerks, draftsmen, etc., which require no special military training, and of course to be assigned according to civilian experience. This reserve should be locally recruited and maintained, on the basis of 1000 per Regular Army and National Guard division, or 3000 in all in each corps area; perhaps 3500 when the needs of corps and army troops are considered. This would reduce the obligation of each National Guard division for filling the Regular ranks by 500 men, and give it 1000 specialist reservists of its own. Its actual strength on mobilization, after making its contributions to the Regulars, would therefore be 5750 men before it began to recruit. It is hardly conceivable that any attack from outside could produce an initial effort which a mobile force of 200,000 troops plus a G.H.Q. air force of 1000 planes could not destroy. But since military policy always seeks to have something in reserve, these National Guard divisions will certainly take care of all possibilities. Their full war strength would be 288,000 men.

One very useful function they might fulfil is the training of replacements. Even supposing half of them — one division from each corps area — were eventually required to take the field, the other division could train replacements for both the Regular division and the Guard division at the front. Reserve officers could be allotted to the Guard for this duty. This set-up could be enlarged to include replacement-training for harbor-defense and anti-aircraft artillery, air corps, and overseas garrisons.

Such a system will avoid one of the worst errors of our Civil War, in which all the States save Wisconsin filled up their successive quotas of volunteers by organizing new regiments, with new sets of officers, while their veteran units already at the front were allowed to waste away. Wisconsin alone adopted the plan of sending out drafts of recruits to fill the ranks of her serving regiments. The result was that at the end of the war it was the consensus of army opinion that a Wisconsin volunteer regiment was worth a brigade from any other State.

Even if all the National Guard divisions are eventually called upon, there will be time to organize depot units to remain behind and take care of the all-important duty of maintaining a steady flow of trained replacements.

The place of the Officers' Reserve Corps in the proposed establishment is to provide additional officers required on mobilization, and a reservoir of officer personnel to replace losses. Reserve officers could also be used to build up the National Guard divisions. The total strength of the Officers' Reserve Corps in June, 1937 (exclusive of inactive officers) was 96,545. Of these, about 16,000 were World War veterans, who in a few years will be incapable of active service. Some 25,000 of the remainder belonged to the various administrative and supply services, which will absorb a large number of officers in war. There remain about 55,000 officers of the combatant arms, four-fifths of whom were graduates of the various Reserve Officers' Training Corps in our universities. A very great majority of these were in the grade of lieutenant. About 10,000 would be required to fully mobilize the forces above outlined; the rest would be available as replacements, or for training enlisted replacements.

The present strength of the Regular Army (including the increments of officers provided for under present law) is about 180,000 officers and men. The authorized strength under the National Defense Act is 16,000 officers and 280,000 enlisted men, which has been reduced by the annual appropriations of subsequent years. The proposed organization would not reach this total, but would represent a considerable increase over that at present maintained. This increase (from 180,000 to 238,000) should not be made all at once, but by annual increments of 15,000 men, reaching the full strength in four years. There need be little increase in officers.

The proposed establishment of the National Guard represents an increase of but 9800 men over the present establishment.

Certainly this organization will cost more than the one we have now, yet not so much more as might be supposed. For pay the Regular Army will cost about $25,000,000 extra per annum at present rates; if these are increased to equal the navy's average rates, as they ought to be, it will cost something over $45,000,000 more. For subsistence it will cost $9,600,000 extra per annum. For clothing the extra cost will be an average of $4,170,000 per annum. These sums do not seem very formidable, when it is considered that in return we will get, not a skeleton army requiring weeks of preparation before it can take the field, but an army ready instantly to meet any emergency, an army each officer and man of which will be giving the nation a full return, in insurance against the perils of war and the terrible consequences of defeat in war, for the money spent on him. The increase in the size of the Regular Army will be about 32%; the increase in its cost, about 25%; the increase in war-efficiency, reckoned in degree of readiness, rises into infinity. This is the truest of economies; if so much can be purchased at so reasonable a price, we should be foolish not to pay that price cheerfully.

No nation, contemplating aggression against us or our neighbors; no nation, contemplating the challenge of our rights and vital interests by armed force, will fail to take such an army into account. There is all the difference in the world, in such calculations, between an army that cannot bring its full force into action for 30 days or 60 days, and an army which can strike *now*.

Moreover there must be considered that at present, to partly compensate for the low establishment at which the Regular Army is maintained, the creation of a Regular Army Reserve of 150,000 is contemplated, and a start has been made toward raising it. Under the suggested system, this will be reduced to a specialist reserve of about 32,000.

Compare this proposed army with the forces maintained by some of the European powers.

France, with one-third our population, maintains in France and North Africa an army and air force with a peace strength of 660,000. Germany, with a little more than half our population, maintains a peace strength of 950,000 (including the air force). Soviet Russia's peace establishment (with a population about one-third greater than ours) is 1,300,000. Poland, with less than one-fourth our population, has a peace strength of 266,000. All of these countries have, literally, millions of trained reserves for which they must keep up stores of weapons, ammunition, clothing and equipment: except, of course, Germany, whose trained reserves have not yet caught up with the "lag" caused by the abolition of compulsory military service from 1919 to 1935, but are being feverishly increased now. In a warring world, it is surely not too much to ask the people of the richest of its nations to maintain a home peace establishment of 194,000: to have a total of one regular and one citizen soldier for every 600 of its total inhabitants, when France has a soldier, active or reserve, for every 8 inhabitants!

Let us also remember that on June 30, 1937, there were 261,000 young men in the Civilian Conservation Corps, being paid at rates averaging more than we pay our soldiers. The army needs but 58,000 men more than it has to give us a far better return in security. An adjustment of national expenditure here is obviously indicated: and an army job is a permanent job if its holder wants to make it so, with retirement pay in old age assured.

The proposed organization would not greatly disturb the present arrangement of units of the Regular Army. For example, it would require 27 infantry regiments, and there are 28 available in the Continental United States. It would require 40 field and mobile coast artillery regiments, and there are 25 available. It would require 12 cavalry regiments, and there are 14 available. The principal increases would be in the filling in of the inactive battalions and batteries of existing units, and the organization of new artillery regiments.

The National Guard's regimental arrangement would be far more profoundly disturbed, but with the coming of a new divisional organization this is inevitable anyway. Many regiments would have to be consolidated. We might lose some of the old traditions. But this could be kept to a minimum by transforming excess infantry regiments into regiments of harbor-defense or anti-aircraft artillery, and by preserving the identity of the older units as far as possible. The 19 cavalry regiments could be transformed into 18 divisional reconnaissance squadrons; and perhaps one or two horse cavalry regiments might be retained where local conditions make available a full supply of mounts.

The result: a Regular Army still very small in comparison with the armies of foreign powers, composed of highly trained professional soldiers, with immediately available reserves of citizen soldiers to bring it to its war establishment; an army capable of striking a terrific *and immediate* blow against any enemy force that could conceivably reach our shores, and one also well organized for expeditionary service of a limited nature. Behind it, a sufficient skeleton on which to build up a citizen force of reinforcing troops.

BUT — this is not an army capable of indefinite expansion. The utmost fighting strength it could ever reach, including the overseas garrisons, would be about 600,000 officers and men. This is wholly insufficient for any overseas expedition on foreign continents. Our whole military policy should be oriented toward maintaining an army invincible on our own shores and in our own overseas possessions, and we should completely forget about any organization, tentative or otherwise, seeking to create an army of millions which could only be needed for transoceanic adventurings. The greatest effort we seem likely to be called upon to make may be a war with Japan in which we will have to extend our sea-power far enough westward to bring an intransigent Japanese Government to its senses. For this, the suggested army is sufficient. For an invasion of Japan, it is nowhere near enough; nor is it enough for an expedition to the Philippines to fight the Japanese army there.

It does provide an army which can defend us against any form of attack, and which can support our navy in keeping command of the oceans to east and west. This is all we need. But — this we *must* have. There can be no trifling with minimum requirements. In war, to be second best, to have almost enough, is to be defeated.

Chapter XIV

THE ARMY AND THE NATION

The stature of the Army increases, and we think of it not as a fighting machine only, but as an integral and essential part of the Government of the Nation. We realize that it is not a mere aggregation of men, not even an aggregation of regiments. It has a soul of its own, over and above the souls of its component individuals.

COLONEL OLIVER LYMAN SPAULDING, U. S. A.,
The United States Army in War and Peace.

THE PRESIDENT is the constitutionally designated Commander-in-Chief of the army as he is of the navy. He exercises this duty through the medium of the Secretary of War, to whom the Chief of Staff is principal military adviser.

The Chief of Staff is selected from the general officers of the line. "He shall cause to be made," states the National Defense Act, "the necessary plans for recruiting, organizing, supplying, equipping, mobilizing, training and demobilizing the Army of the United States and for the use of the military forces for national defense. He shall transmit to the Secretary of War the plans and recommendations prepared for that purpose by the War Department General Staff and advise him in regard thereto; upon the approval of such plans or recommendations by the Secretary of War, he shall act as the agent of the Secretary of War in carrying the same into effect."

This in practise makes the Chief of Staff the direct inheritor of the powers which for a century were exercised by the Commanding General of the Army. It places the chiefs of the bureaus and branches of the War Department in a relation to him analogous to that of a staff officer to a commander.

Under the Chief of Staff there is a Deputy Chief of Staff, and five General Staff Divisions: Personnel (G-1), Military Intelligence (G-2), Operations and Training (G-3), Supply (G-4) and War Plans (WPD). Each has a chief (usually a general officer) with an appropriate number of assistants. The duties of the General Staff are of a general and co-ordinative nature; they are not administrative. Formerly appointments to the General Staff were made from an "eligible list," to which admission was gained by qualification at the Command and General Staff School at Fort Leavenworth. Recent legislation has opened these appointments to other officers, an admirable measure: as many highly qualified officers are unable, by reason of the limited capacity of the school, to attend the Leavenworth course. The capacity ought, however, to be increased, so that all officers may have the benefit of this excellent training.[1]

The "overhead" of the army may be said to consist of the first seven departments named in Appendix "B", and of officers and men on detached service: at present some 33,000 officers and men all told. Many of these are maintained on the theory of being ready for a great war-time expansion, something like that which took place in 1917. This overhead can be somewhat reduced if the contrary theory — that of having a small, highly-trained professional army for the defense of our own country and its possessions — is adopted.

[1] For administrative organization of the War Department, see Appendix "B."

Under the plan suggested in the two previous chapters, about 9000 of this overhead would be absorbed by the nine divisions and four cavalry divisions, each of which would require its proportion of quartermaster, medical, ordnance and other services. Another 5000 would be in the overseas garrisons and is included in the figure given for them. Recruiting service (1000) and National Guard duties (800) would be performed locally by regimental and other units. The remainder of these "overhead" duties can be performed by about 12,000 officers and men even with the proposed increase in total strength: as long as we are not planning a great war-time increase in the army. While we have the present skeleton organization both in the army and the National Guard, while we talk in terms of millions of wartime soldiers, we need all the overhead we have, and more. When we get down to a small, mobile army for the purposes for which we actually need an army, we do not need so much overhead.

It will be easy enough for us, in war, to enlist truck drivers, clerks, bakers, plumbers, carpenters, medical attendants, and the thousand and one other trades and callings which will be needed. These men do not, in general, have to be trained as soldiers. Certainly work of this sort needs to be done in the army in time of peace, but the peace establishment should be exactly related to peace-time needs and not to a war need which can be rapidly and easily filled. So far as possible, money spent on Regular Army enlisted men in time of peace should be spent in training them to handle weapons and war equipment and to acquire the qualities of leadership and not to perform the duties of tradesmen.

Where special needs arise, civilian employees can be used to fill them, temporarily, at less actual cost than by using soldiers.

The Chemical Warfare Service has been specially excepted

from the "overhead" in this discussion, as it requires separate examination. It is all very well to say that the United States is not going to use poison gas in the next war: but we used it in the last, and will in the next if it be used against us. We need not set up a vast peace establishment on this basis, but we do need to continue experiment, to provide for the gas-defense of harbor forts and mobile troops, and also for defense against such gas as might be used by air raiders. The tactical use of smoke requires study and preparation. Special gas-defense measures in our overseas possessions must be considered. For this purpose, our Chemical Warfare Service should have a modest expansion from its present establishment of 866 officers and men. A small chemical unit in each division (about 60 officers and men) should be part of this increase. A similar unit should be assigned to each coast artillery district.

The procurement and promotion of officers of the army has already been examined. The army officer, unlike the officer of the line of the navy or Marine Corps, is a specialist: that is, he enters a particular branch or arm and remains in it, save for the possibility of transfer, from the grade of second lieutenant to the grade of colonel. The very close cooperation required of the several arms in battle is raising a question of the advisability of continuing this venerable arrangement. An infantry officer, for example, must in action depend for support upon the field artillery, with the capabilities and limitations of which arm he is acquainted only in theory. In modern warfare he must also depend upon air support in many situations. Within his own arm, not only must he know the duties of a rifle company officer, but he must also understand the tank, the heavy machine-gun, the anti-tank gun, the infantry mortar. He learns about these things in the Infantry School, but he may never serve in a company which handles them, for the natural tendency of a regimental commander when a junior officer reports is to look at his record, and assign him — for the efficiency of the regiment — to duties similar to those he has already been performing.

When an officer comes to be appointed to the General Staff, or when he comes finally to the grade of general officer, his experience is limited to a single arm of the service. He must to a large degree depend on his associates, or his staff, for accurate information as to the others. With the navy officer, this is not true. He has rotated between deck, engineer and communications duties as a junior officer; he has likewise rotated between battleships, cruisers, destroyers, submarines and in some cases aviation. The Marine Corps officer, by the time he becomes a colonel or a general, has served ashore and afloat, has served with infantry and artillery units and ships' batteries.

The army might do well to adopt a similar principle. An officer now serves three years in the grade of second lieutenant and seven in the grade of first lieutenant. Every infantry lieutenant might be required to spend six months or a year as a battery officer of field artillery, and a similar period with attack aviation. His infantry duties should take him into a rifle company, a machine-gun company, a tank company, and a battalion staff. Field artillery officers might similarly be required to serve with the infantry and perhaps with observation aviation. Air officers should spend some time with the various ground arms which they must support. Coast artillery officers should rotate between harbor-defense, anti-aircraft and heavy mobile artillery; a few months with the navy and with aviation would do them good.

Every officer, under this plan, on reaching the grade of captain, in which he may be assigned to the command of a company, troop or battery or to a regimental staff, and may in war be called to the command of a battalion, would find himself not only with theoretical but practical knowledge of the other arms with which his unit would be associated in battle. The unifying effect, the elimination of friction, would not be the least valuable feature of such a plan. The writer well remembers occasions during the World War when, as a company and battalion commander of infantry, he expected of the supporting artillery accomplishments which were wholly out of reason; his reaction thereto being in his youthful ignorance a feeling, which sometimes found vocal expression, that the artillery was not up to its job.

The educational system for officers and men is very thorough.[1]

Like the navy, our army is preeminent in this respect among the nations of the world. There is not a system of military education anywhere to equal ours, both in efficiency and in results. The army's greatest lack in this field is the ability to make practical application of the theoretical knowledge thus acquired, as the navy can do in the fleet, and as foreign armies can do because of the great numbers of men available.

The troops of the army are scattered among 157 posts and stations, of which 131 are in the continental United States. The average strength at a continental post is about 900 officers and men; the largest, Fort Sam Houston, Texas, has but 7477, and the next largest, Fort Benning, Ga., 6216. Many of these posts were outgrowths of the dispersion incident to the Indian wars; others are maintained by local or political pressure. Yet this dispersion of the army is not wholly a bad policy. The small post has its advantages. It affords experience in independent command for officers of comparatively junior grade, increases initiative, permits training of additional personnel as key-men (staff, noncommissioned staff, etc.) distributes facilities for training civilian components of the army, spreads the army's contacts with the civil population, and is strategically good for the purpose of dealing with internal disorder if necessary. The administrative

[1] For details see Appendix "C."

overhead, however, is likely to be excessive; no training or association with the other arms is locally possible, except in the
rare cases where a small post includes troops of two or more
arms; for war purposes the small post violates the principle
of concentration. The large posts provide better training for
general officers and higher staffs, and training of the associated arms; they have larger facilities for training civilian
components; for war purposes, tactical and strategical concentration in large posts is to be preferred; mobilization and
distribution of supplies is expedited; and administrative
overhead is lowered. On the other hand, the large post tends
to predominate its civilian community, not always to the
army's eventual benefit; it eliminates the possibility of independent command and the development of initiative except
in the highest ranks; and adequate training areas for large
commands are difficult to obtain.

No system based on posts of a single size, therefore, is
ideal; the present system, which, like Topsy, "just grew," has
on the whole turned out fairly well; it gives varying experience to officers and men, and fits well into the peace-time
training and general life of the army. Its greatest fault is
that it does not offer the best set-up for combined training,
mobilization and war concentration. This should be rem-
edied, and can be. In each Corps Area, a mobilization and
training center should be established. The headquarters of
the Regular Army division should be here located, and such
troops as might be convenient. Here training for the combined arms could be carried out, even though the entire
division might not often be assembled. There should be
sufficient space for mobilizing at least one division; if the
Regular Army division were to be concentrated at this center for mobilization, it probably would not stay long, and
then one of the National Guard divisions could be brought
there, and could use the center for training recruits and replacements. This system would afford many of the advan-

tages of the "large post" idea, while leaving the smaller regimental and battalion posts, on which a great deal of money has, after all, been spent, as they are.

New posts should of course be provided for the infantry regiments now quartered in harbor-defense posts, and for the new field artillery regiments that will be required. This will require a careful survey, and can partly be attained by enlarging old posts, where room is available.

Funds should be provided for yearly divisional maneuvers for the Regular Army and half the National Guard. The National Guard divisions should alternate their 15-day active training periods, every other year, between maneuvers and their regular camps of instruction. In the maneuver years, opportunities should be arranged for the National Guard troops to fire the annual range practices.

The condition of the army as to armament and equipment is far from satisfactory; this is by all odds its worst deficiency. It may be examined seriatim:

Rifles. There are sufficient Springfield rifles, model 1903, for all probable needs. This is the best military bolt-action rifle in the world. It is, however, to be superseded by the Garand semi-automatic rifle, which has a higher rate of fire and the advantage of firing each shot of the clip after the first without the soldier having to disturb his aim by working the bolt. It is considered about $2\frac{1}{2}$ times superior in volume of aimed fire to the Springfield. This rifle is being produced very slowly, at Springfield Arsenal. Only about 7500 will be ready during the fiscal year ending in June, 1939. To arm 27 regiments of infantry, about 50,000 are needed, and twice that many for the National Guard, besides, of course, enough for the regiments in the overseas possessions.

Light machine-guns. At the present time the army's light machine-gun is the Browning automatic rifle, with bipod, hinged butt plate and butt rest added. Manufacture of these guns is progressing. A new type of light machine-gun is being considered.

Heavy machine-guns. The heavy Browning machine-gun is highly satisfactory; World War stocks of these weapons are still available.

Anti-tank guns. Of these there are few; the model type has but recently been developed. Meanwhile the .50-caliber machine-gun is being used as an anti-tank gun, for which it is poorly adapted.

Anti-aircraft machine-guns. This is the proper role of the .50-caliber machine-gun. There is a severe shortage of this weapon, especially in the machine-gun batteries of the anti-aircraft artillery. As many more such batteries will be required, production should be speeded up.

Anti-aircraft guns, 75-mm. This is the mobile gun. Some of the Regular Army regiments have but one battery each. The National Guard has one gun per battery for training purposes. Contracts have been let for 333 new anti-aircraft guns.

Field artillery. There are enough guns, but modernized carriages and high-speed adapters to enable the guns to be towed by motors are needed.

Tanks. 162 medium tanks of the new model are required for the Regular Army; 18 are being produced this year as a first installment. There are some, but not enough light tanks for the Regular Army; the National Guard tank companies (18 of them) have but one old tank each for training purposes.

Armored cars. A beginning only has been made in producing these.

Ammunition. There is an absolute necessity for quickly building up the war reserves of all classes of small arms and artillery ammunition and airplane bombs. The World War stocks are dwindling fast, and what is left of them is beginning to deteriorate at an accelerated rate.

Other very serious deficiencies are in fixed anti-aircraft guns for harbor defenses, anti-aircraft fire-control equipment (of which each National Guard regiment, for example, has but one set), infantry mortars, grenade tubes, motor ammunition and weapon carriers, critical items of medical supply, and gas masks.

It is useless to build up the man power of the army unless it is to have weapons to fight with. The smaller the army, the greater the necessity that its weapons should be the very best available. The whole idea of a small highly mobile professional army is to be able to strike heavy blows very quickly, to produce a high concentration of fire-power against an enemy before he can effect a like concentration. Unless our army is thoroughly armed and equipped, it loses much of its advantages of training and mobility.

Some of the delay in procuring weapons has been due to delay in experimenting and making decision on the best types. Some has been due to insufficient appropriations. Some has been due to the lack of capacity of Government arsenals, coupled with difficulty in obtaining bids from private industries on certain items.

A word may be said as to the employment of the army in dealing with civil disturbances. The army does not like this type of duty, but it has always performed it faithfully and well when called upon. We must not overlook the fact that the technique of modern war frequently includes the attack from within — the attack upon the national unity of an enemy state. Ideological and racial sympathies are exploited to the full, as they are being exploited today in Spain, in Czechoslovakia, as they may be tomorrow in the United States. The activities of Communists, of Nazis, of various so-called Fascist groups in this country are almost daily in the headlines. Propaganda is today as much a weapon as high explosive. If we are ever involved in a war with a nation which is the center and birthplace of any of these "isms," we may expect internal trouble. If war comes in Europe in which we are not involved, we may expect a passionate taking of sides, not only by present devotees of foreign ideologies, but by some of our loose-thinking citizens who are attached to, or blindly prejudiced against, one or the other of them. We may also expect trouble from the racial minorities involved; and if we are engaged in trade with any belligerent power, we may expect a thoroughly-planned and wholly ruthless campaign of sabotage and destruction by the agents of and sympathizers with that power's enemies. Our defense against these attacks, whether they come in war or peace, may be primarily the responsibility of the civil authorities, but in the end, and especially as to possible outbreaks of actual violence, may become the responsibility of the army.

That the army will well discharge this duty, its long record of loyal service bears witness. Today as never before in all its history, the nation is conscious of its army, the army is part of the warp and woof of national life. No longer is it out on the vast frontier, or cooped up in distant, isolated posts. Its posts are scattered over the whole nation. Some of them are in the midst of our great cities. Officers and enlisted men are employed in the training of the citizen soldier — the National Guard, the Organized Reserves, the R.O.T.C., the Citizens' Military Training Camps. Few indeed are the cities of any consequence which do not have one or more army activities stationed in them. The National Guard is also widely scattered, and reserve officers are to be found in every community of the country. The nation has come to know its army better these post-war years.

The army's traditions are long and honorable. Much is now being done to preserve and foster regimental tradition; the provision of regimental badges to be worn on the uniform and displayed on regimental colors and bugle-tabards has helped greatly to impress these traditions on old and young soldiers alike. The heraldic arrangements of these badges are based on the history of the regiment, and the mottoes are expressive of some feature of its past. That of the 21st Infantry, for example, is "I'll try, sir!" — words uttered by its colonel at the Battle of Lundy's Lane, in the War of 1812, when asked by Major General Brown whether he could take a battery of British guns which was inflicting heavy losses on the Americans. The thick sheaves of battle streamers on the colors of our older regiments are eloquent of more than a century of service over half the world — from the Niagara Frontier to the jungles of Cuba, from the walls of Peking to the forest of the Argonne. Through good years and bad, whether nurtured or neglected, the army has given of its best, without complaint, without ostentation. Its officers and men have died in the face of the enemy; they have died in fever-ridden camps, too, and in frozen bivouacs. They have fought half-armed and half-trained against foes superior not only in numbers but in every other appointment of war; and they have dragged out long weary years of peace, ill-paid, ill-clothed, ill-housed, without a murmur or a whimper.

As with the navy, the army's tradition is in the fighting sense an offensive tradition. In the war of 1812, we attacked again and again along the Canadian frontier; in the Mexican War, we were continually on the offensive; the Civil War was marked by alternate assumptions of the offensive by both sides, and was brought to an end by this means, just as the Confederacy made its brightest bid for victory by the offensive which was but barely stopped at Gettysburg. In the World War our troops were particularly remarkable for the offensive spirit which activated them from the commanding general downward. This is not to say that American troops do not fight well on the defensive when it is forced upon them by circumstances: New Orleans, Buena Vista, Gettysburg, the Marne are successive examples in point. But the

American officer has an almost innate belief in the offensive principle, and the American soldier's normal battle-cry is "Let's go!" It is notable throughout our military history: whether one considers Lundy's Lane or San Juan Hill, Chapultepec or the Meuse-Argonne, the underlying American idea has ever been to get the matter done and over with by *going after* the enemy. This quality must be borne in mind in considering the employment of the American Army in war.

The officers of the army do not all come from West Point, but the traditions and spirit of the Academy pervade them all — are perhaps its greatest gifts to the army of which it is a part. No better epitome of the army's spirit could be found than in the West Point motto — "Duty, Honor, Country." The standard is a high one, but it is rigidly adhered to. It is possible for a man in other walks of life to be a scoundrel and yet retain a certain place among his fellows, even to be a pillar of the church and a member of fashionable clubs; but it is not possible for such a man to retain a commission in the United States Army. One of the very few offenses for which, under the Articles of War, the punishment is mandatory — dismissal from the service — is "conduct unbecoming an officer and a gentleman."

The officer corps of the United States Army is unsurpassed. This is saying a great deal; for the French officer corps, in particular, stands very high, in education, in efficiency, in spirit and intelligence. Moreover the French officer has far more opportunity to practise his profession, not only in maneuvers, but in colonial warfare, which is a veritable school of application for captains and lieutenants. The American officer does not have these advantages; he has no colonial wars nowadays, his maneuvers are less frequent and extensive. But he has one greater than them all — he is closer to his men. He does not leave the details of interior discipline to the sergeants, as the French do. He has to deal with the same men year after year, and not with successive classes of conscripts. He is of course the product of the American military system, just as the French officer is the product of the French military system; *chacun à son métier.*

The British officer is a fine leader, as a rule; though with all the changes in the British army, there is still too much of the "carry on, sergeant," spirit there too. But in professional education, he is far behind. He spends but a year and a half in Sandhurst or Woolwich as a cadet; his subsequent education is about half that of the American officer. He is bound, rather than inspired, by a tradition which instinctively recoils from that which is new; a spirit well expressed by the Duke of Cambridge when, as Commander-in-Chief, he introduced a lecturer who was to speak on the subject of foreign cavalry. "I'm sure I don't know, gentlemen," said he, "why we should wish to know anything about foreign cavalry when we have very good cavalry of our own. I fear the Army is in danger of becoming a debating society." That was many years ago; but it was only the other day, comparatively speaking, that in the Staff College entrance examinations the examiners had occasion to remark with pain upon the extraordinary fact that many officers, in presenting solutions of a tactical problem involving the location of a hostile partisan force in the deserts of Trans-Jordan, had completely failed to make any use whatever of the squadron of observation planes which was among the forces at their command. The writer will venture the assertion that to any American officer of comparable rank and service, such an omission would have been impossible.

These things are not here set down to depreciate the officers of any foreign army. They are set down to show the American people that they possess, in the officers for whose education and training they have paid, the finest military asset in the world — guardians who will not fail them in their hour of need.

[320]

The enlisted men of the army are today very carefully selected. No longer is it just a case of taking anyone who can get by the doctor. The background, moral, mental and educational, of the prospective recruit is investigated. The physical standards are high. The preliminary training in recruit depots is thorough and well supervised. When the recruit joins his unit, everything possible is done to prepare him for advancement — either to noncommissioned rank, or to some "specialist" duty. The great need is for better pay — pay which will at least put the soldier on a level with the sailor or the C.C.C. enrollee. Given this (coupled with better chances for promotion), the fine young men who are entering the army today can be retained in the service. Lacking it, they will go back to civil life.

But, better pay or not, of one thing the citizen of this nation may be sure: in war or peace, his army will loyally do its duty as it has always done. Whether he neglects it or not, it will protect him when he needs protection; whether he takes an interest in it or not, it will take an interest in his safety when the bugles sound "To Arms!"

Only — it can do a much better job, and at far less cost not only in the citizen's tax-dollars, but in irreplaceable American lives, if the citizen will see to it that it is given the tools and the men it needs wherewith to serve him.

Chapter XV

COORDINATED MILITARY PLANNING

Naval preponderance and warfare on land are mutually dependent, if the one is to assert itself conclusively and if the other is to be carried out with vigor and effect.

> COLONEL C. E. CALLWELL,
> *Military Operations and Maritime Preponderance.*

IN ALL OUR wars, we have seen the necessity for army and navy working together. The Revolution was brought to an end by a combined naval and land campaign which contained and ruined Cornwallis. The War of 1812 showed us to our cost the formidable offensive qualities of amphibious warfare when used against us. The decisive stroke of the Mexican war began with Scott's landing at Vera Cruz, aided by the navy both in getting his army to the spot, and afterward in the siege operations. The navy's blockade was one of the decisive factors of the Civil War, and the amphibious operations on the western rivers, at Mobile and at Fort Fisher, were among the great accomplishments on the Union side. Two joint operations — that of Merritt and Dewey against Manila, that of Shafter and Sampson against Santiago — brought us victory over Spain. In the World War our army could not fight until the navy had escorted it across the Atlantic Ocean, maintaining thereafter the sea-communications by which it lived.

We have discussed how, in the strategy of our "insular" state, this interdependence must continue: how the navy is our offensive arm, with power to strike at enemy fleets within our waters, at the sea-communications of enemy states, and to inflict upon them such injuries as shall bring the war to a close. We have seen how, meanwhile, the army must make safe the ports from which the navy operates, secure our shores against raids, provide that firm and unshakable defensive base upon which all offensive action must be founded. In the future as in the past, the two services must work side by side, each in its own sphere, but each with due regard for the needs and operations of the other.

This interdependence may in particular operations become even closer, extending into the tactical field; as in a case when the navy might have to reach out into the Pacific, and the army might be needed to seize an advance base there. The navy would then convey the army to the place selected, would cover its landing with fire, would supply and support it after the landing had been accomplished. The army might equally have to support the navy in such a case, for example, as a transit of the Panama Canal with a hostile fleet waiting on the other side; when it would devolve upon the bombers and long-range coast guns of the army to see that our fleet had free exit without being exposed to piecemeal attack.

These are but examples of how, in a state whose military policy is pronouncedly maritime, the control of the shore conditions naval preponderance, helps naval supremacy to protect the shore from direct attack.

Such considerations, and others arising from the complete regimentation of certain states of the European continent for war purposes, have given rise to the theory of "totalitarian war," and have led the nations of the Continent to consolidate their navies, armies and air forces under a single command in order to insure, to the greatest possible degree, unity of control and concentration of power.

France, for example, has set up a Ministry of National Defense, under which function the old Ministries of War and Marine, and the new Air Ministry. Germany and the Soviet Union have similar arrangements; and the concentration in the single person of Signor Mussolini of the offices of Minister of War, of Marine and of Air produces the same effect under a different form in Italy. Even Britain, while maintaining her separate departments, has a "Minister for the Coordination of Defense."

One reason for this, of course, is that each of these countries has an air force which is separate in administrative control and military command from the army and the navy. This is perhaps essential to nations whose chief military apprehension is air attack, and who are aware that the best immediate reply to air attack is a vigorously delivered air attack of one's own (that is, of course, between nations living close enough to each other to make such attacks possible). The whole question of national defense for a European country is so intimately bound up with air operations that it is not to be wondered at that separate Air Ministries and separate Air Forces with their own staffs, schools and systems of training and preparation have been thought advisable. But since the air forces so created must nevertheless cooperate with surface forces, both by sea and by land, the complications to be envisaged in war might be considerable; and it is to ameliorate and smooth out these complications, as well as meet the threat of totalitarian war, that the combined Ministries of National Defense have arisen.

We have in this country an unfortunate penchant for copying European ways of doing things, often without critical examination. It is well enough to adopt somebody else's successful methods if they fit your own problems; as Britain's strategical policy of the 19th century fits ours today. But in this matter of the unified Departments of National Defense, it is to be remembered that these establishments are experiments, upon which success in war has not set its seal. In fact, where similar systems have been tried in war, they have uniformly failed. "We have had," says Vice Admiral Darlan of the French Navy (*Revue Militaire Générale*, January, 1938), "two previous examples of the unified command: that of Louvois and that of Napoleon. The results are known as La Hogue and Trafalgar. . . . The British did not think of putting, let us say, Nelson under Wellington's command, or vice versa; but to the British the names of La Hogue and Trafalgar are the names of victories."

In the World War the Russian Navy in the Baltic was placed under the command of the Grand Duke Nicholas, the Commander-in-Chief of the Army, and even though Nicholas was the best of the Russian generals, and even though Admiral von Essen, who commanded the fleet, was a capable and energetic officer, the Russian fleet was thereby all but paralyzed. The Austro-Hungarian fleet was under military control, the Naval Bureau being an adjunct of the Imperial and Royal Ministry of War; and this fact more than anything else accounts for its miserable record of accomplishment, though it had fine, well-armed ships and excellent officers and men.

Nevertheless, there is arising in this country a school of opinion which seeks to have us adopt this method of administering our military forces. The proposition as presented here is to have a Secretary of National Defense, with Under Secretaries for the Army, Navy and Air. We are told that this will avoid friction, effect great economies, produce greater efficiency in peace and in war. This, of course, is mere rationalization, based on European and not American conditions. It further ignores the universal failure of such a plan in war. There is no instance in all history, since the days of the rowing galley at any rate, in which such a unified command succeeded; there are plenty of instances of failure.

But from the American viewpoint the worst indictment of the combined command and administration is that it is wholly unadapted to American strategical requirements.

Take the matter of a separate air force. In Europe, as we have said, the air comes first. In this country, the navy comes first. The principal objective of all our strategy is the control of sea-communications—denying them to an enemy while we preserve them for our own use. This must continue to be so while the Atlantic and Pacific oceans continue to exist and cannot be spanned by military airplanes. It is the fundamental basis of all American strategical thought, of every plan of national defense. It is therefore vital that the navy be complete in every part, including its aviation. To set up a separate control of that aviation, even though a part of it then be graciously handed back to the navy for operation (as has been done in Britain) is simply to introduce a fresh complication into the most important and immediately vital part of our defense system. Naval aviation is so essential a part of the fleet, and its control and coordination so essentially a naval problem, having to do with the control of the sea in just as great a degree as the operation of surface ships, that to take the air personnel out of the navy, to make the whole air force a thing apart, owing allegiance to a different authority, supplied and administered by a different agency, would be a handicap equal to taking our Admiral's destroyers away from him and putting them under the Coast Guard, in the Treasury Department. It would be just about as sensible, too.

But if the navy is to retain control of its aviation, what about the rest of our flying force? Its primary mission, of course, is the defense of our coasts and outlying possessions. In so doing, it must work very closely with such activities as harbor defenses, anti-aircraft guns, mobile ground troops. It is as much a part of this military machine as naval aviation is a part of the naval machine. The naval aviation has floating bases which must be supported and protected by the fleet; land aviation has land bases which must be supported and protected by the army. Here again, to set up a separate system of control for the air force would be to fly in the face not only of experience but of common sense.

The one remaining plea might be that it is necessary for all aviation to work together, and that this will be achieved by having a separate air force. This may sound plausible, but it does not bear examination. Naval aviation is part of the fleet and must be able to accompany the fleet wherever the latter goes; which is the reason for aircraft carriers, seaplane tenders and catapults. Army aviation is tied to the land; it can fly over the sea only to a limited extent. The occasions for actual cooperation between army and navy aviation in war may well be fewer than the occasions for cooperation between ships and land forces; thus when the latter are borne in ships to some distant scene of operations, it will be upon naval aviation that they must depend in the first instance. Their own will not be available until they have landed and created a base for it. Patrol-plane squadrons operating in a theater from which the fleet is absent may indeed have to work closely with army aviation; but this possibility seems hardly sufficient reason to change our whole system of military administration.

As to the elimination of friction, it is surely a curious way of achieving this to begin by setting up a third component of the armed forces with its own hierarchy and the vested interests which it will presently acquire. It is further to be considered that it will be necessary for the Secretary of National Defense to have a military staff, since he can hardly discharge his onerous duties without competent military advice. Such a staff would of course be a mixed staff, chosen from Army, Navy and Air Force. No one with the smallest knowledge of human nature would upon reflection recommend this as a means of eliminating friction and inter-service jealousy. Yet such a staff is indispensable if the plan is to function at all. The French have found it so: and the result has been, again to quote Vice Admiral Darlan, that they have acquired "a fourth staff to quarrel with the other three." A notable plan, indeed, for eliminating friction.

And what about economy? It will be observed that the old Departments would have to continue to function much as before, with about the same setup and arrangement under different names. The new Department of Air would require a complete staff and administrative services of its own. Above it, the super-staff would also require its own controlling and operating machinery. Some economy in purchasing might be arrived at, of course; but we can do that anyway. We do not need to combine the departments for that. Then we hear something about using the same bases for army and navy planes. People who talk of such things do not seem to understand that an air base has a limited capacity for its various functions. It has enough mechanics, machinery and equipment to take care of such a number of planes. It cannot handle twice that many without being given twice the facilities. An army air base designed to take care of two army pursuit squadrons cannot also take care of the squadrons of some navy carrier when these happen to be ashore. It makes no difference by what names you call things; the fact remains that for so many planes you have to have so much in base facilities.

As for efficiency in war—the unified command—it may perhaps be noted that Napoleon, the greatest soldier of history, never did and never could understand the methods of sea warfare. In his famous *Maxims of War* he writes: "The art of land warfare is an art of genius, of inspiration. On the sea nothing is genius and inspiration," (and this from the man who had Nelson as an opponent!) "everything is positive and empiric. The admiral needs only one science, that of navigation. . . . An admiral needs to divine nothing; he knows where the enemy is, and his strength." (Napoleon should have been on Nelson's quarterdeck when the latter was frantically searching for Brueys from Toulon to Alexandria and half-way back again.)

But the point is this—if Napoleon could not command a knowledge of sea war as well as land war, what assurance has this nation that in her hour of need Fortune will raise up for her a genius able to do that which was denied the great Corsican?

The fact is, as Napoleon recognized without realizing it, that land war and sea war require different schools of training; not different "geniuses" or different principles. A general and an admiral make war according to the same basic principles of concentration, offensive action, security and all the rest of it. But they make war with different instruments, which operate in different ways. There is no use trying to make a man who has served all his life with a fleet, operating over the trackless plain of the sea at speeds of 15 to 30 knots, carrying with it supplies sufficient for many days or many weeks, conduct war on land with armies which (at least as to their primary component) march on their feet at two or three miles an hour and must have fresh supplies every day or every other day, and are continually obstructed by rivers, mountains, swamps and other obstacles.

To attempt such a thing is to throw away the experience which, applied to its own problem, is so vitally important. Yet this is what will happen in a Department of National Defense, for either the views of the naval contingent of the staff will prevail, or those of the army, or those of the air force. One will obtain a greater degree of confidence from the Secretary than another. Or if not, then there will be endless debate and nothing done.

The fact is, that the idea of a Department of National Defense, for this country, is appealing only from the administrative point of view, and that only in theory and not in fact. From the point of view of command in war, it is not only fallacious but dangerous: yet it cannot be divorced from command and applied only to administration, for the two are so linked as to be indissoluble. From the point of view of American strategical requirements, this idea presents nothing but a vision of inextricable confusion, charged with the menace of defeat.

One very appealing argument put forward in connection with this scheme does however deserve further examination: and that is the matter of *planning* the national defense. Plans when made must be carried into execution; as far as peacetime preparations for defense are concerned, this means that Congress must appropriate the necessary money. There are at present six Congressional committees which deal with these matters: the Naval Affairs, Military Affairs, and Appropriations Committees of each House. As a matter of fact, there are really eight, as each Appropriations Committee has sub-committees on Naval Affairs and Military Affairs. It is only necessary to read the various hearings before these committees to realize how little those which deal with military affairs know of naval requirements, and vice versa. This can and should be corrected. The Committees on Naval and Military Affairs ought to have an interlocking membership extending to at least one-third of the membership from each of the two principal parties. The Appropriations subcommittees might be worked on the same principle or might be wholly merged.

This however would be only a beginning.

The present arrangements for joint naval and military planning include two principal bodies: the Joint Board and the Joint Munitions Board. The Joint Board consists, for the army, of the Chief of Staff, the Deputy Chief of Staff, and the Assistant Chief of Staff, War Plans Division; for the navy, of the Chief of Naval Operations, the Assistant Chief of Naval Operations, and the Director, War Plans Division, Office of Naval Operations. Its duties are the conferring upon, discussing and reaching common conclusions concerning all matters calling for the cooperation of the two services in war; conclusions which are then translated into the war plans of both. It will be noted that the members of this Board are all busy men with plenty of responsible duties to occupy them within their own respective services. They cannot give a great deal of their time and attention to the work of the Joint Board.

There is however as a subsidiary to the Joint Board a Joint Planning Committee, to which officers from the respective War Plans divisions are detailed to make extensive studies of problems affecting cooperation of the two services; there is also a Joint Aeronautical Board which operates in much the same manner, and both submit their conclusions to the Joint Board for approval.

The Joint Munitions Board, which consists of the Assistant Secretaries of War and Navy and their representatives and technical members of both services, concerns itself with matters of procurement and supply. It also submits to the Joint Board for approval its conclusions affecting joint war plans and policy.

All this, however, is merely interdepartmental planning between the two defense departments. When it comes to matters of higher policy, there exists no planning agency, other than the President himself and such commissions (like the Baker Board on air policy) as he may from time to time appoint for the purpose of collecting information and aiding in the formulation of policy. There ought to be a permanent planning body, concerning itself with matters of national defense in their broadest aspects, a body similar in purpose to the British Committee of Imperial Defense.

This Committee consists of the Prime Minister and certain Cabinet members, together with the chiefs of staff of the armed services. It has a permanent secretariat, including military members; and working in conjunction with it is the Imperial Defense College, where matters affecting the defense of the Empire as a whole are studied and threshed out.

The work of this Committee has been immensely valuable; and it affords the germ of a plan by which the United States might greatly benefit.

We might well consider the setting up of a Committee of National Defense, to consist of the President as chairman, the Vice-President as the vice-chairman and the usual officiating head (since the President would rarely have time for this), the Secretaries of State, Treasury, War, Navy, and Commerce, the Chief of Staff of the Army and the Chief of Naval Operations. Since in Great Britain the members of the Cabinet are all members of Parliament also, Parliamentary representation is taken care of in their plan. We would require additional members to represent the legislative branch, and these might be the chairmen and the senior minority members of the various committees affected, or each committee might select one member of each party to represent it.

Since the various Cabinet members could not always be present, the Secretaries of State, Treasury and Commerce might each appoint a suitable official of his Department to take cognizance of national defense matters as affecting that department, and to be the permanent representative of the Secretary on the Committee. The Secretaries of War and Navy might be allowed each an additional Assistant Secretary whose duties would be wholly concerned with the work of the Committee, and with the coordination of the national defense. Similarly there might be an additional Assistant

Chief of Staff and Assistant Chief of Naval Operations devoting all their time to this work.

The Committee should have a permanent secretary, appointed for a long term of years by the President on the joint recommendation of the Secretaries of War and Navy. This official should have a proper clerical staff. A certain number of officers of the army and navy should also be appointed as assistants and technical advisers to the Committee.

Working with the Committee, under the direct supervision of the President, should be a national defense college, with a staff of very carefully selected officers of both services, including air officers and Marine Corps officers. The students should also be carefully chosen, in equal numbers from the two services, and should always include a proper proportion of air and Marine Corps officers. Officers of the Coast Guard, of the State Department's Foreign Service, and of the Department of Commerce should also be admitted as students; and the State and Commerce departments should contribute to the faculty. The President of the college should be chosen alternately from the army and the navy for a four year term. The students should not be more than twenty-five or thirty in number. It should be the work of this college to study the national defense as a whole and work out plans for dealing with its problems in their broadest aspects. The results of its studies would of course be available to the Committee of National Defense for the latter's guidance.

The Committee itself should be a consultative body only. It should have no executive authority. Its function should be study and planning, not administration and command. It should prepare reports for the President, and for the appropriate committees of the Congress. It should have the right to call into consultation not only any officer of the Government, but leaders of industry, business, transportation and labor, economic experts, and so forth, as to particular phases of its work. Aside from the intrinsic value of its planning, it would have the tremendous merit of inspiring public confidence, of assuring the citizens of the nation that their defense was being given the attention it deserves; and of building up that enlightened public opinion upon which sound military policy depends.

While the majority of the members would of course represent the party in power—and necessarily so, since responsibility cannot be divorced from authority—there would still be the non-partisan military members, and the minority members from the Congressional committees; thus the suspicion of political bias would be avoided. From time to time —perhaps annually—the Committee should make a public report on the state and needs of the national defense. It should also hold occasional public hearings, at which any citizen who desired to express his views on defense matters should be permitted to appear. No better way of answering the irresponsible and uninformed clamorings of fanatics and propagandists could possibly be devised than to allow them to come before such a Committee and speak their minds, being thereafter subject to questioning. Nor could a better way be devised of assuring a full hearing to any citizen who might have ideas and suggestions of a constructive nature — which such persons, if unable to appear, could of course submit in writing at any time. The reports of these hearings should be made public documents, naturally omitting any matter which might require secret consideration because of its character.

Such a Committee on National Defense, with its National Defense College and its secretariat, would give the nation something it has long needed and has never had: coordinated defense planning extending into every angle and ramification of the subject, and bringing to bear upon the problem the thoughtful study of expert opinion in every related field.

Army and navy cooperation could be furthered in other

ways: notably by increasing the number of officers of each service attending the schools and War College of the other. Nor should this be all; selected army officers should from time to time spend six months or a year with the fleet, as extra members of the staff of the Commander-in-Chief, or elsewhere: and selected navy officers should be sent to serve with division headquarters of the army, especially during maneuver periods.

Local cooperation — in the outlying possessions, and between the commanding generals of corps areas and those of naval districts — already exists, and detailed plans for local cooperation have been prepared.

Joint maneuvers have been held from time to time, such as those in Puerto Rico and the Virgin Islands early this year; there should be more such maneuvers, for only in actually working together can the two services solve many of the problems which will confront them in war. Joint maneuvers ought to be an annual feature of the training schedules, and should be so arranged that as many ships, troops and Marine Corps organizations as possible might participate in some operation of this sort each year.

Nor should this matter of coordination of defense planning be confined to this country. We have assumed certain obligations for the defense of the Western Hemisphere against external aggression: obligations which only the other day were reaffirmed, as to Canada, by the President. There seems no reason why the problems of mutual defense against such aggression should not be made the subject of practical consultation amongst the army and navy staffs of the various American countries. A start has already been made in this direction, by the sending of American naval missions to aid in the work of the Argentine, Brazilian and Peruvian navies, and an American military mission to Haiti. Latin American cadets frequently are admitted to our Military and Naval Academies, and Latin American officers to our service schools.

[335]

This practice should be encouraged and increased; and we should send our officers to their schools, some of which are exceptionally fine institutions. If possible, joint naval and air maneuvers should be arranged. This matter of military and naval cooperation with our neighbors, begun in a small way, would soon grow—if handled on the proper basis—and would be mutually beneficial, tending toward a mutual confidence and respect which could not but make for closer ties between all the nations of the New World.

Not long ago we proposed to lend to Brazil six of our older destroyers for the purpose of training crews for the new destroyers now building for the Brazilian navy. This was the occasion of considerable agitation in some other Latin American countries, who felt that our aid in expanding the Brazilian navy was giving the latter an unfair advantage. Much of this feeling could be relieved by closer relations between the military authorities of all the American powers. There should, for example, be no reason why we should not make a loan to Brazil for the purpose of constructing a naval base at Belem or Recife which our fleet could use if it had to extend its power southward for the defense of South America, while meanwhile such a base would be of great value to the Brazilian fleet. Probably such a move would be ill-advised now; but the way toward this and other contributions to mutual aid in time of need can be smoothed if some means of working together on these matters is evolved.

In all our defense planning we must remember that it is not the army or the navy that is primarily responsible for our safety, not even the President or the Congress: it is the citizenry at large who in the broad sense make and unmake our policies, military, foreign and domestic alike. We could not have an army or a navy at all if our people did not want one. We can use our army and navy only to effect objects which the people who create and pay for them find desirable.

The military arms of the Government need the support,

not only of public confidence but of public appreciation of their problems and requirements. In war, they must have the active aid of every citizen, doing his or her part in the furtherance of the national effort. Particularly, in modern war, must they have the support of industry: which means not only of "big business," but of the workers without whom big business could not exist. How this nation-wide cooperation may be furthered, and how it may contribute to the defense of the freedom which is the priceless heritage of us all, will be the subject of the next and concluding chapter.

Chapter XVI

THE DEFENSE OF FREEDOM

The condition upon which God hath given liberty to man is eternal vigilance.

JOHN PHILPOT CURRAN,
Speech upon the Right of Election, 1790.

MODERN WAR takes its character from the age in which we live — the machine age. It is a war of men, and it is a war of machines. Without the men, the machines are useless. Without the machines, the men are helpless.

A modern army or navy, in war, uses vast numbers of machines, consumes enormous quantities of the munitions which feed the machines. The machines, the munitions must be fabricated by the industry of the nation which is defended by the army or navy. The extent to which the national industry will be absorbed in discharging its military obligations depends therefore upon the number of the war machines, and the rate of their consumption of munitions, in proportion to the normal, or peacetime capacity of that industry.

But there is this to be noted — that even a very great navy has far fewer machines, and therefore requires far less industrial support, than a great army. All the fighting ships of our present fleet, for example, possess together only some 1700-odd pieces of artillery of various calibers. At the close of the World War, the French army alone had 11,638 pieces of artillery in organized batteries. Naval guns fire only intermittently, on those comparatively rare occasions when an enemy is within sight and range; army artillery may be called upon for continuous effort lasting many days. During the Meuse-Argonne battle the American army fired 4,214,000 rounds of artillery ammunition, or about ten times the total ammunition capacity of our entire fleet. And this is considering artillery only, and not the astronomical figures into which small-arms ammunition expenditures by an army ascend; while for a navy, aside from anti-aircraft machine-gun fire, there is little or nothing of this sort.

In Europe, where potential antagonists lie side by side on a crowded continent, there can be little doubt that, as in the last war, the whole industrial effort of any nation at war will be taken up with the furnishing of machines and ammunition to its fighting forces. Indeed that industrial effort, in a war of any duration, will have to be greatly expanded. Such a struggle is not only a struggle between the fighting forces, it is a struggle between whole nations. Every man and woman, yes, and every child capable of doing a little work, will be pressed into the service of the State in the struggle for survival. Every man, woman and child will also be in some sense on the firing line, exposed to danger of battle and sudden death; for the air weapon will be used, and ruthlessly used, to interrupt the vital industrial life which feeds the fighting forces. Even though there be no outright attack on great cities, as a means of terrorizing the people, the centers of industry, the forges of the armorers, will assuredly be assailed by night and by day.

In such a conflict, survival becomes the paramount object of all. Victory must be attained. The whole energies of a people, whatever their original state of political freedom, must be ordered, regimented, directed by a single authority to a common end. Of this there can be no smallest doubt.

Everything—man-power, industrial power, wealth, production, transportation, liberty itself—must be at the service of the government. It makes no difference by what name such a government is called: in war, it must assume absolute power over the life and property of every citizen. It must do this, or perish.

The less degree of preparedness for war such a nation has attained in time of peace, the greater must be its sacrifices in war. If it has provided itself with adequate armaments, it will be able to begin a war with some degree of confidence. It will be able to continue orderly and intelligent efforts to gain victory, without undue confusion, without frantic and wasteful struggles to make up for anterior neglect. To this extent, the coming of war may be a lesser burden to such a provident nation than to one which has allowed its defense mechanism to fall into decay. But a European war is so vast a business, in any case, calling for the maintenance in the field of the greater part of the young men of any nation— millions of them—by the industrial labors of the rest, calling for thousands of guns and tanks and airplanes, for continual replacement of the wastage of battle, dragging ever fresh contingents of men from forge and lathe to handle machine-gun and armored car, and all the while consuming such enormous quantities of shells, cartridges, explosives and other munitions, that nothing less than the full and ordered effort of a whole nation can suffice for victory.

This is so true, can be so clearly demonstrated to be true, that it has come to affect American thought on the subject of American effort in war. The experience of the World War, in which this nation created an army of four million men, and sent more than half of it across the Atlantic Ocean, while creating also a transport fleet of more than three million tons to carry and supply it, and providing naval escort for it as well as other forms of naval effort, has in sum total reaffirmed the idea that in any future war America must adopt even more stringent controls than she used in the last; indeed, that her industry, her commerce, her citizens must be subject to the same sort of centralized command that those of any European nation at war must endure.

Plans to accomplish that end are already well in hand. Laws have been drawn up, laws which require only the insertion of a date and a few details to be presented to a Congress fired with the war spirit, perhaps blinded by war hysteria; laws which would take away the individual rights and liberties of every American citizen and convert this country, in a single day, into a totalitarian dictatorship, under the sole control of the President, for the duration of the "emergency."

Let us consider some of these laws a little more carefully.

First, there are the laws which are printed as appendices to the Industrial Mobilization Plan. This plan has been prepared by the office of the Assistant Secretary of War, who is charged with the duties of procurement and supply by the National Defense Act, to enable the industrial effort of the nation to be aligned behind the fighting forces in war. In time of peace, the work of industrial mobilization consists in a continuing survey of the possible needs of war and of the industrial resources of the country, and an attempt to keep the two in harmony. The nation is divided into "procurement districts," and in each of these districts the industrial facilities are carefully checked over to determine how far they could be used as, or converted into, war-supply agencies. In this work the War Department, with the assistance of the Navy Department, has accomplished a remarkable achievement; and in so doing, has had the hearty cooperation of industrial management. The last Congress made a great advance when it permitted certain funds to be used by the War and Navy Departments in giving what are called "educational orders" to selected plants to enable the latter to acquire experience in the production of certain critical items of munitionment; formerly this was not possible, as every Government contract had to be let, on the basis of advertised bids, to the lowest bidder, which was naturally a firm already equipped for turning out the desired product. All this part of the Industrial Mobilization Plan is necessary and will make a great contribution to our effectiveness in war.

But to secure compliance with the requirements of the fighting forces, the Industrial Mobilization Plan goes further. Directing itself to the ends of "procurement planning, control of economic resources and mobilization of industry," it asserts that war will require the extension of the "war powers of the President" to the control of prices, foreign trade, manufacturing facilities, raw materials, labor, financial resources, power and transportation: in a word, to the regimentation under dictatorial power of the daily life of every citizen and his work and property.

To this end, the Industrial Mobilization Plan presents drafts of certain bills "deemed necessary to carry into effect this plan"; bills which are to be presented to a war Congress as essential ingredients of victory.

The first is entitled: "A Bill making available to the President the man power of the Nation." It is a selective service law, calling for the registration for military service of various age-classes of our young men. It is based on the sound principle of the universal liability of every citizen to defend the republic in war.

The second is entitled: "A Bill making available to the President the material resources of the Nation."

It authorizes the President to fix the prices of any commodity or service (i.e., wages), to regulate, limit or prohibit the purchase, sale, use, transportation, manufacture or distribution of any commodity or service, to buy and sell any commodity or service on such terms as he may deem desirable, to requisition any commodity on such terms as he may deem desirable, to license any sort of business or commercial enterprise and forbid engaging in it without such license, to prescribe the accounting methods of and reports to be rendered by the licensees, to have the right of entry and inspection of all such licensed businesses by means of his duly authorized agents, to promulgate rules against waste, destruction, hoarding, speculation and profiteering in any commodity or service, and to delegate any authority or power conferred by the act to any person or agency he may think proper.

Another section of this law contains the following provision: "That whenever the President shall find it necessary for the national security and defense in the prosecution of the war, he is authorized to suspend in whole or in part the operation of the following listed laws of the United States insofar as, in his opinion, they restrict or impede the procurement activities of the Government or the successful prosecution of the war."

Blank spaces are then provided for the insertion of the titles of the various statutes thus to be placed at the executive mercy.

The law concludes with the usual provisions of fine and imprisonment (amount and term left blank) for violators, and with a clause providing that if any part of the act be held unconstitutional, the rest shall not be affected.

Other laws provide for the commandeering of property, the control of capital issues, the control of foreign trade, the creation of a War Finance Corporation, and a system of marine insurance.

So much for the bills printed in the official Industrial Mobilization Plan, which doubtless represent the policies which are considered necessary and desirable by the Government agencies which cooperated in drawing them up.

There are certain other measures which have been introduced in Congress looking toward the same ends. The motive behind most of these bills is "to take the profit out of war."

[343]

One such bill, called the May bill after its sponsor, the present Chairman of the Military Affairs Committee of the House of Representatives, has already been favorably reported by that Committee and will doubtless come before the next Congress for consideration. It includes wage and price fixing, the regimentation of all labor, the registration of all engaged in industrial management, the licensing of all business — in short, it goes even farther than the Industrial Mobilization Plan's legislation. The bill sponsored by Senator Nye is principally concerned with taxation and profit-elimination, though it contains most of the May bill's provisions for the control of economic resources. It also goes a little farther in the way of giving the President power to spend the public money without accounting until after the war.

All these bills and plans are based on one idea, or rather one memory: that of the last war. All of them assume that the next war will be just like it — one in which we shall build up a huge army of millions, in which there shall be demanded of us an effort which will strain every national resource to the utmost.

All of them, therefore, stand on a false foundation.

For this is exactly the sort of war in which the United States should never again engage, and need not, at least in our time, again engage if her citizens have the wisdom and the vision, now, in time of peace, to make such a war as impossible as anything can be in this uncertain world.

All this vast machinery of control, all these dictatorial powers, will be unnecessary in a war fought mainly at sea, a war in which our main effort will be directed toward maintaining the control of maritime communications by means of a navy, and in which we will not propose and will not be required to send millions of men overseas, or to enlist millions of men to defend our soil.

If we Americans go to war again, we shall be fighting to

preserve our free democratic institutions, our right to live and govern ourselves as we see fit and to be secure in our own home against aggression from without.

Why should we go to war to defend freedom, if we must begin by destroying it with our own hands?

We need not do this. There is no earthly reason why the war effort of our navy, supplemented by that of an army of the size and missions already mentioned, should require of us any such sacrifice.

Our navy, when at full strength, will require 135,000 men. An organized naval reserve of 35,000, backed by a volunteer reserve of say equal strength and a proper merchant marine reserve, can immediately fill all mobilization requirements. The navy can begin functioning at once. Additional men will be needed, of course; but they will not be needed in great numbers. It is doubtful whether — if the navy be maintained at a level which will permit those vigorous offensive measures necessary to assure victory — it would ever require more than another hundred thousand all told.

The army (including the National Guard) begins with 44,500 men in our overseas possessions, and 423,000 at home. Another 200,000 will be needed to bring the National Guard to war strength, plus a few thousand specialist reserves.

If our military establishments be maintained in a condition to produce such a fighting force quickly, and to strike with it without loss of time, the result will be that few nations will challenge its power; and if any does, we shall be the deliverer and not the recipient of the terrible hammer strokes of war.

The forces enumerated are well within the power of this nation to create and to maintain at full strength in war, without regimenting all our vast resources under a single control, without wiping out our democracy, without abandoning our American ways of life and government.

If, however, we are going again to send an army of millions to fight on distant continents; or if we are going to deprive ourselves of the instruments of offensive war on the sea, and thus make it possible for war to be brought to our shores, for our country to be forced into a frightful defensive struggle for existence, then we shall need all the controls and centralization of authority envisaged by the laws above noted, and more into the bargain. It is this sort of war that those who wish us to depend only on defensive measures are in fact demanding.

Certain measures of control we shall need anyway. No one need suppose that a nation can engage in war without inconvenience to its citizens. The obligation of every citizen to defend his country in war is asserted in the Constitution. To this obligation, the Selective Service Act gives expression; the principle is sound. But there is another principle which is also sound, and that is the principle of making full use of the moral value of volunteer service in war. That we could easily obtain sufficient volunteers for the comparatively modest establishments needed by a war of the character made possible to us by our geographical position, there can be little doubt. It would be better to use such volunteers rather than impose selective service, as long as the number of men needed was not a large one. Care should be taken, of course, to prevent the enlistment of men occupying key positions in essential war industries. The Selective Service Act ought to be enacted at the very beginning of any war, in order to reaffirm the principle on which it is based; but its actual operation should be withheld until required — which, if we be strong enough at sea, it probably would not be.

Taking the profits out of war deserves consideration. No one has a right to amass a vast fortune at the expense of the blood of his fellow countrymen. An excess-profits tax will take care of this; price-fixing may also prove to be necessary, but probably will not, because of the fact that our war-effort will be limited, and will therefore not disturb the normal

economic life of the country to the extent that the last war
did. The "mobilization" of the country's industry, the due
apportionment of effort, is right and proper; but a sufficient
degree of efficiency can be attained through the voluntary
cooperation of industry and the pressure of public opinion.
It is childish to assume that every industrial manager, every
business man, is lacking in patriotism and even in common
honesty. The majority of them will be just as anxious to do
their part in the common cause as all the rest of us; there
are means of dealing with a recalcitrant minority without
taking away the rights of others.

Nor is there any assurance that the creation of the vast
bureaucratic machine needed to operate this whole country
and all its enterprises under Government control would conduce to efficiency. The chances are that the reverse would
be the case. Our war supplies must come from our industrial
machine; the needs of war cannot possibly be met by Gov-
ernment-owned agencies created in time of peace. This being true, will it not be safer and wiser to allow industry
to produce what is required of it by its own means, the
means which have made American industrial management
the model for a wondering world, than to attempt to super-
impose upon it a system of Government control, a maze of
red-tape and a horde of more or less competent inspectors,
agents, administrators and committees?

Certainly there must be plans, very careful, precise and
detailed plans, as to the requirements of our fighting forces
under the various conditions of war which may confront
them, and as to the sources which are to supply these requirements. There must be peace-time arrangements between the procurement agencies of the Government and
the various industries. There must be a clear understanding
of what each industry, each plant is to contribute. There
must in wartime be firm dealing with those who fail, or
haggle, or hang back. In extreme cases there must be com-

mandeering. Profiteering cannot and should not be tolerated.

But why must we assume that the last war is the pattern for the next? Why must we suppose that it will find us with our industry already clogged with foreign contracts, ourselves required to make a great over-seas military effort, no plans laid, no army ready, our navy inadequate, our air force all but non-existent? These things need never happen again. We can make reasonable preparations. We can do those things which we ought to do, and leave undone those things which we ought not to do.

It is unnecessary, and it is dangerous, to make up our minds in advance that at the outbreak of any war, we must immediately convert our government into a complete dictatorship. We ought rather to divide our planning into sections: to make one plan which we might call an Industrial Protective Plan, and which would go hand in glove with the Protective Mobilization Plan which would include the use of the navy, the Regular Army and such National Guard troops as might be needed. This Industrial Protective Plan would include only such degree of centralized control as might be absolutely essential to the supply of these fighting forces, and no more. It should be designed with the idea of disturbing the normal life of the country, so essential to our well-being and so contributory to national morale, as little as possible. The readjustments after the war, in which lie so much of perilous possibility, will thereby be greatly ameliorated. The Industrial Mobilization Plan should be the second installment and should accompany a General Mobilization Plan for the production of our full military effort, if and when that ever becomes necessary. This is the sensible, American way of doing things. There is no occasion for hysteria. There is no occasion for destroying ourselves because others seek to destroy us.

Nor is there reason for assuming that if a general European war occurs we shall necessarily be drawn into it. We were involved in the last war through a variety of causes, which it is needless to review here. Infinite controversy has raged about this subject, and will continue to do so. Our present need is for less of speculation upon the past, and more of clear vision as to the possibilities of the future. A war in Europe, today, would almost certainly include Britain and France on the one side, Germany and Italy on the other. The disparity in naval power is so enormous that there would be little peril to our shipping, whatever trade we might engage in with the Western powers. Means for controlling the operation of submarines have vastly improved since the last war; they will not roam the seas unchallenged and unhindered. Nor are airplanes operated from Italy and Germany across hostile land and sea any great peril to the Atlantic shipping lanes. The amount of war-trade we will have with the Western powers will be seriously affected by their inability to obtain credits here under the Johnson Act. To this wise and just law we should rigidly adhere, whatever our sympathies. It is worth a dozen Neutrality Acts for keeping us from becoming too deeply involved, our industries too greatly compromised by foreign orders. But there is no necessity for otherwise confining our future policy within rigid limits. The necessity is that we shall make up our minds that whatever betide, we send no more great armies to fight in a European war. This resolve once deeply imbedded in American hearts, and with it the determination to command the sea-approaches to our own country against all comers, and we may view, if not with serenity at least with security the struggle for power which has through all recorded history made of the continent of Europe a battlefield and a shambles.

Certainly we may have to shut off some avenues of trade; our trade into the Mediterranean, for example, under certain circumstances; our trade into the Baltic under others. It may be advisable for us to sharply curtail even our trade with the Western Powers. These are matters of policy to be decided under the conditions which may in future confront us. Certainly we may assume that our neutral rights will be little respected by belligerent powers except insofar as we are prepared to defend them. The degree to which we should defend our right to unrestricted trade with other nations, and the degree to which we should temporarily abandon that trade, will become matters for grave consideration. Our safety probably lies in not becoming too deeply committed — becoming the economic partners of one side or the other. This is controllable in part by policy, in part by the purchasing power of those nations which have free access to our ports by sea. Again it is this vital matter of sea-communications upon which our security rests. It is for us to say what ships and what goods may pass safely in our waters. It is for us to say to what degree we shall supply the needs of belligerent nations, whoever they may be. There is no reason to assume that we shall blindly repeat all our errors of the past. We are not a nation of fools. If it is to our advantage that certain powers shall be victorious, we may help them — to a degree. If it is to our advantage to remain completely aloof, that too we may do — while the command of our waters is securely in our hands.

If war comes to us unbidden, we can and should meet it on the sea, far from our cities and our firesides; we can and should be able to direct such immediate and vigorous offensive measures against the sea-communications of our enemy and against his naval forces, with which and only with which he may initiate an attack against us, that he will find himself far too occupied with immediate and pressing concerns of the moment to dream of attempting any serious assault on our homeland.

The most serious effort which under present conditions seems likely to be demanded of us, as previously noted, is a war with Japan. If we do have to extend our seapower so far to the westward that we can bring the pressure of blockade to bear on Japan, we may have to undertake certain control measures beyond those normally to be envisaged in a sea-war. Even then we probably would not need to regiment everything and everyone. But the requirements might be severe, before we were through. For this reason we should avoid such a war if we possibly can do so. For this reason we should dispose of the Philippine problem as soon as we can honorably accomplish that end. For this reason we should make our Pacific armaments sufficiently formidable to give pause to the most militaristic of Japanese. For this reason we should give up any idea of interfering in the present or any future struggle in the Far East, between Far Eastern nations. These things are not our concern, they do not involve any of our vital interests, they are Asian affairs in an Asian theater, too far away for our military power to reach save at an effort beyond any possible compensatory reward of victory.

Providence, in its infinite mercy and wisdom, has been very good to this nation. We have been given a geographical position far removed from dangerous neighbors. The genius of man has not yet created instruments of aggressive warfare which can span the oceans which protect us on either hand, save as those instruments may move upon the surface of those oceans. But the sea, while it is in this sense a protection, is in another sense a highway, free to all, by which navies and armies may travel. Fortunately the laws which affect its control in war, and the instruments by which that control is maintained, are limited by the capacity of man to construct fighting ships, and by the very nature of such ships themselves. As they become constantly more complicated and more costly, the building of them is thereby more restricted. They become available in any numbers only to the greater nations: and ours is happily so great in wealth and resources as to be able to maintain a naval superiority ample for our defense.

Given this, with all that it implies — not only a navy but a sufficient army and air force to make that navy free to act — we are secure. It makes no difference what vast armies may march beyond the seas at the command of some dictator or emperor. It makes no difference with what vast armadas of airplanes he may darken the skies. If he have not a navy superior to our own in fighting power upon the sea, all the rest is nothing we need regard.

An army of a million men, complete with every instrument of aggressive land warfare, is, on the sea in transports, helpless before a single cruiser — unless it have naval escort. Ten thousand fighting planes, securely packed in the holds of cargo-vessels, but unguarded by warships, may be sent to rest forever in the ooze of the ocean's bottom by a destroyer manned by a hundred seamen. War on the sea can be successfully prosecuted only with instruments precisely adapted to the purpose. The fighting ship is now so vastly more formidable than any other ship can possibly be made even by the addition of armament, that there is no comparison whatever between the conditions of today and those of a century ago in this respect.

Of course conditions may change; and of course our military policy must change with them. For the present, the conditions are as stated. For the present, America need not in peace stagger under the burdens of vast armaments, nor suffer in war the horrors of invasion and the perils to liberty which war must bring to less fortunate peoples; if only she make sure of this, that she commands the seas which divide her from all possible sources of attack.

Nor is this all; for the sea being the great highway of nations, every great power with which we might be involved in conflict is in greater or less degree dependent on the sea for its supplies and for its trade. While we possess in sufficient number the instruments of offensive sea-war, we can inflict upon any such power injury differing in degree in proportion to its dependence on sea-communications; injury, in the case of any power with which we are at all likely to come into conflict, of so serious and distressing a nature as to enable us to compel our enemy to sue for peace. And this is our true war-policy: this is the key to our security, that we be able to do this, and that we be ready to do it if we must, and that all shall know in advance that we have not only the power, but the will to use the power.

Why, then, in Heaven's name, should we plan for any other sort of war? Why should we blindly assume that we must make war according to the plans, and laboring under the necessities of others who have not our advantages? Why should we deliberately prepare in advance to destroy the freedom which we would, if we fought, be fighting to protect?

Let us not deceive ourselves. Let us not say, these powers that we propose to grant to a single man will be politely handed back when the war is over, as a matter of course. They may be, and they may not be. The risk that they may not, or that the reclaiming of them might plunge this nation into the horrors of a civil strife to which foreign war would seem but a pleasant dream, is far too great to be taken if it need not be taken.

It need not — if the American people understand the principles on which their security rests. It need not, if they will implement those principles with the necessary military policy and establishments. The financial sacrifices they will be called on to bear for this purpose are not great. They are as nothing to the cost of a war fought on our own shores, or those of other continents. They are as nothing to the cost, not only to our treasury, but to our national way of life, our institutions of democratic government, our personal and precious liberties, of war in the European sense of that terrible word.

To all the familiar arguments that have been made in favor of reasonable military preparation in times gone by, arguments which Americans have often heard and as often disregarded, there is now added this: that modern war bears so heavily upon an unready people that they must subject themselves to iron-fisted dictatorial rule if they are to have any hope of victory.

The degree of readiness demanded of us is far less in degree than is demanded of others less securely emplaced upon this planet. It is a price which we should gladly pay in defense of freedom. But it is a price which must be paid, if we are to escape the necessity of beginning our next war not as a free people but as a people under the yoke of arbitrary power. It is no matter that we may assume that yoke voluntarily. Assume it we must; a yoke is a yoke, and such yokes have this eternal quality, that they are not to be cast off as lightly as they may be assumed. We are accustomed to talk of our inalienable rights as free men; we do not as often think of the responsibilities which those rights impose upon us. "No man is free," said Epictetus, "who is not master of himself." To retain our freedom, it is not enough that we assert our rights, our privileges, that we lean upon the accomplishments of past generations and make no sacrifices of our own. The degree and nature of the sacrifices which we must make, that war may be avoided or that it may be quickly followed by victory if it comes, will be exactly conditioned upon the degree of instant readiness for action of the means we possess of offensive operations upon the sea, and of the defensive measures securing the base from which those operations must proceed. If we compromise with these minimum military necessities, we are compromising with disaster. By such a policy, the people of Great Britain kept themselves at peace for a century, made themselves secure in their homes and means of livelihood for two centuries. Today we alone may pursue such a policy: but only if we provide ourselves with its essential instruments.

We alone may so arm ourselves as to be able — if compelled to do so — to inflict grievous hurt on others, while taking little hurt ourselves. In this is all our safety. In this is all our hope of being left in peace, to pursue our own way untroubled by the sound of distant war-drums. In this is all our hope, if war does come to us, of being able swiftly and certainly to bring it to a victorious conclusion.

We cannot bring peace to a warring world; but we can keep the peace of our own part of that world. We cannot settle the troubles of distant continents; but we can prevent the peoples of those continents from transporting their wars to the Western Hemisphere. We cannot shut ourselves off from every contact with other nations; but we can make sure that we command the seas which are the medium of those contacts — the seas which are our ramparts, and upon which we must stand our watch.

Appendices

APPENDIX A

THE BUREAUS OF THE NAVY DEPARTMENT

(1) The Bureau of Navigation (personnel and records).

(2) The Bureau of Ordnance (guns, torpedoes, small arms, ammunition, mines, and armor).

(3) The Bureau of Engineering (steam and electrical machinery, engineering experiment, fuel inspection, radio and sound apparatus).

(4) The Bureau of Aeronautics (aircraft and their operation).

(5) The Bureau of Construction and Repair (design and construction of ships, and all matters relating to their hulls and sea-equipment).

(6) The Bureau of Yards and Docks (shore stations and their equipment).

(7) The Bureau of Supplies and Accounts.

(8) The Bureau of Medicine and Surgery.

The chiefs of each of these Bureaus are chosen from the captains or rear admirals of the navy, and have the rank of rear admiral while so serving. Those of the first four Bureaus mentioned above are chosen from the line; the others as follows: Construction and Repair from the Construction Corps; Yards and Docks from the Civil Engineer Corps; Supplies and Accounts from the Supply Corps; Medicine and Surgery from the Medical Corps.

APPENDIX B

The administrative work of the army is performed by several bureaus:

(1) Adjutant General's Department (personnel and records),

(2) Inspector General's Department (routine and special inspections and inquiries),

(3) Judge Advocate General's Department (legal matters),

(4) Quartermaster Corps (purchase and procurement of general supplies not pertaining exclusively to any other supply department; construction and maintenance of buildings and utilities; storage and issue of supplies; operation of utilities; transportation),

(5) Finance Department (disbursements and accounting),

(6) Medical Department,

(7) Ordnance Department (weapons and ammunition),

(8) Chemical Warfare Service (gas, smoke and flame, and defense against these agencies).

The Corps of Engineers and the Signal Corps are part of the "line of the Army," but also perform administrative duties appropriate to their titles. The Corps of Engineers is charged with the various duties of military engineering (fortification, railways, roads, mapping, camouflage, water supply, bridges, etc.) and also performs civil functions in connection with our navigable waterways (rivers, harbors, inlets, etc.). The Signal Corps is charged with all military communications by radio, telegraph, telephone, visual signalling, and cable.

The Air Corps has many administrative, experimental and supply duties.

The Chiefs of arms — Chiefs of Cavalry, Infantry, Field Artillery, Coast Artillery — exercise general supervision over the progress and organization of their arms, and prepare plans and recommendations for the Chief of Staff, but do not exercise command of troops.

All these branch and department chiefs are chosen from the colonels or lieutenant colonels of the appropriate branch of the army, and have the rank of major general while serving. Most of them have one or more assistants with the rank of brigadier general.

APPENDIX C

WAR DEPARTMENT SCHOOLS

First there are the schools of the various arms (Infantry School, Fort Benning, Ga.; Cavalry School, Fort Riley, Kan.; Field Artillery School, Fort Sill, Okla.; Coast Artillery School, Fort Monroe, Va.) at which there are two courses, basic and advanced, each lasting for a year with a period of troop duty intervening. There are many special schools (Quartermaster School, Quartermaster Motor Transport School, Army Medical School, Army Dental School, Army Veterinary School, Medical Field Service School, School of Aviation Medicine, Engineer School, Ordnance School, Ordnance Field Service School, Signal Corps School, Chemical Warfare School, Finance School). All these schools have courses for officers of the Regular Army, and shorter courses specially arranged for National Guard and Reserve officers. Most of them also have various special courses for enlisted men.

The Air Corps has a whole battery of schools of its own (Primary Flying, Advanced Flying, Tactical, Technical, Engineering).

The general service schools are three in number: The

[359]

Command and General Staff School at Fort Leavenworth, Kan., where officers of all branches are trained in the tactics and technique of the combined arms and qualified for General Staff duties; the Army War College, at Washington, the seat of higher military learning; and the Army Industrial College, also at Washington, where the subjects are related to industrial mobilization and procurement of supplies and services.

There are many schools for bakers and cooks, and a well-organized system of unit instruction for enlisted men of all branches. Army Correspondence Courses are available to all officers of both regular and civilian components.

Selected Bibliography

(1) GENERAL.

If War Comes, R. E. Dupuy and G. F. Eliot (Macmillan).
Armaments and Arbitration, A. T. Mahan (Harpers).

(2) FOREIGN POLICY OF THE UNITED STATES.

Neutrality for the United States, Borchard and Lage (Yale University Press).
America Goes to War, Tansill (Little Brown).
The Road to War, Millis (Houghton Mifflin).
Powerful America, Young (Stokes).

(3) ECONOMIC AND MILITARY FACTORS.

The Strategy of Raw Materials, Emeny (Macmillan).
America's Stake in Foreign Investment, Lewis (Brookings Institution).

(4) STRATEGY AND WARFARE, NAVAL.

Naval Strategy, Mahan (Little Brown).
Naval Warfare, Creswell (Sampson Low, Marston & Co.— London).
Sea Power in the Modern World, Richmond (Reynal & Hitchcock).
Sea Power in the Pacific, Bywater (Houghton Mifflin).
War in the Pacific, Denlinger and Gary (McBride).

Selected Bibliography

(5) Strategy and Warfare, Land.

Principles of War, Foch (Chapman & Hall—London).
Military Operations and Maritime Preponderance, Callwell (Blackwood—London).
The Caissons Roll, Baldwin (Knopf).

(6) Strategy and Warfare, Air.

Air Power and Armies, Slessor (Oxford University Press).
Air Warfare, Sherman (Ronald).

(7) American National Defense.

We Can Defend America, Hagood (Doubleday Doran).
Fighting Fools, Edmonds (Appleton Century).
The Interest of America in Sea Power, Present and Future, Mahan (Little Brown).
History of the U. S. Army, Ganoe (Appleton Century).
The U. S. Army in War and Peace, Spaulding (Putnam).
The Navy, Pratt (Doubleday Doran).
History of the U. S. Navy, Knox (Putnam).

Index

[363]

INDEX

INDEX

INDEX

INDEX